The Metamorphoses of Don Juan

STANFORD STUDIES IN
LANGUAGE AND LITERATURE, XVIII

THE METAMORPHOSES OF
DON JUAN

LEO WEINSTEIN

AMS Press, Inc.
New York
1967

AMS Press, Inc.
New York, N.Y. 10003
1967

Library of Congress Catalog Card Number: 59-5050

Preface

"The subject of Don Juan has been turned one way, another way, a thousand ways, in prose, in poetry, in music. It has been used and abused, but in spite of all this, is it not as new as ever?" So wrote Théophile Gautier on January 27, 1845.[1] The past one hundred years have confirmed Gautier's view, for the literary market has been swamped with so many Don Juan versions that not even Leporello could keep a complete list of them.

As literary production on the Don Juan theme increased, so did critical writings; both are of necessity uneven and range from brilliant insights to mere verbiage. Among this wealth of material the reader will be surprised at the relative dearth of informative and scholarly works on the history of the Don Juan legend itself. So far as I have been able to ascertain, no full account is available at the present time in any language; the only book in English that might be placed in this category is the very limited study by John Austen,[2] which deals primarily with the origin of the legend and with English versions of it.

Among the scholars who have dealt with the Don Juan subject one name stands out—Georges Gendarme de Bévotte.[3] His is the only work constituting an actual history of the Don Juan legend up to the early twentieth century. Bévotte not only did the painful spadework to which all subsequent critics are indebted but also brought into his treatment of the legend a quality that had been lacking in nationalist-minded critics—a high degree of impartiality. Being a pioneer effort, Gendarme de Bévotte's study suffers, of course, from some shortcom-

---

[1] Théophile Gautier, "Italiens: *Don Giovanni*," in *Histoire de l'art dramatique en France depuis vingt-cinq ans* (Paris, 1858–59), IV, 35.

[2] *The Story of Don Juan: A Study of the Legend and the Hero* (London, 1939).

[3] *La Légende de Don Juan* (2 vols., Paris, 1911).

ings,[4] but all things considered it remains the outstanding critical work on the Don Juan legend and a classic study in comparative literature.

Several works provide information on Don Juan versions in individual countries. Besides the already mentioned study by John Austen, Hans Heckel[5] contributes to our knowledge of Don Juan's fate in Germany, and J.-G. Magnabal[6] collected and translated the writings of three Spanish critics on the subject.

The story of Miguel Mañara, which became fused with that of Don Juan in the nineteenth century, has been treated by Lorenzi de Bradi[7] and, more recently, by Esther van Loo.[8]

In recent years some very signal contributions to the study of the Don Juan legend have been made by American scholars. Martin Nozick, in his dissertation "The Don Juan Legend in the Twentieth Century" (Columbia University, 1954), brought Gendarme de Bévotte's work up to date, and Mabel P. Worthington's dissertation, "Don Juan: Theme and Development in the Nineteenth Century" (Columbia University, 1952), treats the subject from a psychological point of view. Most important perhaps are two excellent bibliographies: Armand E. Singer's *A Bibliography of the Don Juan Theme* (Morgantown, West Virginia, 1954) and Everett W. Hesse's *Catálogo bibliográfico de Tirso de Molina* (Madrid, 1949) and its supplements, which devotes a special section to the Don Juan legend.

Thanks to these works, an attempt can now be made to consider the Don Juan subject from a wider perspective. It was found that certain versions constitute definite turning points in the evolution of the legend, and these were selected as landmarks around which related works could be grouped. We shall cross frontiers freely, for if any subject is truly

---

[4] Primarily the relatively little space devoted to such crucial versions as Mozart's *Don Giovanni*, E. T. A. Hoffmann's interpretation of Don Juan, and Zorrilla's *Don Juan Tenorio*; also the lack of a clear distinction between the Don Juan and Mañara legends.

[5] *Das Don-Juan Problem in der neueren Dichtung* (Stuttgart, 1915).

[6] *Don Juan et la critique espagnole* (Paris, 1893). Contains translations of the following: (1) Don Manuel de la Revilla, *El tipo legendario de Don Juan Tenorio y sus manifestaciones en las modernas literaturas*; (2) F. Pí y Margall, *Observaciones sobre el carácter de Don Juan Tenorio*; (3) Felipe Picatoste, *Estudios literarios: Don Juan Tenorio*.

[7] *Don Juan: la légende et l'histoire* (Paris, 1930).

[8] *Le Vrai Don Juan: Miguel de Mañara* (Paris, 1950).

international, it is that of Don Juan. From Spain it was taken to Italy, from Italy to France, then to England, Germany, the Scandinavian countries, Russia, Hungary, Poland, and the Western Hemisphere.

It is not surprising that in the course of his wanderings Don Juan has undergone so many transformations that at times we can scarcely find any resemblance in him with Tirso de Molina's hero; in fact, not infrequently serious doubts arise whether a personage called "Don Juan" is really entitled to that name. In all such doubtful cases, I included the particular work if a reasonable connection could be detected between the hero and the Don Juan legend as it had crystallized by the time Mozart and Da Ponte treated it.

In quotations from works in foreign languages the original is reproduced only when needed for greater clarity. Unless otherwise stated, translations are mine.

Acknowledgment is made for permission to quote from the following: Søren Kierkegaard, *Either-Or*, Vol. I, translated by David F. Swenson and Lillian Marvin Swenson (Princeton University Press, 1946); Edmond Rostand, *La Dernière Nuit de Don Juan* (Fasquelle, 1921); Albert Camus, *The Myth of Sisyphus and Other Essays*, translated by Justin O'Brien (Alfred A. Knopf, 1955).

I wish to express my gratitude to all those who have aided me in this work and without whose kindness and interest it could not have been accomplished. My research was made possible by a Fulbright grant which enabled me to visit libraries in France, Italy, and Germany. It would be impossible to name all those who aided me in one way or another in the course of this study; however, special thanks are due to Professors Frederick Anderson and Aurelio M. Espinosa, Jr., of Stanford University, for advice and suggestions; to Professor René Jasinski of the University of Paris and Harvard University for his aid during my research in France; to Lawrence Margolis of New York City for his untiring interest and valuable criticism; to Claire Clouzot for last-minute information from Paris; and to J. Christopher Herold, of Stanford University Press, for placing his experience and literary insight at my disposal.

LEO WEINSTEIN

Stanford, January 1959

Contents

The Metamorphoses of Don Juan

CHAPTER ONE

The Don Juan Problem

Oui, don Juan. Le voilà, ce nom que tout répète,
Ce nom mystérieux que tout l'univers prend,
Dont chacun vient parler, et que nul ne comprend;
Si vaste et si puissant, qu'il n'est pas de poète
Qui ne l'ait soulevé dans son cœur et sa tête
Et pour l'avoir tenté ne soit resté plus grand.[1]

ALFRED DE MUSSET,
Namouna, II, xxxviii

Whenever during a literary discussion the participants are asked to pick out the four greatest heroes in modern literature, their choice is most likely to include Hamlet, Faust, Don Quixote, and Don Juan. All four have enjoyed universal renown and given rise to innumerable studies, commentaries, and interpretations. So vast is each of them that together they seem to encompass the greatest problems and aspirations of mankind.

None of these four can ever be completely defined. They defy any attempt to put them into the straitjacket of a brief classification, and even logic must yield when two diametrically opposed views of them are presented both of which seem to be at least partially right; for, to be truly representative, a character must be such as to include those apparently irreconcilable features which can be observed in human

[1]   Don Juan, the name resounds within my mouth;
       Mysterious name, that takes the universe,
       Not understood but spoken North and South;
       The greatest poets oft the name rehearse,
       Keep it in mind and meditation late,
       Make bird thereof and seem to grow more great.

Translation by Marie Agatha Clarke, in *The Complete Writings of Alfred de Musset* (New York, 1905), Vol. I.

beings of flesh and blood—without, however, falling into the artificial pattern of mechanical antithesis.

This does not mean that *any* interpretation is acceptable or that we can discuss them without a firm basis of knowledge. At this point, however, Don Juan parts company with the other three, for in their case there is no doubt as to which work serves as basis for discussion: for Hamlet we go to Shakespeare's drama; while there are various Faust versions of merit, Goethe's work has definitely eclipsed all the others; and where but in Cervantes' novel would we look for the portrait of Don Quixote?

But what of Don Juan? His name has become a household word; everybody is talking about him, but nobody can be quite sure of what he is talking about. To the mythical "man in the street" he is the handsome fellow who knows how to attract and seduce women;[2] yet how many people outside Spain have so much as heard of *El Burlador de Sevilla* or of Tirso de Molina? Not even the informed critics can agree on a definite text for Don Juan: the Spanish are divided between Tirso de Molina and Zorrilla; the French prefer Molière or Musset; the Germans choose Mozart or Hoffmann; and the English are likely to think of Byron and Shaw.

The absence of a universally accepted Don Juan version accounts for both the strength and weakness of the legend. On the one hand, new authors have felt encouraged to try their hand at a subject that apparently has not been closed to further exploration, and thus the figure of Don Juan has given rise to almost continuous interpretations and commentaries; on the other hand, the subject has been invaded by a kind of anarchy which permits any publicity-conscious author to baptize his hero Don Juan, just so long as he is attractive to and successful with two or more women.

Anarchy in a literary field presents the conscientious critic with a painful problem but opens up magnificent opportunities for the imaginative essayist. A brief survey of commentaries will show quite clearly that Don Juan is indeed all things to all men.

To Théophile Gautier[3] Don Juan represents "the aspiration towards

---

[2] Frank Sedwick, "*El Burlador, Don Giovanni* and the Popular Concept of Don Juan," *Hispania*, XXXVIII (1955), 173–77.

[3] "Italiens: *Don Giovanni*," in *Histoire de l'art dramatique en France depuis vingt-cinq ans* (Paris, 1858–59), IV, 38.

the ideal. It is not vulgar debauchery that drives him on; he seeks the dream of his heart with the obstinacy of a Titan who fears neither thunder nor lightning. . . . Not only does Don Juan not go to Hell but he goes to Paradise and to the most beautiful place besides; for he has sought true love and absolute beauty with all his might, and no human being could have a nobler occupation."

Stendhal,[4] quite on the contrary, claims that "Don Juan reduces love to an ordinary affair. . . . He thinks like a general about the success of his maneuvers and, in short, kills love instead of enjoying it more than anyone else, as is commonly believed. . . . Love in Don Juan's manner is a feeling somewhat like a fondness for hunting. It is a need for activity which must be aroused by different objects and which places our talent incessantly in doubt."

Another debate concerns a matter which at first view would seem beyond doubt: Don Juan's virility.

Here the negative is represented by Dr. Gregorio Marañón,[5] who attempts to prove Don Juan's lack of virility by a scientific examination of the legend and of living Don Juan types. Marañón studies their morphology and finds that it is the opposite of the "hypergenital" type. Stressing the point that, contrary to normal relations, it is Don Juan and not the woman who is the center of attraction, Marañón states: "Masculinity can be accentuated until all sexual energy is spent on social activities, the love act itself being reduced to a minimum. Life offers us numerous examples of men of paradoxical masculinity who, absorbed by intense work, live in a state of almost absolute chastity. On the other hand, the normal type deviates in the other direction, towards femininity, when the contrary happens, when all his sexual energy is converted into love properly speaking, at the expense of a precarious social activity, as happens in the woman. That is the case with Don Juan."

José Ortega y Gasset's interpretation of Don Juan[6] is strongly opposed to that of Marañón. Ortega sees in Don Juan the personification of virility, the man who makes a woman truly a woman. According to Ortega, "Don Juan is the man who before the woman is nothing but

[4] De l'Amour (Paris: Ed. de Cluny, 1927), pp. 253, 257.

[5] "Notas para la biología de Don Juan," in Cinco ensayos sobre Don Juan (Santiago de Chile, 1937), p. 38.

[6] "Meditación del marco," in Obras completas (Madrid, 1947), II, 300.

man—neither father, nor husband, nor brother, nor son. . . . Most women are fully women only one hour in their lives, and men usually are Don Juan for only a few moments."

It would be easy to multiply these commentaries on Don Juan, but the foregoing examples demonstrate the most frequently found issues of the dispute: Don Juan the ideal-seeker *versus* Don Juan the cold, calculating seducer; the virile Don Juan *versus* the effeminate Don Juan; Don Juan the egoist *versus* Don Juan the bringer of happiness; Don Juan the carefree individualist *versus* Don Juan the symbol of revolt against bourgeois society.

Should we be astonished if Ramiro de Maeztu labels Don Juan a myth? "I do not believe," Maeztu writes,[7] "that the figure of Don Juan can have arisen in Spain or any other country, because the elements that make up his psychology cannot be reduced to a common denominator. He runs after women yet does not fall in love; he is a libertine yet does not lose his strength; he is a spendthrift yet does not ruin himself; he disavows all ideas of social and religious duty yet always remains a nobleman proud of his stock and his pure Christian blood. Don Juan is a myth; he has never existed, he does not exist and will never exist except as a myth. But the imaginative consistency of the Don Juan figure depends precisely on his condition as a myth. The figure of Don Juan is more popular than literary. It was the people who really created him by realizing in him the fusion of two old legends—that of the Deceiver and that of the Stone Guest—and by finding in Don Juan the imaginative solution of their problems."

Are all these commentators speaking of the same Don Juan? And if so, of which Don Juan? Tirso's, Molière's, Mozart's, Hoffmann's, Byron's, Zorrilla's, or some synthetic Don Juan concocted from common features found in these highly diversified works? This brings us right back to the initial difficulty. So long as we speak of a specific Don Juan, a firm basis for discussion can be established, but when a critic or commentator speaks of Don Juan without further specification, we cannot be quite sure that he is not indulging in pure fantasy.

There is certainly no lack of Don Juan versions. Beginning his career in Spain as a carefree deceiver, he becomes a determined and sometimes brutal "galantuomo" in Italy; in France, Molière endows

[7] *Don Quijote, Don Juan y la Celestina: ensayos de simpatía* (Madrid, 1926), p. 151.

him with an amorous, religious, and aesthetic philosophy; Mozart and Da Ponte combine what has preceded them into an opera which, in turn, inspires Hoffmann's romantic interpretation of the ideal-seeker and the *révolté*. Byron uses his Don Juan for social satire, Musset lends him poetic wings, and Zorrilla makes him find the right woman. Mérimée describes the legend of Miguel Mañara, which eventually becomes fused with that of Don Juan; and from Shaw to Montherlant ever-new, ever-changing interpretations of Don Juan continue to appear.

And now we see more clearly what Musset meant when he spoke of Don Juan as a "mysterious name . . . not understood but spoken North and South." His metamorphoses have been such that one does not always readily recognize him. Is he that youthful Spaniard climbing under cover of darkness into the bedroom of a noble lady whom he is about to deceive? Is he that French nobleman who fools two peasant girls at the same time? Or that Italian lover who tosses his glass over his shoulder after singing a wild and sensuous aria? Or that handsome but pensive German who is in search of the one woman he once beheld in a dream?

Don Juan is all of these and more. His name has become a symbol, ill-defined yet so powerful that its very sound makes the heart beat faster.

CHAPTER TWO

The Origin of the Don Juan Legend

"No vengo por verte a ti,
ni por comer de tu cena;
vengo a que vayas conmigo
a media noche a la iglesia."[1]

Old Spanish romance

The origin of the Don Juan legend remains an unsolved problem about which much has been written and conjectured but little has been satisfactorily proved.[2] The evidence at our disposal is so incomplete that only the discovery of new documents could dispel the doubts which must necessarily greet every new speculation on this subject. In the

---

[1] "I have not come to see you, nor to eat at your table; I have come so that you will go to church with me at midnight."

[2] The following works may be consulted on the origin of the legend: A. Farinelli, "Don Giovanni: note critiche," *Giornale Storico della Letteratura Italiana*, XXVII (1896), 1–77; 254–326. (Farinelli, basing his argument on a statement in Riccoboni's *Histoire du théâtre italien* [Paris, 1731], that around 1620 an Italian version of the *Festin de Pierre* existed, attempts to prove that the legend is of Italian origin and denies that Tirso is the author of the *Burlador*.) Víctor Said Armesto, *La leyenda de Don Juan* (Madrid, 1908), defends the view that the legend was born in Spain. T. A. E. Schröder, "Die dramatischen Bearbeitungen der Don-Juan Sage bis auf Molière einschliesslich," *Beihefte zur Zeitschrift für Romanische Philologie*, XXXVI (1912), 1–215, claims that the legend originated in Germany. Karl Engel, *Die Don-Juan Sage auf der Bühne* (Oldenburg and Leipzig, 1887). François Henri Blaze (called Castil-Blaze), *Molière musicien* (Paris, 1852), I, 189–339. Gustave Reynier, "Les Origines de la légende de Don Juan," *Revue de Paris*, XIII, Part 3 (1906), 314–38. Ramón Menéndez Pidal, "Sobre los orígenes de *El convidado de piedra*," in his *Estudios literarios* (Madrid, 1920). J. Boelte, "Über den Ursprung der Don-Juan Sage," *Zeitschrift für Vergleichende Literaturgeschichte*, XIII (1899), 374–98. Gendarme de Bévotte, *La Légende de Don Juan* (Paris, 1911), Vol. I.

absence of such evidence, many more or less unsubstantiated theories, at times dominated by national prejudice rather than scholarly integrity, have been advanced, only few of which are worthy of serious consideration.

Any attempt to trace the Don Juan legend to its origin inevitably leads to the play *El Burlador de Sevilla y convidado de piedra,* commonly attributed to the monk Gabriel Téllez who is best known by his pen name Tirso de Molina. The play first appeared under Tirso's name in 1630,[3] but it may actually have been performed as early as 1613. The action of the *Burlador,* which will be discussed later, can be divided into two parts: (1) the amorous exploits of a young Spanish nobleman, Don Juan Tenorio, and (2) the punishment of Don Juan by the statue of the Commander Gonzalo de Ulloa.

At this point our investigation into the origin of the legend bogs down, for it is impossible to ascertain the sources of *El Burlador de Sevilla.* The battle of the critics over this question has been raging with such fury that one might think it involves a matter of territorial dispute rather than one of purely academic interest. Although most of the argument revolves around the second part of the *Burlador,* only a source containing the two parts of the play can be considered as a valid predecessor. To go one step further, the proof of the original source would not become final until it has been shown that Tirso was acquainted with that source or with one of its derivations. Unfortunately, the little that is known about Tirso's life does not help us much. Some critics,[4]

---

[3] In a collection of plays entitled "Doze comedias nuevas de Lope de Vega Carpio, y otros autores. Segunda parte. Impreso con licencia. En Barcelona por Jeronimo Margarit, año de 1630."

[4] Notably Farinelli and Schröder (see note 2 above). The main arguments presented in support of their thesis are: (1) The fact that the play appears under Tirso's name in the 1630 edition is no conclusive evidence of authorship, since it was a common practice to use the name of a famous author in order to increase the appeal of plays by lesser-known dramatists; (2) the *Burlador* is not contained in the collections of Tirso's plays published during his lifetime; (3) certain favorite stylistic constructions of Tirso's are absent in the play; (4) Tirso usually gives the most important roles to women, whereas in the *Burlador* women are insignificant compared to Don Juan.

The counterarguments, as summarized by Gendarme de Bévotte, retort that: (1) Tirso should be considered the author of the *Burlador* until it can be proven that someone else wrote it. (2) Tirso wrote more than four hundred plays and only fifty are contained in the editions of his plays published from 1627 to 1636;

attempting to prove that the legend is not Spanish in origin, have denied Tirso's paternity of the play (which does not make it any less Spanish), but the various arguments presented in favor of this thesis, while raising legitimate doubts, are not conclusive.

Of the many theories regarding the sources of Tirso's play, we shall review only those most frequently advanced: the historical theory, the theory of the *auto sacramental*, and the theory that Tirso combined a theme he found in folklore with borrowings from Spanish literature.

The historical theory was apparently first proposed by Louis Viardot,[5] who claims that the play is based on a historical event described in the chronicles of Seville. According to Viardot, Don Juan Tenorio was a member of a distinguished family in Seville. He killed the Commander de Ulloa, whose daughter he had abducted, and the Commander was buried in a chapel at the Convent of San Francisco. The Franciscan monks, desiring to put an end to Don Juan's excesses, managed to lure him into an ambush and killed him. They then spread the rumor that Don Juan had boldly entered the chapel to insult the

---

in the Madrid edition of 1635, it is stated that of the twelve plays in it only four are by Tirso, and he cared so little about receiving credit that he did not even indicate which of these plays he had written. (3) The editions of the *Burlador* which have come down to us are probably bad copies; besides, the stylistic construction absent in the *Burlador* is likewise not found in other uncontested works of Tirso. (4) The nature of Don Juan requires that he conquers women quickly and leaves them just as hastily, so that the women necessarily play a minor role in the drama.

The controversy received new fuel when, in 1878, the Marquis de Fuensanta del Valle discovered a play entitled *Tan largo me lo fiáis*, attributed to Calderón de la Barca but containing no indication of date or place. *Tan largo* is obviously the same play as the *Burlador*, except that a number of clarifying changes can be found in it. Joaquín Casalduero, "Contribución al estudio del tema de Don Juan en el teatro español," *Smith College Studies in Modern Languages*, XIX, Nos. 3 and 4 (April, July, 1938), 17–44, claims that *Tan largo* is posterior to the *Burlador*, and that it was produced between 1650 and 1660. Casalduero presents a strong case in defense of his thesis; however, Doña Blanca de los Ríos, "El viaje de Tirso a Santo Domingo y la génesis del 'Don Juan,'" *Raza Española* (Madrid), VI (1924), 4–35, sets the date of *Tan largo* between 1623 and 1625 and that of the *Burlador* between 1625 and 1629. She also claims that Tirso was born in 1583 rather than 1572 and denies the frequent assertion that he led a dissolute life and was married before his entry into the priesthood.

[5] *Etudes sur l'histoire des institutions, de la littérature et des beaux-arts en Espagne* (Paris, 1835), p. 344n.

statue of the Commander and that the statue had thrown him into Hell. Other authors even supplied the information that Don Juan lived in the fourteenth century, the son of Admiral Alonso Jofre Tenorio and a contemporary of Peter the Cruel. The view that the legend is based on a pseudo-historical event was further strengthened by the fact that names such as Juan and Pedro Tenorio, de Ulloa, and de la Mota, which appear in the *Burlador*, are not fictitious but those of families which actually existed in Spain. However, subsequent investigations by Farinelli and Bévotte revealed that the chronicles of Seville contain no such account. Since the matter would certainly not have been omitted from the chronicles, it seems reasonable to assume that Tirso merely borrowed the names of historical families for his imaginary heroes, a common practice in Spanish literature.

Another theory claims that the elements of the *Burlador* were already contained in an *auto sacramental*—that is, a play with a religious theme—supposedly performed in the fifteenth and sixteenth centuries, the *Ateista fulminato*. Castil-Blaze, who advances this view, presents no evidence to support it; but Shadwell, in the preface to his *Libertine* (1676), mentions an *Ateista fulminato* which is said to have been performed for many years in the churches of Italy. This seemed to be confirmed when Simone Brouwer discovered an *Ateista fulminato*, with author and date unknown, among a collection of forty-eight scenario manuscripts in Rome. The scenario recounts the adventures of Count Aurelio who, having abducted the young Leonora from a convent and being pursued by her brother, disguises himself as a hermit and thus escapes his pursuers. He is finally punished by the statues of Leonora's parents, whom he has insulted and who drag him off to Hell while lightning crashes upon his head. Yet this drama, far from having inspired the *Burlador*, contains numerous borrowings which prove that it dates from about the end of the seventeenth century. We might add to this that the hero of the *Burlador* cannot be called an atheist.

Since neither the historical theory nor that of the *auto sacramental* rests on satisfactory evidence, we may find it more profitable to turn our attention to medieval folklore. The theme of the dead man who, upon being invited by a carefree young madcap, makes an appearance can be found in the folklore of many nations. Usually the invitation is extended to a skull and the young man who has kicked and mocked it either gets off with a severe admonition thanks to some relic he is wearing or else has to pay with his life.

A variation of this theme provided the plot for a scenario which appears in print under the title *Leonzio, ovvero la terribile vendetta di un morto* and which was first performed at the Jesuit school of Ingolstadt in the fall of 1615. The scenario relates the fate of Count Leonzio who, perverted by Machiavelli's doctrines, finds a skull near a cemetery. He kicks the skull and jokingly invites it to dinner. At the appointed time a huge man knocks at the door. Leonzio has the door bolted, but the mysterious visitor simply tears it down. He is Leonzio's grandfather, sent by Heaven to prove that there is a life beyond this one. The apparition then smashes Leonzio against the wall with such force that his head cracks open, and finally takes him to Hell.

Although the Leonzio scenario antedates the publication of the *Burlador* by fifteen years and probably is of even earlier Italian origin, it cannot be considered the source of Tirso's play, because Leonzio bears no relation to Don Juan, the invited dead man is not a statue but a skull, and the return invitation by the dead man is lacking,[6] to mention only the most important dissimilarities.

A new ray of hope appeared with the discovery of popular Spanish romances by Spanish scholars (especially R. Menéndez Pidal and Menéndez y Pelayo) in the provinces of Segovia, León, and Burgos at about the turn of the century. Two of these romances contain features which bear a certain resemblance to the Don Juan legend.

The first of these was discovered by Juan Menéndez Pidal in the village of Cureña, province of León. It tells of a young man who goes to church "not to hear Mass but to look at the pretty girls." On his way, he sees a skull. He kicks it and jokingly invites it to supper. To the "galán's" horror, the skull accepts the invitation, appears at mealtime, and in turn invites the madcap to come to its tomb at midnight. There the young man is let off with a warning thanks to the relic he is wearing.

The second popular romance was recited to Ramón Menéndez Pidal in Riaza, province of Segovia, in 1905. It resembles Tirso's play more closely, for here the young ladies' man goes to church, where he pulls a statue by the beard. "My venerable old man," he sneers, "who would

---

[6] Strictly speaking, only those versions containing the double invitation of the *Burlador* enter into the question. For an interesting account of this, see Dorothy Epplen McKay, *The Double Invitation in the Legend of Don Juan* (Stanford, 1943).

have thought that one day I would twist your ridiculous beard with these hands of mine?" This implies a previous, hostile relationship between the two, such as exists in *El Burlador de Sevilla*. Otherwise this romance does not differ substantially from the first one, except that the young man is saved from punishment, because he went to confession before heeding the statue's return invitation.

Both these romances contain at least the outlines of both the "Burlador" and the double-invitation themes. It is quite likely that these Spanish romances antedate Tirso's *Burlador*, since, as Menéndez Pidal points out, otherwise features of Tirso's play would probably be present in them. Even though the two romances and their variations seem to be the strongest evidence yet presented with regard to the origin of the Don Juan legend, they are far from the last word on the subject, for (1) their date cannot be established with certainty; (2) there is no evidence to prove that Tirso was acquainted with them; (3) the young caballero who invites the dead man bears only a very vague resemblance to Don Juan; and (4) there may well be, as Menéndez Pidal admits, a Seville legend on the subject which has not yet been discovered or which is completely lost.

Tirso did not necessarily have to go to popular romances or obscure Jesuit plays to find a model for his drama. The Spanish theater of his time contained ample material to draw from. Thus we find an animated statue in Lope de Vega's *Dineros son calidad* (1623), although the circumstances are quite different from those in the *Burlador*. As for characters resembling Don Juan in impetuous passion and disregard of conventions in their dealings with women, a long list of heroes from Golden Age plays could be cited. There are, however, two who are rather closely related to the Burlador: Leonido, in Lope de Vega's *Fianza satisfecha* (1612-15), and especially Leucino, in Juan de la Cueva's *Infamador* (1581).

In the involved controversy about the origin of the Don Juan legend one point is only too frequently forgotten: that, regardless of what the original sources may have been, the Don Juan legend owes its popularity and success—for all practical purposes, its existence—to the man who first combined these various elements into one coherent play and who created the character of Don Juan Tenorio. No matter who this man was, the glorious career of the Don Juan legend, which was to inspire so many writers all over the world, received its initial impetus from *El Burlador de Sevilla*.

CHAPTER THREE

Tirso de Molina's *Burlador de Sevilla*

CATALINON: ¿Donde vamos?

DON JUAN: Calla, necio, calla agora;
adonde la burla mía
ejecute.

CATALINON: No se escape
nadie de ti.[1]

El Burlador de Sevilla, ii, 500–504

"All Seville calls me 'the Burlador' and my greatest pleasure is to deceive a woman and leave her dishonored."[2]

This is the "Burlador" theme in Tirso de Molina's play *El Burlador de Sevilla y convidado de piedra*, written at some time between 1613 and 1630. What kind of man is this Don Juan Tenorio? Why does he bend all his efforts to deceive women? What kind of game is this "burlar una mujer"? Is he a passionate, oversexed maniac or a cold, calculating seducer? Does he hate women or does he love them too much? And if the latter, what kind of love is it that enjoys the shame of a deceived woman?

To the modern, Freud-oriented reader, Tirso's hero is likely to remain enigmatic, at least in part, for the author very rarely explains the motives behind the Burlador's actions. "My greatest pleasure is to

---

[1] CATALINON: Where are we going?
DON JUAN: Be quiet, you fool; to the place where I'll play my trick.
CATALINON: Not one escapes you.

[2] Sevilla a vozes me llama   es burlar una mujer
el Burlador, y el mayor   y dejalla sin honor.
gusto que en mí puede haber   (ii, 269–73)

The text used is *El Burlador de Sevilla*, edited by Américo Castro, in Tirso de Molina, *Obras*, Vol. I ("Clásicos castellanos," Madrid, 1952).

deceive a woman and leave her dishonored," he says just as a new opportunity for deception comes his way. He has never seen the woman
before; she is loved by a man with whom he seems to be on quite
friendly terms—a man, in fact, who has just offered to let Don Juan in
on a trick he plans to play on a prostitute. Why? the reader asks; is
no woman excepted from this virtual declaration of war? Apparently
not, for among his victims we find women of high and low birth.

The key to Don Juan's role with women, I believe, is contained in
the very title of the play: Tirso does not call him "el Seductor" or "el
Galán" but "el Burlador"—the practical joker, the mocker, the jester.
The seducer and the ladies' man, in general, are subject to at least
temporary emotional attachments and may eventually settle down with
one woman; their seductions are to a considerable extent designed to
satisfy their sexual desires and they will make every effort to have the
desired woman fall in love with them, if for no other reason than to
heighten their erotic pleasure.

With Don Juan, the Burlador, we cannot be so sure of this. Not
that he lacks passion—far from it. Not that he lacks strong sexual
urges; quite on the contrary, they seem to be so impetuous that he looks
for the quickest satisfaction of them. But, as he states himself, the most
important part of his amorous adventures is the trick, the joke he plays
on the woman. He does not, like the experienced seducer, prepare carefully planned tactical maneuvers, advancing step by step and making a
frontal attack when the time is ripe. Rather, he is an excellent impro-
viser, ever ready to take quick advantage of an opportunity. But his
improvisations are limited to proven and repeated maneuvers; in fact,
compared to the refinements of seduction employed by the eighteenth-
century *roué* or by nineteenth-century "Donjuanism," his methods appear coarse and uncomplicated. Yet these methods are not so unreasonable, considering the circumstances in which he finds himself. Here is
a young madcap, living in a society in which women are closely guarded
by parents, duennas, or husbands. Deceiving his prey under the cover
of darkness seems the easiest way of gaining his goal, and he unhesitatingly chooses this method. He might write sonnets, hoping to gain
the affection of the woman; he might work out elaborate schemes for
achieving his conquest, like Lovelace. But Don Juan cannot wait.
"¡Esta noche he de gozalla!" Tonight, no later—this is what distinguishes Don Juan from Lovelace and from the sophisticated, almost professional seducer of the eighteenth century. But when he at-

tacks, he strikes like lightning. And afterwards he laughs. "That was a good one," he roars—and he means the trick he played, not the woman.

If we may assume that *El Burlador de Sevilla* reflects in some way the manners of Tirso's time, it appears that this game of "burlar una mujer" was rather fashionable among the noble dandies of seventeenth-century Spain. Arriving in Seville after a prolonged absence, Don Juan runs into an old companion of his, the Marquis de la Mota. Don Juan inquires about several women of light virtue and learns that the Marquis has planned two deceptions for that night. It is in preparation for these deceptions that Don Juan manages to have Mota give him the bright-colored cape he needs to deceive Doña Ana; but what distinguishes him from his fellow burladors is that they limit themselves to a definite type of woman while he has extended his deceits to any woman he encounters.

During the action of the play, Don Juan has four adventures, two with ladies of rank and two with girls of the lower classes. In his amorous enterprises he displays no particular originality; he rather follows a set pattern which apparently has proven successful in the past.

His first victim is Duchess Isabela at the court of Naples. Don Juan has deceived her under the cover of darkness by pretending to be her lover, Duke Octavio. Isabela discovers her error when she wants to strike a light, and her screams bring to the scene the King, guards, and Don Juan's uncle, who is the Spanish ambassador at the court. Because of the latter's complicity Don Juan is able to escape, while Octavio receives the blame for the whole affair. Since the play opens *in medias res*, we are not told explicitly how Don Juan had managed to deceive Isabela, but his attempt on Doña Ana, later on, provides a clue to his method. In this case Don Juan intercepts a message from Ana to the Marquis de la Mota, whom she invites to a rendezvous at eleven with the specification that he is to wear a colored cape. Don Juan relays the message but changes the hour to twelve; he then manages to exchange capes with Mota and appears at Ana's at eleven. But this adventure, which was to be a masterstroke, ends disastrously, for Ana discovers the deceit and her screams bring her father, the Commander Gonzalo de Ulloa, to the scene. Don Juan reluctantly fights a duel with the old man, whom he wounds fatally and whose curses accompany his flight. Again another man is at first accused of the crime—this time Mota, who arrives just as Don Juan has fled.

With ordinary women, such as the fishergirl Tisbea and the peasant bride Aminta, Don Juan uses a different approach. He begins with passionate declarations of love, then sweeps aside all arguments of social inequality or even the obligations of a marriage vow, and finally overcomes the girl's resistance by swearing that he will marry her. When Don Juan pronounces his lyrical love verses, he seems carried away by passion. After being saved from drowning in a shipwreck, he regains consciousness and finds himself in the arms of Tisbea. He is still dazed, but that does not prevent him from courting the fishergirl in terms strongly tinged with the conceits of Gongorism:

Would to God, my lass, that I had drowned in the sea, so that I would have ended sane instead of driven to madness by you. For the sea could engulf me in its silvery waves that crash beyond their bounds, but it could not set me aflame.[8]

Don Juan does even better when, after discouraging Aminta's bridegroom, he boldly enters her bridal chamber. There he bursts into these lyrical verses:

I saw you, I adored you, I was aflame with love. My only wish is to marry you. And even if the kingdom should grumble, if the King himself objects, if my father threatens to interfere—I shall be your husband.[4]

These declarations would sound very convincing, if the same man had not, a few moments earlier (as he had before joining Tisbea in her cottage), ordered his servant Catalinón to hold two horses in readiness for their escape and if, after Aminta's tender assent, he had not jeered in an aside: "How little you know you are dealing with the Burlador of Seville!"

Why all these deceptions? Don Juan has no time to stop and explain. He considers his attitude toward women perfectly natural. "So

[8] A Dios, zagala, pluguiera
que en el agua me anegara
para que cuerdo acabara
y loco en vos no muriera;
que el mar pudiera anegarme
entre sus olas de plata
que sus límites desata;
mas no pudiera abrasarme.   (I, 621–29)

[4] Vite, adoréte, abraséme
tanto, que tu amor me anima
a que contigo me case;
mira qué acción tan precisa.
Y aunque lo mormure el reino
y aunque el rey lo contradiga,
y aunque mi padre enojado
con amenazas lo impida,
tu esposo tengo de ser.   (III, 247–54)

you intend to possess Tisbea?" Catalinón asks him. Don Juan is annoyed that anyone could ask such a stupid question. "Why do you ask?" he replies. "You know that deceiving is second nature with me." (I, 890–94) Don Juan goes after women like Harpagon after money. His motives are a combination of passion and vanity—factors present in most seducers. Yet, like all great literary creations, he is at the same time an individual such as might well have existed in seventeenth-century Spain.[5]

There is another theme in *El Burlador de Sevilla*, one that was to enjoy less fortune than the "Burlador" theme but which was without doubt considered of greatest importance by Tirso: this is what might be called the "¡Qué largo . . . !" or procrastination theme. Because of the subsequent transformations of the Don Juan legend, it is often forgotten that Tirso's play is essentially a religious drama. The presence of God and His judgment dominate the entire play, hovering over it like an ominous cloud—and every character, including Don Juan, is constantly aware of this. Time and again, the Burlador receives admonitions to repent and warnings of punishment in the hereafter; but he brushes them aside with his mocking "¡Qué largo me lo fiáis!" (That is a long way off!).

The two themes are tightly woven together by this recurring "¡Qué largo . . . !" phrase, which appears like a foreboding fate-motif at the very moment when the Burlador seems to be enjoying his greatest triumphs. "You will pay for these tricks with your life," Catalinón cautions when Don Juan is about to deceive Tisbea. (I, 901–3) Again, just as his master prepares Ana's deception, Catalinón sounds his warnings. (II, 311–14) But Don Juan merely laughs: "¡Qué largo me lo fiáis!" His father's position at the Spanish court protects him against severe punishment, and his sword can take care of those who might challenge him.

But matters take a turn for the worse when, after their escape from Aminta's village, Don Juan and Catalinón take refuge in a church. The master is still chuckling over the trick he has played on the naïve peasant girl, but his servant annoys him with bad news: Octavio has

---

[5] Those interested in probing the question of Don Juan's verisimilitude more deeply may consult my unpublished Master's thesis, "The Don Juan of Téllez and Molière" (Stanford University, 1948), in which an attempt is made to demonstrate that individuals such as those two Don Juans could well have existed in their respective times and countries.

found out who has deceived Isabela, and the King of Castile has decided that Don Juan must marry her; also, Mota is demanding Don Juan's punishment. They come upon Don Gonzalo's tomb, over which the dead man's statue towers. "What is written on the pedestal?" Catalinón asks, and Don Juan reads the inscription: "Here the most loyal knight waits for the Lord to wreak vengeance upon a traitor."[6] Don Juan, his sense of honor offended, pulls the statue's beard and invites it ironically to come to supper that night if it is so anxious to obtain vengeance. So occupied is he by the present moment that he has already forgotten the oath he swore to Aminta only a short time before: "If, perchance, I fail to keep my promise, I ask God that I be killed for treachery and deceit by a man—(aside) a dead man, not a living one, God forbid!"[7]

The meal at which the statue appears is dominated by Don Juan. Rising to the height of recklessness, he has the stone guest entertained with verses that join the "Burlador" and the "¡Qué largo . . . !" themes:

> If you ask me to delay
> What so fervently I pray,
> Since I'll live yet many days,
> Let us hope my patience pays.
> If you force my love to wait
> Till I stand at death's dark gate,
> Then, dear lady, I must say,
> "Why wait till that far-off day?"[8]

The statue remains silent but before leaving asks Don Juan to shake hands as a sign of agreement that he in turn will come to supper at the

---

[6] Aquí aguarda del Señor
el más leal caballero
la venganza de un traidor. (III, 450–52)

[7]   Si acaso
la palabra y la fe mía
te faltaré, ruego a Dios
que a traición y alevosía
me dé muerte un hombre . . . ([Ap.] muerto:
que, vivo, ¡ Dios no permita!)   (III, 277–81)

[8] Si ese plazo me convida   Si de mi amor aguardáis,
para que gozaros pueda,   señora, de aquesta suerte
pues larga vida me queda,   el galardón en la muerte,
dejad que pase la vida.   ¡ qué largo me lo fiáis!   (III, 594–601)

statue's chapel. For the first time in his life Don Juan experiences terror; his body is bathed in cold sweat, but he soon recovers.

At the statue's tomb the roles are reversed. Now it is Don Juan's turn to listen while mysterious voices proclaim the divine countertheme which dominates ominously above Don Juan's *Leitmotif*:

> Let those young fools be swayed
> Who think God's judgment late:
> No debt remains unpaid,
> No due will miss its date!
>
> .   .   .
>
> While living in this vale of tears,
> Let no one dare to say:
> "Of life I have yet many years,"
> Because the living die each day.[9]

Don Juan courageously shakes hands with the statue; feeling the infernal fire which begins to burn him, he asks to have a priest called for his confession. But it is too late. Twice the statue thunders the severe moral of the play: "This is God's justice: As you act, so you pay."

Despite his immoral behavior, the Burlador can in no way be considered an atheist. He may be a bad Christian, he certainly does not share the popular superstitions of Catalinón, he does not think that the statue can become animated and appear at his supper, but at all times is he aware of the presence of God and of His power. So deeply ingrained is this belief in him that he instinctively asks for confession when death is upon him. Nor is Don Juan unduly surprised when the statue enters his dining room: to a Spaniard miracles form part of the atmosphere he lives in. He does entertain his guest with mocking songs but as soon as they are alone, he inquires anxiously: "Are you enjoying the presence of God? Did I kill you in a state of sin?" (III, 637–38) Even Don Juan's false oaths contain casuistic reservations; to

---

[9] Adviertan los que de Dios
   juzgan los castigos tarde,
   que no hay plazo que no llegue
   ni deuda que no se pague.
          (III, 930–33)

Mientras en el mundo viva,
no es justo que diga nadie:
¡qué largo me lo fiáis!
siendo tan breve el cobrarse.
          (III, 938–41)

Verse 931 in the Castro edition ends in "grandes"; I have used instead "tarde," as found in *Tan largo*, which seemed preferable.

play safe, he swears by Tisbea's eyes and by Aminta's hand. (1, 940–42, and 111, 273–75, respectively) To quote Felipe Picatoste:

[The Don Juan of Tirso] is not an unbeliever but a madcap; he is not impious but wild; he is not in revolt against society and family but a young man drunk with gaiety. Like most youngsters, he keeps his religious and moral beliefs in a corner of his mind and he assumes that a great amount of time will have to go by before he may need them. He does not deny that at some time he may be punished for his actions; but the remoteness of justice keeps that thought out of his mind.[10]

Don Juan possesses several traits which will ingratiate him with the spectator, who is not likely to applaud the culprit's punishment as strongly as he ought to. One factor which helps to create this reaction, at least in this spectator, is the manner in which the Burlador is made to die. After he has finished the ghastly meal at the Commander's tomb, the statue says:

Give me your hand; be not afraid, give me your hand. DON JUAN: What do you mean? I afraid? Oh, fire is devouring me! Do not burn me with your fire![11]

There is something in this procedure of the statue that seems unworthy of a messenger from the beyond. Don Juan is its guest and a handshake is an expression of confidence, agreement, and mutual good faith. However effective this scene may be dramatically, it leaves one with the uncomfortable afterthought that Don Juan has been ignominiously tricked by the very man who, just a few lines above, has accused him of having behaved cowardly when he fled after the duel. One would think that mighty, supernatural forces would not have to resort to such means; yet an alternative solution seems to be difficult to find, for Molière and Da Ponte also have the handshake preceded by words that lead the hero to believe he is shaking hands as a sign of accepting the statue's invitation.

There are additional factors that show the Burlador in a sympathetic light. He is handsome, young, and dashing; he is brave without being

[10] Picatoste, "Estudios literarios: Don Juan Tenorio," in J.-G. Magnabal, *Don Juan et la critique espagnole*, p. 186.

[11] STATUE: Dame esa mano;   DON JUAN: ¿Eso dices? ¿Yo temor?
no temas, la mano dame.   ¡Que me abraso! ¡No me abrases
con tu fuego! (111, 946–49)

a ruffian; he has a haughty sense of honor, he keeps his promises (with men only, to be sure); but, above all, he rises to unexpected heights in his two meetings with the statue.

When that moment arrives [writes Manuel de la Revilla], the madcap, until then vulgar and mean, becomes transfigured before the danger; his courage rises and takes on sublime proportions, and the traditional Don Juan Tenorio, the fiery and bold libertine who is not afraid to defy even God, appears in all his splendor. None of Tirso's imitators can rival him in this scene; none has been able to understand the personage in these terrible moments so well as he did.[12]

And it is in this conflict between his lust for pleasure and his unquestioning acceptance of divine power with its direct effect on his life that Don Juan ceases to be a merely interesting psychological study but attains the stature of a truly great dramatic hero.

Now, if Don Juan is a believer, why is he denied the comfort of confession and consequently his only chance of salvation? In order to understand Tirso's message fully we must consider Don Juan's punishment in a somewhat wider framework.

The problem of human salvation, free will, divine grace, and predestination is a knotty one and has haunted theologians throughout the ages. For our purposes the two sides of the argument may perhaps best be summarized thus: One side maintains that our fate is predestined and almost entirely dependent upon the grace of God. This is the view maintained by Saint Paul, Saint Augustine, Saint Thomas Aquinas (in a slightly milder form), and by Luther and Calvin during the Reformation; it was to receive a new impetus by the Jansenist movement during the seventeenth century. These religious thinkers do not necessarily maintain that it is not advisable to do good works, but if they were hard pressed, they would probably agree that, in the long run, good works do not amount to much. This view, then, essentially denies, or at least limits severely, the existence of human freedom. It is also inclined to view God as stern and just rather than as merciful.

The opposing camp ranges all the way from those who, while in no way denying the importance of divine grace in our destiny, ascribe a more or less great efficacy to our good works, to the radical opinion that our actions alone determine our fate. In this group belong Saint Peter, Pelagius, the compromise view known as semipelagianism, Duns Scotus,

---

[12] In Magnabal, *Don Juan et la critique espagnole*, p. 13.

Luis Molina and the movement of Molinism which gave rise to grave religious controversy around 1600. Opponents of this view have objected that the emphasis on human free will tends to deny God's omnipotence. The partisans of good works often counter this argument by pointing to the magnitude of God's mercy.

It is almost impossible to find a way out of this theological labyrinth, and debate had become so heated in Tirso's time that the Church prohibited further arguing of the problem.

In his plays Tirso de Molina was less concerned with the strictly theological dispute than with the practical aspects of the problem. What he seemed to fear most were the extremes on either side. If grace is the all-important factor in our salvation, then the believer may take the least sign of divine disfavor as an indication of his doom, lose all hope of salvation, and abandon moral restraint. If, on the other hand, man is the author of his own salvation, then God is reduced to the position of a benign bookkeeper or to that of a father so kind that He will forgive automatically if asked to do so.

The Spanish people were strongly in favor of the view which made God's mercy the decisive factor in determining man's destiny; in fact, most Spaniards would have readily subscribed to the opinion expressed in Don Quixote: "Although all of God's attributes are equal in strength, we feel that His mercy excels and shines more brightly than His justice." (Part II, Chap. 42) A general belief prevailed that even a great sinner could be saved, provided he repented sincerely and received the final rites; therefore the opportunity for confession was extended, if at all possible, to the mortally wounded opponent of a duel, even to the victim of a secret murder. We are told that a Madrid notary, intending to strangle his wife for her infidelity, waited until a day when she had gone to confession.[18]

Thus, for all practical purposes, the problem of salvation could be reduced to this: how much trust can we place in God's mercy? Tirso dealt with this question in two plays, which we may call companion pieces.

In the first of these, El condenado por desconfiado ("Condemned for Lack of Faith"), Paulo, a saintly hermit, is told by the Devil (disguised as an angel) that his fate will be the same as that of a certain

---

[18] Noticias de Madrid, April 18, 1637, quoted in Ludwig Pfandl, Spanische Kultur und Sitte des 16. and 17. Jahrhunderts (Kempten, 1925), p. 96.

Enrico. To Paulo's horror this man turns out to be an incorrigible thief and murderer. Paulo, losing all hope of salvation, begins to lead the same kind of life as Enrico. But the difference between the two men is that, unlike Paulo, Enrico has faith in God's mercy; he also takes care of his old, ailing father. As a result Enrico is saved while Paulo is damned for his lack of faith.

The other play is, of course, *El Burlador de Sevilla.* Here the hero waits literally until the last moment to repent, confident that his final confession will erase all his past sins. But Don Juan is no Enrico—he has not even one good deed to his credit.

It would be presumptuous to read into these two plays, in which the moralist and the dramatist play an equally important role, a systematic expression of Tirso's philosophy. His moral lesson is primarily negative in warning of excesses in either direction.

Just why *El Burlador de Sevilla* has been so greatly neglected is a fact that I find difficult to explain. The play has been completely eclipsed in Spain and Latin America by Zorrilla's *Don Juan Tenorio,* and performances of it anywhere have become a rare event. Tirso's play has never received the recognition it deserves, not merely for being the first Don Juan creation but on its own merits. The worst offenders in this respect have been French critics; just as they have deprecated Guillen de Castro's *Las mocedades del Cid* in order to praise Corneille's *Le Cid,* so they have berated Tirso de Molina's *Burlador* for the sake of applauding Molière's *Dom Juan.* In both cases the critics concerned have often made wild claims that can only be based on a nearly complete ignorance of the Spanish originals.

We need not dwell on Calvet's claim that Molière's hero killed the Commander in an open duel but that the Burlador assassinated him,[14] or on Gauchez's description of the Spanish deceiver as "a coarse materialist, an impious braggart,"[15] but even Gendarme de Bévotte, usually so impartial, expresses some severe judgments on Tirso's drama:

. . . the *Burlador* is not one of his best plays. The subsequent success of the Don Juan legend, the innumerable imitations of it, have given to the

[14] J. Calvet, *Les Types universels dans la littérature française* (Paris, 1928), 2ᵉ série. The author apparently has not read Tirso's play, or else he might be confusing it with Zorrilla's.

[15] H. Gauchez, "Essai sur Don Juan," *La Flandre Littéraire,* 1926, VIIIᵉ cahier.

first drama a reputation which it does not entirely justify. . . . The play is composed of two very unequal parts: the first is merely a banal adventure story, the second a stirring religious drama.

The hero offers the same contrast; in the first two acts he only repeats himself; he remains fixed in the same role of the debauchee without originality or depth. Then, in the third act, he suddenly becomes transformed and takes on an air of unexpected vigor and greatness. Certainly, the theatrical conditions in Spain and the Spanish temperament explain this contrast which shocks our logical requirements; but we must add that the author of the *Burlador* did not attempt to do what we look for in vain in his play and what Molière achieved in his *Festin de pierre*: the portrayal of a character.[16]

The admiration we may have for the classical French theater should not make us forget that a character can be portrayed by action as well as by words. The Burlador's "Esta noche he de gozalla" tells us as much about him as we learn about Molière's hero in his long apology of inconstancy. And "¡Qué largo me lo fiáis!" defines an attitude toward religion as effectively as the dialogue between Dom Juan and Sganarelle on the same subject.

El Burlador de Sevilla, as we have seen, is a firmly constructed drama[17] whose themes are woven together so masterfully that it must be ranked among the great morality plays of all times; moreover, Tirso's language is not only highly poetic but also is endowed with a flexibility ranging from elaborate conceits to crisp dialogue.

What most commentators have overlooked is that, in retrospect, we can find in Tirso's Burlador practically all the future interpretations of Don Juan, either directly or *in spe.* But in order to lend itself to infinite variations, a literary theme must be both simple and rich, clear and yet subject to varying interpretations, general and universal but embodied in a highly individualized personage.

Tirso's work is one of those rare achievements. The Burlador can be turned into a French nobleman by adding refinement to his methods, wit to his expressions, and skepticism to his religious attitude. He can be transformed into a romantic hero by explaining his inconstancy

[16] Gendarme de Bévotte, *La Légende de Don Juan,* I, 36f.

[17] Only three scenes, all in the first act, interfere seriously with the flow of the action, and two of these are obvious hors-d'oeuvres: the conversation between Octavio and his servant, followed by Don Pedro's entry (I, 191–374), Tisbea's long monologue (I, 375–516), and the Commander's recital of his mission to Portugal (I, 721–857).

as being caused by the noble search for the ideal woman. By changing the second part of Tirso's play, the Burlador can be converted as a result of miraculous events and end his life as a saintly monk; or else he can be saved (even after his death) by an ideal woman. On the other hand, this same personage may be considered the supreme realist who refuses to be deceived by intangible moral and religious taboos, thus illustrating a type of "absurd hero" as described by Albert Camus.

These are but a few of the variations and interpretations that will be derived from Tirso de Molina's *El Burlador de Sevilla*. It would seem that such a creation deserves not lip service and patronizing footnotes but the highest compliment a play can receive: frequent performance.

Tirso's *Burlador* was first imitated in Italy. It probably was introduced there as one of the many translations made during this period of active literary exchange between the two countries. The oldest extant Italian version is that of Jacinto Andrea Cicognini, whose *Convitato di pietra*, in prose, seems to have been written before 1650. It is significant that this play bears Tirso's subtitle: in Italy neither the character of Don Juan nor the religious message supply the main interest of the subject; it is Don Juan's servant whose *lazzi* and comical remarks steal the spotlight from his master; the statue, losing any moral or religious meaning, provides merely a spine-tingling stage effect.

Cicognini follows Tirso's version rather faithfully; in fact, some passages are outright translations. The Italian author arranges a more orderly presentation of the play, but nowhere does he approach the excellence of his model. Don Juan undergoes some changes by becoming less gallant and more brutal than his predecessor. Among the added scenes, two deserve our attention: that in which Don Juan's servant Passarino ironically recites a list of his master's conquests to the fishergirl Rosalba, and Passarino's cry for his wages as Don Juan is dragged off to Hell.

In 1652 Onofrio Giliberto published a *Convitato di pietra* which has disappeared. The loss of this play is regrettable, because it may have been the basis of the version which Italian actors introduced in France, probably in 1658; but since they played in the impromptu fashion of the *commedia dell'arte*, it is likely that their performance consisted of a mixture of various Italian scenarios. The notes of the actor Biancolelli,[18] who played the part of Don Juan's valet Arlequino, indicate that in the Italian scenario the servant carried the major role and that the comical elements far outweighed the serious ones. Let us note in passing the scene in which Don Juan orders Arlequino to speak for him when Rosalba demands an explanation of his conduct, and Arlequino's throwing the list of his master's conquests into the orchestra while saying: "Take a look, gentlemen, and see whether someone of your family is on it."

The success of the Italian actors induced two French author-players to produce Don Juan plays—Dorimon in 1658 (printed in 1659) and Villiers in 1659. Both plays are entitled *Le Festin de Pierre ou le Fils criminel*,[19] and both lean heavily on an Italian original, perhaps a lost Italian scenario or possibly even Giliberto's lost play.[20] In these first French versions Don Juan becomes more and more wicked; especially his treatment of his father is shocking. He is not yet an out-and-out atheist, but he insults God and the statue; he also loses much in dignity by acts of cowardice and hypocrisy; finally, in him the sensuality of the Burlador has given way to brutality and perverseness. The only new feature worth noting in these two plays is that Don Juan is in revolt not only against his parents but against society as well; moreover,

[18] The original text is not extant; a translation into French made in the eighteenth century by Thomas Gueulette, a lawyer and playwright, is reproduced in Gendarme de Bévotte, *Le Festin de Pierre avant Molière* (Paris, 1907). Bévotte speculates that the scenario was probably performed in 1662.

[19] The confusion between *pierre* (stone) and the proper name Pierre was practically unavoidable. Dorimon's subtitle was replaced by *L'Athée foudroyé* in 1665.

[20] In an article in *PMLA*, XXXVIII (1923), 471–78, H. C. Lancaster describes a pastoral play by La Croix, *L'Inconstance punie*, published first in 1630, which features an inconstant nobleman who, washed ashore by a shipwreck, successively seduces the three daughters of a poor but ambitious shepherd. The culprit is finally struck by lightning.

Lancaster concludes that this play presents evidence of the influence exerted by Tirso's *Burlador* and the Italian *Ateista fulminato* in France around 1630; he also feels we have reason to infer from La Croix's play that the *Burlador* was produced prior to 1627–30. With all the respect which the views of such an excellent scholar command, it must be pointed out that the evidence in La Croix's play is at best inconclusive. While the shipwreck, the nobility of the seducer, and his final celestial punishment do give rise to legitimate comparisons with the *Burlador*, it would be difficult to account for the omission by La Croix of such striking features as the statue, the servant, the peasant wedding, and other scenes that seem far too tempting.

Dorimon and Villiers deserve credit for having changed the legend back from farce to drama by returning the servant to his secondary position.

In most of these Italian and French plays several personages of the *Burlador* have been eliminated: the two kings, Don Juan's uncle, de la Mota, Octavio's valet, and Isabela; and consequently the action has taken on a more orderly aspect. These versions, however, threatened to cause an early degeneration of the subject; it was fortunate that Molière saved it from this fate with his *Dom Juan ou le Festin de Pierre,* first performed on February 15, 1665, at the Théâtre du Palais-Royal.

CHAPTER FOUR

Molière's *Festin de Pierre*

Un grand seigneur méchant
homme est une terrible chose.
MOLIÈRE,
Dom Juan, I, i

Only some thirty-five years separate the publication of Tirso's *Burlador* from Molière's *Dom Juan ou le Festin de Pierre,* yet one might think the two plays had been conceived centuries apart. The Burlador is a giant who stands with one foot in the Middle Ages which accept miraculous events unquestioningly, and with the other at the edge of the modern world which begins to rebel against the restrictions imposed by religious authority; Molière's Dom Juan, by contrast, is a thoroughly modern hero, highly refined, highly sophisticated, a past master in psychological subtleties.

If one of the difficulties in the interpretation of the Burlador was caused by a lack of self-explanation, Molière's Dom Juan has a tendency to go to the other extreme with several speeches of penetrating self-analysis. Even if this deprives him of the unceasing activity of the Burlador, we must be grateful to Molière for this information, for Dom Juan is too complex to express himself in action alone.

Dom Juan has married Elvire, after abducting her from a convent, but he has left her, and he has killed the Commander before the play opens. We receive a first appraisal of the hero from Sganarelle, who is describing his master to Elvire's servant as "a grandee but a wicked person . . . a man who marries right and left . . . the greatest scoundrel on earth . . . a heretic who fears neither Heaven nor Hell." (I, i)

Scarcely has Dom Juan entered when he supplies us with a key to his character through an apology of fickleness:

"What?" Dom Juan exclaims in reply to Sganarelle's criticism of his inconstancy;

do you expect me to swear faithfulness to the first woman who makes an impression on me, to renounce all other women, to have eyes only for her? What does it profit us to turn faithfulness into a virtue, to bury ourselves forever in one passion, and to be blind from youth on to all other beauties who may attract our attention? No, no: let us leave constancy to fools; all beautiful women have the right to charm us and there is no reason why the one we happen to meet first should deprive all the others of their claims to our hearts to which all of them are rightfully entitled. As for me, beauty delights me wherever I encounter it, and I yield easily to its sweet charms. If I have pledged my heart, what of it? The love I feel for one beauty does not oblige me to do injustice to all the others; I still have eyes to see the merit of all of them and to pay each one the tribute which nature demands of us. Whatever the case may be, I cannot refuse my heart to anything lovable, and once a beautiful woman asks me for it, if I had ten thousand hearts, I would give them all. After all, budding inclinations offer inexplicable charms and all the pleasure of life lies in change. There is a great delight in conquering by a hundred attentions the heart of a young beauty, in watching the progress one makes day by day, in combatting by emotional outbursts, by tears and sighs, the innocent modesty of a soul that finds it difficult to surrender, in pushing back foot by foot the timid resistance she puts up, in overcoming the scruples to which she feels honor-bound, and in leading her gently to where we want her to go. But once the battle is won, there is nothing left to wish for, all the pleasure of our passion comes to an end and the peaceful regularity of such a love makes us doze in boredom, until the prospect of a new adventure happens to arouse our senses by presenting us with the attractive charms of a new conquest in sight. In short, there is nothing more exciting than to triumph over the resistance of a beautiful woman, and on that subject I have the ambition of conquerors who cannot resolve to limit their longings. Nothing can stop my impetuous desires: I feel that my heart is capable of loving the whole world, and like Alexander, I wish there were other worlds to which I could extend my amorous conquests. (I, 2)

Sganarelle, who has listened open-mouthed, echoes our sentiments by saying: "My goodness, how you hold forth!" How far we are from the Burlador! This Dom Juan has a philosophy of, a justification for, seduction. He sounds like a man whose senses have been so dulled by the easy satisfaction of his basic sexual desires that he has to make a cat-and-mouse game out of love in order to find new thrills in it. He goes about his amorous adventures the way a general plans a battle, he notes down his daily progress—not as a lover impatient for the fulfillment of his desires but rather like an over-refined sensualist who tries to prolong the preliminaries as much as possible and for whom fulfillment and satiety have become synonymous. Someone has put it very aptly by saying that "he takes less pleasure in making women fall than in seeing how they fall."[1]

It cannot be denied that Dom Juan's tirade retards the flow of dramatic action, but in the Don Juan legend it is a landmark that points far into the future and constitutes a deep insight into the sophisticated seducer. We have here the first sketch of the eighteenth-century *roué*, of Hoffmann's lover in eternal search of perfect beauty, of Musset's idealist in love with love, of the intellectual dandy of the Second Empire, even of the hero in Lavedan's *Marquis de Priola*, whose greatest triumph consists in overcoming the last resistance of a lady and then ironically refusing to enjoy the fruits of his victory. Or, looking backward, we can see in Dom Juan the reflection of a Maréchal de Retz (1396–1440), whose senses finally became so satiated that he required the thrill of violating and killing innocent children in order to rouse his dulled passions.

We expect, of course, to watch Dom Juan put his theories into practice, but here Molière disappoints us. Dom Juan's only attempt of seduction during the play occurs with two peasant girls both of whom he has promised marriage and whom he very skillfully plays against each other without stating which one he prefers. Prior to that we see how Dom Juan behaves with a woman of whom he has tired. Elvire, who finally catches up with him, gets a very cold reception and is told hypocritically that he has realized their union was sinful. In the last act when, veiled and determined to return to the convent, she exhorts him to repent, Dom Juan's interest is momentarily revived, but this is due merely to the new aspect she presents and perhaps also to his vanity which may be piqued at the thought that a woman has been able to tear herself away from him.

Thus, during the entire play, Dom Juan does not carry out one successful seduction. The reason for this is quite obvious: the slow day-by-day attack which Dom Juan employs cannot conveniently be demonstrated in the confines of a play. The only possible way of showing Dom Juan's strategy in action would have been to limit the portrayal of his character to a relationship with one woman, but in that

---

[1] Jules Lemaître, *Impressions de théâtre* (Paris, 1888), I, 67.

case Molière could not have used Dom Juan to depict a social type—the libertine.

Manuals of history and literature are prone to describe "le Grand Siècle" as a period of order and discipline, but that myth explodes upon closer investigation. Religion, for example, was not openly attacked, yet in 1625 Father Mersenne estimated that there were fifty thousand libertines in Paris alone.[2] Although this figure is probably exaggerated, the fact that Pascal addressed his *Pensées* to libertines, and repeated attacks by Bossuet, Bourdaloue, and others on freethinkers indicate that even during the reign of Louis XIV a real problem of "libertinage" existed.

The term "libertine" underwent some changes in the course of the seventeenth century. Until about 1650, the word denoted religious skeptics such as La Mothe Le Vayer and Gassendi, whose personal lives were usually beyond reproach. In the second half of the century, a libertine was likely to be a freethinker not only in religious but also in sexual matters. The gatherings at the home of Ninon de Lenclos, enabled Molière to observe many a model for his Dom Juan. These men were not philosophers searching for a doctrine to guide them in their moral behavior; if they called philosophy to their aid, they were likely to select only those passages which could *a posteriori* justify their disregard of moral restraint.

It is in this light that Molière's Dom Juan must be viewed. Early in the third act Sganarelle is shown trying to find out just what his master believes. At first Dom Juan answers evasively, but when Sganarelle presses him, he states: "I believe that two and two are four, Sganarelle, and that four and four are eight." (III, i) And there he lets the matter rest. It is not enough to explain Dom Juan's reluctance to expand and justify his attitude by pointing out that he is conversing with his servant; he had gone to great lengths in exposing his apology of fickleness to Sganarelle earlier and, if he had as much to say on the subject of religion, he would probably take great delight in disturbing his servant's peace of mind; in fact, he attempts this unsuccessfully with the beggar they encounter shortly after. Dom Juan rejects religion as he reasons away everything else that stands in the way of his pleasures: God, marriage, parental authority, conventions. He is not

---

[2] Le Père Marin Mersenne, *La Vérité des sciences contre les septiques* [sic] *ou pyrrhoniens* (Paris, 1638).

a rebellious dissident who has studied these matters; any argument will do: two and two is four, as easy as all that. He is a superficial Cartesian dilettante who either has not read Descartes's proof of the existence of God or who chooses to ignore it.

Three more scenes shed light on Dom Juan's character. He unhesitatingly comes to the aid of a nobleman attacked by three bandits (III, iii), which shows that he is not only brave but also adheres to the code of honor when it does not interfere with his pleasures. But he ignores this code when it comes to paying debts. His creditor M. Dimanche receives many a witty and insincere compliment—but no money. (IV, iii) Finally, when faced with too many obstacles, Dom Juan feigns a hypocritical conversion so that he may be able to pursue his enjoyments in greater tranquillity.

It is then primarily as a socio-psychological study that we must view Molière's *Festin de Pierre,* and only to a lesser degree as a morality play. The author obviously did not feel at ease with the statue and retained it only because the stage effects it produced had been one of the main reasons for the success enjoyed by the Italian actors. Because of his concentration on character rather than plot Molière fails to tie up the two parts of the play, for he does not provide Dom Juan with a strong motive for inviting the statue.

As they stand gazing at the Commander's stone image, Sganarelle exclaims: "It seems as if he were alive and about to speak. He casts glances at us that would frighten me if I were all alone, and I think he is not pleased to see us." "He would be wrong," Dom Juan replies, "and would receive with ill grace the honor I do him. Ask him whether he wants to come and sup with me." (III, v) So the invitation is issued as a mere joke, for Dom Juan in no way takes Sganarelle's fears seriously. The statue appears very briefly at Dom Juan's meal and in the final scene it acts as scarcely more than a convenient and effect-producing *deus ex machina,* which is comically offset by Sganarelle's cry for his wages.

We have no definite evidence which would reveal whether or not Molière knew Tirso's play, but since all the resemblances between the two plays can be ascribed to borrowings from other sources with which Molière was definitely acquainted, the answer appears to be negative; it would indeed be surprising that Molière, had he known the *Burlador,* should not have made a more extensive use of it. The sources of his play are primarily Dorimon, Villiers, and, to a smaller extent, the Italians.

Molière's Dom Juan offers some striking contrasts to Tirso's Burlador, most important of which are his aesthetic philosophy of seduction, his cool reasoning and, above all, his outspoken religious skepticism. Contrary to the active Burlador, "this hero analyzes himself more than he acts; he likes to expose his feelings, to dissect his soul. He manifests his character through words rather than through action."[3]

While Dom Juan has certainly gained in intellect, he has lost a proportionate amount in passion. This man is always master of himself, fully conscious of his actions—and in this lies his true wickedness; next to him, the youthful Burlador is a mere rascal. True, Dom Juan too pretends that he wants to postpone his repentance—but with what irony! To Sganarelle's admonitions he replies: "Yes, indeed. We have to mend our ways; another twenty or thirty years of this kind of life, and then we shall look to our interest." (iv, vii) The nodding of the statue irritates him, for it threatens to upset his entire system of philosophy. But when the specter appears, he has recovered his self-assurance. "If Heaven wants to give me a warning, it will have to speak a bit more clearly if it wants me to understand." (v, iv) Even during his last moments Dom Juan remains a confirmed nonbeliever. Call a priest to repent? He would not think of it! "No, no, whatever may happen, I will not have people say that I am capable of repenting." (v, iv)

The last quotation is in keeping with the courage Dom Juan had previously displayed when he came to the aid of Dom Carlos. (iii, iii) We are willing to accept Dom Juan's defiance of divine forces, we may even admire him for it, but has the undeniable appearance of the statue had no effect on him? Are two plus two still four, and four plus four still eight? Apparently, for Dom Juan's basic attitudes have not changed in the least, even if his means have. He takes recourse to his hypocritical conversion not because his skeptical attitude has been shaken but in order to ward off those who threaten to interfere with his pleasures.

Molière has been severely criticized for finally turning his hero into a religious hypocrite. No doubt, the author was primarily motivated in this by his desire to lash back at the critics of *Tartuffe*; yet Dom

---

[3] Gendarme de Bévotte, *La Légende de Don Juan*, I, 129.

Juan's hypocrisy is forecast throughout the play: his excuses to Elvire (I, iii), his double-dealing with the two peasant girls (II, iv), his treatment of M. Dimanche (IV, iii), all these scenes reveal the potential hypocrite in Dom Juan. While this behavior may lower him in the eyes of the spectator, there is nothing illogical about it; in fact, Dom Juan habitually plays the hypocrite, at least with women. Molière simply extended this trait to Dom Juan's general conduct when his entire way of life was in jeopardy.

In still one more respect the author expanded his hero's implicit tendencies. With dramatic insight he put an end to the wavering attitude which Dorimon and Villiers had adopted regarding Dom Juan's religious beliefs: Molière turned him into an outspoken unbeliever, because he realized that Dom Juan impresses only when he is either a believer in or an enemy of religion.

Aside from the protagonist, two characters stand out in the play: Sganarelle and Elvire.

Dom Juan's servant resembles Tirso's Catalinón in many ways. Sganarelle is a naïve religious believer who is not free from popular superstitions; he is scandalized by his master's conduct and goes so far as to criticize him, even though he has to resort to subterfuges in order to escape a beating. If he aids Dom Juan, he does so unwillingly; he even tries to warn the peasant girls of the danger they are running. Sganarelle is as necessary beside Dom Juan as Sancho Panza is to Don Quixote. In both cases the servant not only serves as a foil but also as the voice of popular common sense which prevents the entire picture from going out of focus.

Elvire represents an important innovation in the legend. None of Tirso's women leaves much of an impression: they are either coarsely deceived or have selfish motives for giving in to the Burlador. Elvire, however, really loves the seducer for himself and, even though she eventually recognizes him for what he is, this pure and unselfish woman rises above her initial indignation and continues to pray for Dom Juan's salvation. Again Molière has led the way in showing the full extent of his hero's wickedness by having him deceive a woman of real worth. It will be but a short step to think of a woman who might have held Don Juan, as Hoffmann suggests, or of Zorrilla's Doña Inés, who will save the seducer.

Molière's contribution to the Don Juan legend cannot be overestimated: he lifted the subject out of the low state into which it had fallen, he modernized the hero and opened up completely new possibilities by concentrating on the psychological study of the seducer and his situation in society, he endowed Don Juan with the intellect which made a more complex character possible, and he de-emphasized the religious problem, which, outside Spain, would have aroused relatively little interest in theater audiences and would probably have met with disapproval from religious authorities in France.

These changes, as can clearly be seen in retrospect, were necessary if the subject was to survive; yet in dramatic action and moral implication Molière's *Festin de Pierre* does not always compare favorably with Tirso's *Burlador*. Not only is the plot of the French play far less exciting but the hero himself has lost in stature. The atheist fights an idea in which he does not believe; his courage consists in daring to face the disapproval of his society, which is not little. But Tirso's Burlador is "a weak mortal measuring swords with God,"[4] with a God in whom he believes, who is ever-present and who makes himself known by tangible acts. And Tirso's entire play is conceived on a scale of that size. When Molière's Dom Juan drops down the stage trap, there disappears a "grand seigneur méchant homme" who has fascinated us and whom we have come to understand well; but when the Burlador falls dead at the feet of the statue, the terrible voice of God's judgment rings in our ears, a judgment that concerns all of us because it speaks of our salvation.

After Molière the seventeenth century added little to the development of the legend. Molière had to withdraw his *Festin de Pierre* after its fifteenth performance and it was not taken up again in its original form until November 17, 1841, at the Théâtre de l'Odéon. In 1677 Thomas Corneille wrote an imitation of the play in verse, omitting certain scenes (for example that with the beggar) to which objections had been raised.

In 1669 the actor Rosimond presented his play *Le Nouveau Festin de Pierre ou l'Athée foudroyé* at the Théâtre du Marais. This work consists largely of borrowings from Dorimon, Villiers, and Molière, to which little is added. Rosimond emphasizes the atheism and the hypocrisy of his hero, who argues at length on his philosophy of liber-

---

[4] George T. Northup, *An Introduction to Spanish Literature* (Chicago, 1923), p. 281.

tinism by calling nature to his aid. While Molière had preserved the necessary tact and moderation to make his Dom Juan acceptable, Rosimond goes to extremes to give his hero an almost completely evil appearance.

Primarily borrowed from Rosimond, but also from Cicognini, Dorimon, and Villiers, is the *Libertine* of Thomas Shadwell, written in 1676,[5] in which Don John has two companions. But while Rosimond had maintained a last shred of tact, Shadwell presents us with a monster. His Don John has not only been married six times and engaged sixteen times in one month, but when his wives claim their rights, he turns them over to his companions; then, having given his servant orders to bring him the first woman he meets in the streets, he rapes this one, an old maid, with obvious displeasure. To these outrages are added assassination, poisoning, and parricide. He preserves, on the other hand, the appeal to nature of Rosimond's hero and his stubborn courage is super-human.

In Italy, where the actors of the *commedia dell'arte* continued to emphasize the role of Don Juan's servant, the *Convitato di pietra* of Andrea Perrucci might be mentioned. It was first played in 1678, then again in 1684, and reworked by the author in 1690 under the name of *Enrico Prendarca*. The play is little more than an imitation of Cicognini's *Convitato*; its only additions are interminable tirades which, while eloquent, lend to it an appearance of erudition and artificiality.

During the seventeenth and eighteenth centuries, we find in Germany and Holland imitations of French and Italian models and especially puppet plays of no literary value in which Hans Wurst, the sly valet of Don Juan who never understands his master, dominates the scene.

---

[5] The first trace of the Don Juan legend in England is apparently found in Sir Aston Cockain's *The Tragedy of Ovid* (printing date: 1662). The author, who knew Italian and was probably acquainted with the Italian *Ateista fulminato*, has a captain invite a hanged man, who shows up for a very pleasant dinner and asks for a return visit at the gibbet, where the captain and his companion find a table set in black. After another gay meal, the specter has songs sung for his guests and then seizes the captain and drags him away. The scenes in question are iv, iv (invitation), iv, v (supper), and v, iii (dinner at the gibbet).

CHAPTER FIVE

Don Juan in the Eighteenth Century

Jugez-moi donc comme Turenne
ou Frédéric. J'ai forcé à combattre
l'ennemi qui ne voulait que tem-
poriser; je me suis donné, par de
savantes manœuvres, le choix du
terrain et celui des dispositions.[1]

CHODERLOS DE LACLOS,
Les Liaisons dangereuses

The eighteenth century produced only one great Don Juan work: Mozart's *Don Giovanni*. The other treatments of the subject during this century, except for possible influences they may have had on later versions, are hardly worth mentioning.

This temporary eclipse of Don Juan seems quite surprising at first glance, for no other period appears more favorable to a seducer of women. Religious authority is increasingly exposed to attack, a far greater liberty (if not licentiousness) of morals reigns than in the preceding century, women are no longer subject to grave restrictions of conduct or to the over-watchful eyes of jealous husbands, gallantry and wit are the most highly prized attributes in this pleasure-craving society where the sexes mingle freely and on nearly equal terms.

The men spent all their time in increasing the authentic list of their mistresses, while the women strove to snatch away lovers from each other in public; and in these matters, lies often had to make up for what reality could not supply. The husbands, reduced to having to permit what they could have prevented only at the price of a great deal of ridicule, had made the wise decision simply

---

[1] "Judge me therefore as you would judge Turenne or Frederick. I have forced combat upon an enemy who only wanted to temporize; by skillful maneuvering I have gained the choice of terrain and position."

not to live with their wives. Although inhabiting the same home, they never saw each other, they never could be seen in the same carriage, they never were encountered in the same house and, still less of course, in a public place. Briefly, marriage had become an institution useful for one's wealth, but an inconvenience that could be overcome only by eliminating all the obligations involved. While morals lost ground thereby, society gained immensely. . . . Liberty was extremely great.[2]

To be sure, Besenval's description was true only of a portion of upper society; in this group, at any rate, a seducer should certainly have enjoyed great success. A seducer, yes; but not Don Juan. Let us for a moment place the Burlador in this society and it becomes apparent that he would be considered coarse and vulgar, for this it not an age which calls for deceit under the cover of darkness, nor is the seduction of peasant girls considered a great accomplishment.[3] Molière's Dom Juan would be far more at home in this milieu; it is he, in fact, who forecasts the kind of seducer that the eighteenth century will develop, but while Dom Juan did little more than explain his system, the roué will carry it out in practice and add considerably to it.

Strange as it may seem, Don Juan is at his best in a society that keeps its women behind barred windows and permits them to go out only in the company of chaperones. That is why Don Juan was born in seventeenth-century Spain, where contact between the sexes is limited to fiery but hidden glances during promenades, and where duennas watch over their precious charges; where balconies have to be climbed on silk ladders and where black veils blend mysteriously with the dark of night.

In order to understand the fundamental change in actual (and, for all practical purposes, officially recognized) standards of sexual behavior which distinguishes much of the eighteenth century from the seventeenth, we must be aware of the difference in the position of women. Few writers depict the "new woman" with more perspicacity than Crébillon fils.

[2] From the memoirs of the Baron de Besenval, quoted in Crébillon fils, *La Nuit et le moment* (Paris: Le Divan, 1929), pp. xvi–xvii.

[3] By this I do not mean to imply that coarse behavior was unknown in polite society or that, in general, the eighteenth century behaved uniformly as described here. I am concentrating on those aspects of society which affected the seducer. For examples of different behavior, see Edmond and Jules de Goncourt, *La Femme au dix-huitième siècle* (Paris, 1907), pp. 188–89.

"If we are to believe old memoirs" [one of his characters says as he compares the old and new times], "women were then more anxious to inspire respect than desire; and perhaps they gained thereby. It is true that men spoke to them of love less promptly, but the kind of love they aroused was only the more satisfying and durable on account of it. In those days women felt they were duty-bound never to surrender and, indeed, they resisted.

"The women of my time thought from the outset that they could not possibly defend themselves, and because of this attitude they succumbed at the very instant they were attacked. You would tell a woman three times that she was pretty; three times, no more. The first time she would certainly believe you, thank you the second time, and usually reward you by the third time. It even happened sometimes that a man did not have to speak . . . or to be in love: in emergencies he was even excused from being likable."[4]

The eighteenth-century woman achieved a freedom that has rarely been equaled in history, woman suffrage notwithstanding. In that age the woman, if only in self-defense, had to learn quickly how to take care of herself in society and in her relations with men. She had to know how to judge the real value of gallant declarations, how to be coquettish without making a bad impression, how to use her fan, above all, in order to encourage or discourage a man, express pleasure or boredom or, if need be, tap on the fingers of an overly forward suitor. Her important task was to avoid scandals—almost everything else was permissible, but she did not rush blindly into her adventures: contrary to the pale romantic ingénue of the following century, she knew that loves come to an end and that men can be treacherous.

It was this unromantic clearsightedness which, while removing almost completely all surface drama from love affairs, established relations between the sexes on the basis of a game between two nearly equal parties. Again Crébillon fils will best serve to convey the mood of the times in one of his most celebrated passages:

Two people please each other, they take each other. Should they get bored with one another? They part as unceremoniously as they came together. Should they happen to regain their former feelings? They begin again with as much fervor as if it were the first time they exchanged love vows. They part once more and always without quarreling. It is true that

⁴ Crébillon fils, Les Egarements du cœur et de l'esprit (Paris: Le Divan, 1929), pp. 14, 15–16.

love never entered in the least into all that; yet what is love but a desire they took pleasure in exaggerating in their minds, a fluttering of the senses which the vanity of men decided to turn into a virtue? Today we know that there is only such a thing as a whim; and if people still tell each other they are in love, it is far less because they believe this than because it is a more polite way of requesting from each other what they feel they need. Just as they have taken each other without love, so they separate without hatred, and from the slight liking that each has inspired in the other they salvage at least the advantage of always being ready to oblige each other again. Should a lover's unexpected fickleness depress a woman? People scarcely leave her time to feel it. Should reasons of propriety or interest make it inadvisable for her to leave a lover who bores her or who ceases to be likable? All her friends take turns in consoling her for her unfortunate situation. Should a caprice strike her? It is satisfied in a minute. Suppose a man is in any of the circumstances I have just described? He finds the same resources in the gratitude of the women with whom he has been intimate; and I believe, all things considered, that there is much wisdom in sacrificing for so many pleasures some old prejudices which bestow little esteem but a great deal of annoyance upon those who guide their conduct by them.[5]

Obviously, this state of affairs called for an entirely different type of seducer. He no longer has to attack a woman who is entrenched behind a definite set of rules; on the contrary, the struggle takes place in the open field of the drawing room, the weapons are wit, skill, and ingenuity, and if he does not watch his step, the seducer may find that the woman has turned the tables on him.

Although France dominates the century in this respect, the English too had produced a seducer, and we find him in Samuel Richardson's epistolary novel *Clarissa Harlowe* (1747–48). Its hero Lovelace is usually cited as the seducer par excellence, but even though he does represent a new kind of Don Juan, a closer look at the novel will show that he does not entirely deserve his reputation; the novel is, in fact, far more the story of Clarissa's steadfast virtue than of Lovelace's seductive skill.

Clarissa Harlowe can be divided into two main parts, the dividing point being the heroine's definite escape from Lovelace. Only the first part concerns us, for in the second Lovelace does little more than implore Clarissa's pardon and accuse himself, with now and then an outburst of impotent threats. This is no longer the same man who

---

[5] Crébillon fils, *La Nuit et le moment*, pp. 18–19.

began so brilliantly by taking advantage of Clarissa's predicament, caused by her family which is about to force a repugnant husband on her. During that time Lovelace displays unusual resourcefulness. He compels Clarissa to elope with him by means of a very carefully conceived plan: having foreseen her reluctance to escape, he has his helper beat at the locked door which makes Clarissa believe her father and brother have discovered them, and before she can recover her wits, Lovelace has pulled her away to a waiting carriage.

Lovelace explains his purpose in a letter to his friend Belford. He is apparently going to test whether Clarissa's reputation as a paragon of virtue is merited:

If she be a *woman*, and *love* me, I shall surely catch her once tripping: for love was ever a traitor to its harbourer: and love *within*, and I *without*, she will be more than woman, as the poet says, or I *less* than man, if I succeed not.

Now, Belford, all is out. The lady is mine; shall be *more* mine. Marriage, I see, is in my power, now *she* is so; else perhaps it had not. If I can have her *without* marriage, who can blame me for trying? if *not*, great will be her glory, and my future confidence. And well will she merit the sacrifice I shall make her of my liberty; and from all her sex honours next to divine, for giving proof, "that there was once a woman whose virtue no trials, no stratagems, no temptations, even from the man she hated not, could overpower."

This letter announces the new eighteenth-century theme, which changes from the unilateral attack by the seducer to a contest between the sexes. Clarissa, to be sure, is a long way from being a Mme de Merteuil, but she is neither so naïve as the victims of Tirso's and Molière's Don Juans nor so ripe for seduction as Madame Bovary. She sees through Lovelace's assurances of love, his cajoling, and his postures, and speculates rather why he has not repeated his marriage proposal after first having been so bent upon "speedy solemnization."

There is, indeed, almost no trial, stratagem, or temptation to which Lovelace does not expose Clarissa. He lodges her with female accomplices, has others impersonate his respectable aunts, intercepts and falsifies letters, keeps her like a prisoner—all this and more; yet Clarissa, though frightened, resists all his advances. Even her eventual dishonor testifies to the strength of her virtue, for although he holds all the trump cards, Lovelace is forced to resort to drugs in order to subdue her momentarily. Needless to say, this loses him Clarissa forever, and no amount of pleading by himself and by his very virtuous family can induce her to marry him thereafter.

Lovelace differs from Don Juan in many ways. Perhaps he resembles him before meeting Clarissa, for we are told that Lovelace "had served twenty and twenty women as bad or worse," but our information goes no further. In the course of the novel, Lovelace devotes his entire energy to seducing *one* woman only; he even falls passionately in love with her—and that Don Juan would not do; nor would he give himself over to regret and repentance.

There is no doubt as to who is the victor in the contest announced by Lovelace. Clarissa has not only withstood all his machinations but she also ends in an apotheosis, pitied by everybody except her family, adored and respected by ex-libertine Belford, and besought by Lovelace and his noble family to marry the repentant seducer.

It is usually claimed that Choderlos de Laclos, in his *Liaisons dangereuses,* lifted what present-day newspaper jargon might have called the "sugar curtain" that had veiled a great deal of eighteenth-century reality behind a pretty series of rococo tableaux in the manner of Watteau and Fragonard. The same claim can be made for a much earlier novelist—Crébillon fils.[6] His novel *Les Egarements du cœur et de l'esprit* (1736–38) contains two characters who anticipate Mme de Merteuil and Valmont of *Les Liaisons dangereuses*: Mme de Lursay and Versac; the former, although more mellow and human than Laclos's heroine, is no less skillful in the delicate task of bringing a younger and inexperienced man to declare his love. Of special interest to us is Versac, who impresses us at first as a consummate fop, a *petit-maître,* but who turns out to be a perceptive Machiavelli in the field of his chosen activity. While initiating the naïve hero of the novel into

[6] It is difficult to understand why modern critics, who take pride in their objectivity, continue to accept the judgment of Crébillon fils as erotic, or even pornographic, a judgment pronounced by nineteenth-century critics who were unable to separate their personal moral attitude from aesthetic considerations. Those who admire Musset's plays and the novels of Constant, Stendhal, and Proust will find much enjoyment in store for them in Crébillon's works.

I am indebted to Robert-Peter Aby for his study, "The Problem of Crébillon *fils*" (unpublished Ph.D. dissertation, Stanford University, 1955).

the art of seduction, Versac exposes his system which is based on six points:[7]

First, one must eagerly embrace all the fads of the moment, no matter how ridiculous they may seem. Fads, Versac explains, "must be assumed while they are in vogue; often it is just as fruitless to take them up when people are beginning to tire of them as to continue them when they are absolutely out of date. . . . But it does not matter what we call it, so long as it serves to make an impression: while a fad is popular, everybody finds it graceful, charming, and witty; and only when people grow tired of it do they call it by the name it really deserves."

"But" [the young man asks] "how can you tell that a fad is beginning to go out of fashion?"

"By the scant attention women pay to it," he replies.

Second rule: you must be different at any price.

You must realize at the outset [Versac continues] that by following well-known principles, you will never be anything but an ordinary man; that there is something new about you only when you deviate from normal behavior; that people admire only what strikes their fancy and that extravagance produces this effect on them. Therefore you simply cannot be too extravagant—that is to say, you cannot go far enough in trying to be unlike everybody else, both in your ideas and in your behavior. A quirk which only you possess will bring you more honor than a merit you share with someone else.

Third principle: study other people without revealing yourself.

You must learn how to disguise your character so perfectly that no one can discover it. To the art of deceiving others you must add that of seeing through them, of always trying to discern, underneath the appearance people want to give, what they really are. People are quite wrong in wishing to judge everything by their own character. Do not appear to be offended by the vices you are shown, and never take pride in having discovered those which people think they have hidden from you. It is often better to give a bad impression of your intelligence than to show all of it, to conceal beneath an inattentive and silly air any worthwhile ideas you may have and to sacrifice your vanity to your interest.

Fourth point: be overbearing and overly self-confident; this does not contradict the third principle which, on the contrary, implements it.

---

[7] The quotations below are taken from *Les Egarements du cœur et de l'esprit*, p. 262 and *passim*.

There must be a certain kind of confidence reflected in our eyes, our tone
of voice, our gestures, and even the respect we pay to others. Above all, let
us always talk and speak well of ourselves; let us not fear to say repeatedly
that we possess superior merit. There are a thousand men whom people
consider superior only because they never cease saying so. Do not be disturbed in the least by the cold and disgusted way people will listen to you,
or even by the reproach that you never step out of the limelight. Any man
who blames you for speaking too much about yourself does so only because
you do not always leave him the time to speak of himself.

Point five, assume the *bon ton* of good society.

Whoever wants to speak in the proper tone of good society must avoid
saying things frequently that show thought: however naturally he may express these things, however little vanity he may derive from them, people
find in them a marked affectation to speak differently from everybody else
and they say of a man who is so unfortunate as to assume this manner not
that he is intelligent but that he *thinks* he is.

Since the spirit of the times is exclusively devoted to speaking ill of others,
people have endeavored to express this in a very particular way and those
who possess good breeding can be recognized more readily by their way of
vilifying others than by anything else. . . . Well-bred people leave to the
common rabble both the task of thinking and the fear of thinking incor-
rectly. Convinced as they are that the more cultivated the mind the less
natural it is, they have of their own will limited themselves to a few frivolous
ideas around which they flutter incessantly; or if, perchance, they know
something, this knowledge is so superficial and they value it so little that they
could not possibly be ridiculed on account of it. As nothing is more base for
a woman than to be virtuous, so there is nothing more indecent for a man
of good breeding than to be taken for learned. The extreme ignorance to
which this custom seems to condemn him is, however, all the more surprising
since he is at the same time required not to hesitate about any decision. . . .

To be ignorant of everything and to believe he knows everything; not
seeing anything, whatever it be, without scorning or praising it to excess;
believing himself equally capable in serious and humorous subjects; never
fearing ridicule yet being ridiculous all the time; turning his phrases with
finesse yet expressing infantile ideas; proclaiming absurd things, maintaining
them, saying them all over again—that is the mark of good breeding in high
society.

Finally, make a noisy display in order to conquer women.

Of all the oddities that rule the day, a noisy display is the one which most
generally overawes people, especially women. They consider as true only

those passions which begin by carrying them away completely. The sort of attachment formed sometimes by the habit of seeing each other regularly appears almost always to them as a mere matter of convenience to which they are obliged to pay but little attention. An impression made upon them gradually never acts vividly upon them. In order to love ardently, they must be unable to know what has aroused their feelings. They have been told that a passion, if it is to be strong, must begin by making them extremely disturbed, and they have believed this too long ever to overcome the idea. Nothing is more apt to create this enchanting disturbance in their soul than that self-intoxication which, as it makes you risk all, animates your charm or covers your defects. A woman admires, is astonished, becomes enchanted, and, because she refuses to reflect, she believes your charm does not leave her enough time to do so. If, perchance, she thinks of the resistance she could put up, she does this merely in order to convince herself that it would be useless to try and that one should not resist something so strong, so unexpected, so extraordinary as love at first sight. This is basically a rather ingenious pretext for surrendering promptly without giving a bad impression of herself, since there is not a man who is not more flattered by inspiring a violent love suddenly than by bringing it about gradually.

These excerpts should suffice to show that Crébillon fils is not a mere writer of frivolous and erotic anecdotes but a perceptive observer and critic of the society he lived in. Apart from Marivaux's best plays, I know of no other literary source which enables us to savor the eighteenth century "tone" as completely as *Les Egarements du cœur et de l'esprit*.

The eighteenth-century *roué* finds his most perfect expression in Choderlos de Laclos's *Les Liaisons dangereuses* (1782). This epistolary novel was for almost a century considered so immoral that public sale was prohibited by law. Only in relatively recent times has the book received its due, and its place as a classic work seems no longer in dispute.

Valmont, the hero, is involved with three women: the virtuous and pious Présidente de Tourvel, whom he wants to add to his conquests; Mme de Merteuil, with whom he once had an affair which he wants to renew; and Cécile de Volanges, a young girl fresh out of convent school who is to marry a man against whom both Valmont and Mme de Merteuil bear a grudge.

It is Valmont, far more than Lovelace, who carries out Dom Juan's plan of day-by-day progress in seduction. When, during the absence of her husband, the Présidente de Tourvel is staying at his aunt's country home, Valmont begins his maneuvers by joining the ladies in a card game; next he arranges a walk during which he is forced to carry the Présidente over a ditch, finally he performs an act of charity to impress her, and only then he declares his love. He might have taken advantage of her momentary confusion, but Valmont eschews an easy victory.

"My plan," he writes to Mme de Merteuil, ". . . is to have her *feel* thoroughly the value and extent of each of the sacrifices she is going to make for me; not to lead her on so quickly that remorse cannot follow her; to make her virtue expire in slow agony; to fix her attention unceasingly on that distressing spectacle; and to grant her the happiness of having me in her arms only after she has been forced to admit this desire freely." (Letter LXX)

By patiently taking advantage of every opportunity, Valmont weakens the resistance of his virtuous victim until she flees in despair. But by then it is too late, and the Présidente has to admit her love. To renew contact Valmont turns her confessor into an unsuspecting go-between; in her belief that he has been converted and disdains her, the Présidente is an easy victim when the seducer visits her. It is true that, as happened with Lovelace and Clarissa, Valmont takes the Présidente while she is in a swoon, but this condition is not brought on by drugs; it is rather the effect of an overly strong emotion, or perhaps it is even a weakness to which the Présidente consciously gives way because her Roman virtue could not unbend otherwise.

The conquest of young Cécile de Volanges, on the other hand, hardly adds to Valmont's glory and is undertaken quite brutally, partly in order to compensate himself for the patience he has to employ with the Présidente, partly because Mme de Merteuil demands it of him.

Valmont may be one of the greatest seducers in literature, but he is no match, either in adroitness or in wickedness, for Mme de Merteuil. It is she who holds the strings that control all the puppets around her. Having formed herself from early youth on, Mme de Merteuil, after her husband's death, has managed to lead exactly the kind of life she wants to while at the same time enjoying a splendid reputation. She changes lovers at will but not until she has found out something compromising about each; as for her reputation, it is assured by keeping assiduous company with old ladies. Having rid herself of emotions, she can nevertheless simulate any of them. What chance has even a famous seducer like Prévan, who counts among his feats the victory over the three "inseparable women," against such an opponent? Far from fleeing this formidable threat, Mme de Merteuil eagerly enters into the contest, leads Prévan on by giving the appearance of demure resignation to defeat, even enjoys his embraces, and then has him thrown out of her home by her servants who quickly spread the story that Prévan hid in the house in order to overcome her by violence.

Even Valmont is but a pawn in her game. She achieves her vengeance on Cécile's future husband through him, she forces him to sacrifice the Présidente, to whom he is more strongly attached than he is willing to admit, and she tops it all off by refusing to give herself to him as the promised reward for this sacrifice. It is she too who directs the foil of the young man who finally kills Valmont in a duel. What does it matter that in the end she loses her lawsuit and much of her wealth, that all is found out, that she has to flee, disfigured by smallpox? She has had her greatest triumphs—there is nothing left for her to conquer.

For us who, whether we like it or not, are the heirs of romanticism, it is almost impossible to recapture the full flavor of the atmosphere which pervades *Les Liaisons dangereuses*. The very terms used by its characters have to be retranslated to fit the attitude of Valmont and Mme de Merteuil. They have certain "principles" of which they are proud and which they consider inviolable. The most important of these is always to maintain self-control, so as never to be overcome by passion; another is to devote themselves to conquests over the other sex in order to prove their superiority and add to their glory. Hence terms such as *gloire, volupté, amour* take on meanings radically different from both seventeenth-century and present-day usage. Love is described by Valmont as "that pusillanimous passion," and Mme de Merteuil declares: "Love, which is glorified as the source of our pleasures, is at best merely the pretext for them."

What then is the actual source of their pleasures? It is to lead a difficult campaign to a successful conclusion, to make use of their gifts the way a general goes about waging an important battle—but for mere personal motives: to satisfy their vanity as well as their physical desires and, perhaps no less important, to escape boredom.

Les Liaisons dangereuses far transcends the mere description of sexual intrigues. According to Turnell, "Laclos' theme is the tragedy of the Rational Man, the man who was carefully conditioned through the removal of all moral scruples and the sense of guilt, but inevitably condemned to action in a very limited field. The novel is a masterpiece because it gives final expression to this phase of human experience."[8] Turnell is to be commended for disputing opinions which see in Laclos's characters representatives of sadism, Satanism, or *le mal*. These certainly are not the charming creatures who play Marivaux's game of love and chance, for we often see the ugly grimace behind their gracious smiles; but, on the other hand, Laclos's characters possess a sense of fun which prevents them from appearing demoniacal.[9]

The over-all atmosphere of the novel is that of a complicated chess game in which two champions, who have once played to a draw, are constantly looking for new opponents to take on. They play the game as only connoisseurs would, even simulating defeat in order to reward an exceptionally good move,[10] increasing the stakes and the obstacles in order to put fresh excitement into the game, flying from victory to victory, until the two champions come inevitably together again for the decisive match.

The stakes are high, indeed, especially for the woman. One wrong move and she will lose her reputation or, worse still, be forced to withdraw from society and spend the rest of her days in a convent. But these very risks lend a new thrill to what would otherwise be a mere frivolous entertainment, and they actually contribute to making the woman a superior player in the game. At least, this is true in the case of Mme de Merteuil, who defeats Valmont with great ease because, whereas she has achieved perfect control over her emotions, in him

---

[8] Martin Turnell, *The Novel in France* (New York, 1950), p. 76.

[9] This carefree sense of gay escapades can be found especially in Letter LXXI and also in Letter LXXXV, which describes Mme de Merteuil's tricking of Prévan.

[10] Cf. Mme de Merteuil's statement: "As for me, I admit that one of the things that flatter me most is a quick and well-executed attack in which one move follows another in an orderly manner but with rapidity; which never places us in the painfully embarrassing situation of having to make up for a clumsiness of which, on the contrary, we ought to have taken advantage; which manages to maintain an appearance of violence even in the things we grant and to flatter skillfully our two favorite passions—the glory of defense and the pleasure of defeat. I admit that this talent, which is rarer than people think, has always given me pleasure, even when I did not surrender to it; and it has sometimes happened that I have given in solely in order to reward the man." (Letter X)

there remains "a rest of sensibility which makes him inferior to Merteuil."[11]

Characteristically enough, it is a commoner who turns out to be
the Don Juan of the last quarter of the eighteenth century: Rétif de la
Bretonne. In his long autobiographical novels, primarily *Le Paysan
perverti* (1775), *La Paysanne pervertie* (1784), and *Monsieur Nicolas*
(1794–97), Rétif parades before us an almost unbroken series of
amorous adventures. Born in 1734 as the son of a rather well-to-do
peasant family, Nicolas-Edme Rétif de la Bretonne became a printer;
the bulk of his exploits took place during his apprenticeship in Auxerre,
around 1755, although they continued after his unhappy marriage in
1760 and during his subsequent life in Paris where he wrote his volumi-
nous production.

Rétif takes great delight in pouring out his confessions. He adores
and idolizes not one but two women (Jeanette Rousseau and Mme
Parangon, his employer's wife) and is haunted by a sense of guilt after
his conquests—but only afterward, for during his fits of passion Rétif
is the prey of his overpowering vitality. Thus, almost crazed by his
long worship of Mme Parangon and her perhaps unconscious coquetry,
he took her by violence, followed by remorse and sincere repentance;[12]
Toinette, the nice and virtuous chambermaid and Rétif's student, is
likewise overcome in spite of his good intentions toward her. "I was
coming back from my father's, it is true," Rétif explains, "but during
the seven leagues covered swiftly by foot, I had filled my mind with
dreams of love; I arrived drunk with the voluptuousness induced by the
open air in anyone who is strong and in good health."[13] And that takes
care of Toinette. The only woman Rétif never touched was Jeanette
Rousseau with whom he had fallen in love in his adolescence. As for
the rest of his women, they pass by monotonously, hardly leaving any
impression at all. Vividly desired at the moment, they surrender almost
without struggle and do not show any anger, even though most of these
affairs result in pregnancies.[14] Fortunately Gaudet d'Arras, Rétif's
wealthy and mysterious friend, stands ever ready to take care of both
mother and child.

---

[11] "Notes de Baudelaire sur *Les Liaisons dangereuses*," in Choderlos de Laclos,
Œuvres complètes (Bibliothèque de la Pléiade), p. 743.

[12] *Monsieur Nicolas* (Paris, 1883), V, 30–43.

[13] *Ibid.*, V, 212.

[14] Rétif enumerates twenty such cases, but he was given to exaggerating.

In a rather curious way Rétif forecasts the nineteenth-century Don Juan who seeks in all women the one he has once perceived, albeit in a dream.

Colette and young Edmée attached me so fully to Jeanette that never, during all the time I loved them, did I cease to feel my heart throb at the memory of my beautiful Rousseau. . . . How many men, if they looked within themselves the way I scrutinize my poor heart, would find that they have never loved but one woman, even though they may have pursued and possessed several![15]

What had happened to the Don Juan legend itself during all this time? It had not altogether disappeared but had rather been relegated to serve for popular entertainment. In France the subject had been taken over by the strolling players of the fairs, where vaudeville productions in the style of the Italian *commedia dell'arte*, with verses sung to popular tunes of the day, enjoyed considerable success. The earliest of these, Le Tellier's *Festin de Pierre* (1713), used a plot made up of the Italian scenario and scenes from Dorimon and Villiers. Le Tellier's production was imitated in numerous versions of equally slight literary value, some of which were still performed as late as the early nineteenth century.

In Spain Molière's play received but scant attention, for the religious attitude of its hero would have scandalized the public; instead, two rather poor dramatic imitations of Tirso continued the Don Juan legend in that country.

The first of these, *La venganza en el sepulcro*, by Alonso Córdoba y Maldonado, variously dated from 1660–70 to the last years of the seventeenth century, exists only in manuscript form.[16] The author generally adopts Tirso's plot but achieves a greater concentration by focusing attention on the rivalry between Don Juan and de la Mota over Doña Ana. Don Juan, however, is not a true Burlador, for he actually falls in love with Ana and attempts to overcome her reluctance to marry him by every means from tenderness to brutality. Ana, in turn, feels attracted to Don Juan, even though she suspects that he, and not Mota, has killed her father. She therefore declares that the man

---

[15] *Monsieur Nicolas*, IV, 85.

[16] A study of this play may be found in José Franquesa y Gomis, "*La venganza en el sepulcro*, comedia inedita de D. Alonso de Córdoba y Maldonado," in *Homenaje a Menéndez y Pelayo* (Madrid, 1899), I, 253–68.

she chooses will have to avenge her father. "None but I can take this vengeance on me," Don Juan brags. He shows a similar attitude by insisting upon a duel with the statue. "It is up to God to avenge me," the statue proclaims, and Don Juan disappears amidst flames.

While Córdoba y Maldonado's play is quite mediocre, it introduces several innovations which point to many of the aspects which the nineteenth century will develop more fully. The fact that Don Juan gives a brief recital of his life indicates a desire to delve more deeply into the motivations of the character; he not only falls in love and seeks marriage, but instead of betraying women, he is held in check by Ana, who at times seems to be making a fool of him. The role of Ana (i.e., the Commander's daughter), already enlarged by Dorimon and Villiers, attains here full size and her wavering feelings toward Don Juan followed by tears over his punishment establish tendencies that will come to a climax in Hoffmann and Zorrilla; finally, remarkable in Spain, Don Juan dies without even an attempt to repent.

Antonio de Zamora, in *No hay deuda que no se pague y convidado de piedra*, returns to the tradition by having Don Juan die at least with a plea for pardon, for his last words are, "If God takes my life, may He save my soul." But before that moment arrives, Don Juan engages in a rather excessive number of duels: with students who disturb his visit to Beatriz, an ex-mistress; with Beatriz's brother, whom he fights several times and finally kills; and with Filiberto, who here is a combination of Tirso's Octavio and Mota. The central plot, which deals with Don Juan's efforts to add Ana to his list of conquests, is well developed, but episodic scenes of no importance distort the action; and the portrayal of Don Juan as a quarrel-seeking ruffian who nevertheless has spells of fidelity leaves much to be desired. The play indicates the tendency to outdo what has been previously produced by exaggerating the spectacular traits in the legend to the point of distortion. Zamora used the *Burlador* as basis for his play, but the importance given to Ana points to Córdoba y Maldonado; the influence of Dorimon, Villiers, and possibly Molière (whose Elvire may have served as model for Beatriz) are also present. Zamora's play, which was published in 1744 but may have been performed as much as twenty years earlier, is condemned by Manuel de Revilla as "the most unfortunate of all the imitations of Tirso."

In Italy the legend did not fare much better. Goldoni's play *Don Giovanni Tenorio ossia il dissoluto* was first performed in Venice during the carnival of 1736. In his play the author makes thinly veiled allusions to a personal experience, for his mistress, the actress Elisabeth Passalacqua, had betrayed him with Vittalba, another actor. Goldoni wanted to replace the supernatural elements by real ones; he even blamed Molière for having maintained the talking statue, which appears in Goldoni's play only as a silent bust, a last concession to the requirements of tradition. The result of this modernization was not a happy one: Goldoni, the creator of middle-class characters, was ill-suited to deal with a nobleman of Don Juan's stature. He reduces the grandiose Burlador to an ordinary, vulgar seducer who does not have the courage to admit his vices, who cajoles women, who even sheds tears; in short, Goldoni offers the portrayal of a seducer on whom he is taking personal revenge. The denouement is modern too: Don Juan no longer dies from the handshake of the statue, but he is struck by lightning (during a clear day, it is true), leaving the spectator with nothing but disgust and contempt for him. Of some interest is the role of Anna who, as Chimène, continues to be attracted to Don Juan even though he has killed her father; but Goldoni does not develop this trait. The main reason for the success of the play was no doubt the public knowledge of the episode from the author's life referred to in the play. The actress Elisabeth Passalacqua, charged with the role of the shepherdess Elisa (Goldoni thinly disguises himself as the shepherd Carino), refused to play it at first and did so only when she was threatened with dismissal. We are assured that she played the part to perfection.

More than a hundred years had passed without an important Don Juan version being produced; the subject seemed dead except for an occasional unimportant play and some operas, most of the latter in Italy. Then, in 1787, a work appeared that was not only to create greater interest in the Don Juan legend than it had ever received before but also to give it a new direction—Mozart's *Don Giovanni.*

CHAPTER SIX

Mozart's *Don Giovanni*

Mi pare sentir odor di femina.
MOZART,
Don Giovanni

"Mozart is the greatest among classic composers and . . . his *Don Juan* deserves the highest place among all the classic works of art."[1]

Mozart's opera *Il dissoluto punito ossia il Don Giovanni* has found many enthusiastic admirers since its first performance in Prague on October 29, 1787, but few have been more fervently devoted to it than were Søren Kierkegaard, who wrote these lines, and E. T. A. Hoffmann, whose interpretation of *Don Giovanni* began a new phase in the evolution of the legend. Time has borne out the judgment of these men, for today one frequently hears the claim that *Don Giovanni* is the greatest opera ever written.

Those who unhesitatingly give their preference to Mozart's opera may not find it equally easy to justify their choice. Some of them will say that the music is beautiful, but the same can be said of *The Marriage of Figaro*; others will state that, like Hoffmann, they are completely carried away by a performance of the work. Impressive as such testimony may be, it is of little value in explaining the superiority of *Don Giovanni* over other operas for which the same statements can be made by equally enthusiastic admirers.

In this dilemma we turn again to Kierkegaard, who, while far from being objective, has probably delved most deeply into the subject.

Kierkegaard sets out by defining what he considers a perfect work

[1] Søren Kierkegaard, *Either-Or*, transl. by David F. Swenson and Lillian Marvin Swenson (Princeton University Press, 1949), I, 52. Subsequent quotations of Kierkegaard are taken from the section entitled "The Immediate Stages of the Erotic or The Musical Erotic," *ibid.*, pp. 35–110.

of art. Such a masterpiece can be created, he says, only when an ideal author finds a subject that is ideally suited to him; hence "it is fortunate that the most distinguished epic subject fell to the lot of Homer; . . . [and] that the subject, which is perhaps the only strictly musical subject, in the deeper sense, that life affords, fell to—Mozart." (pp. 37–38)

Next Kierkegaard poses a number of questions which are obviously so arranged as to prove his point but which, nevertheless, present some penetrating views not only about Mozart's opera but about the arts in general. We may be able to follow Kierkegaard's chain of reasoning more readily if we consider his arguments one by one.

What is a classical work?

It is one that contains "the absolute harmony of the two forces, form and content." (p. 39) While "all classic productions stand equally high, because each one stands infinitely high" (p. 40), a classification among them could be based on uniqueness of such nature that the work cannot be reproduced. This uniqueness, contrary to what we might expect at first thought, is not to be found in works rich in ideas and style; for "the more abstract and void of content the idea is, the more abstract and hence the more poverty-stricken the medium is, the greater the probability is that a repetition will be impossible; the greater the probability is that when the idea has once obtained expression, then it has found it once for all." (p. 43)

This definition gives rise to two immediate questions: Which is the most abstract medium? Which is the most abstract idea?

Regarding the most abstract medium, Kierkegaard replies it is the one farthest removed from language, which is the most concrete medium because it is most closely associated with "history," i.e., with a particular period. Thus "Homer is indeed the classic epic poet, but just because the epic idea is a concrete idea, and because the medium is language, it so happens that in the section of the classics which contains the epic, there are many epics conceivable, which are all equally classic, because history constantly furnishes us with new epic material." (p. 44) Conclusion: the most abstract medium is music.

As for the most abstract idea imaginable, it is sensuous-erotic genius when expressed in all its immediacy. "But in what medium is this idea expressible? Solely in music. It cannot be expressed in sculpture, for it is a sort of inner qualification of inwardness; nor in painting, for it cannot be apprehended in precise outlines; it is an energy, a storm, impatience, passion, and so on, in all their lyrical quality, yet so that it does not exist in one moment but in a succession of moments, . . . for it has not yet advanced to words, but moves always in an immediacy. Hence it cannot be represented in poetry. The only medium which can express it is music. Music has, namely, its moment in time, but it does not pass away in time except in an unessential sense. It cannot express the historical in the temporal process. The perfect unity of this idea and the corresponding form we have in Mozart's *Don Juan.*" (p. 45)

It remains now to prove the last statement, to wit: that Mozart's *Don Giovanni* is the most perfect expression possible of the most abstract idea (sensuous-erotic genius in all its immediacy) by means of the most abstract medium (music).

To begin with, Kierkegaard finds three immediate stages of the erotic in Mozart's operas.

The first is represented by Cherubino in *The Marriage of Figaro.* Considered as a mythical figure rather than as an individual, in Cherubino "the sensual awakens, not yet to movement, but to a hushed tranquillity; not to joy and gladness, but to a deep melancholy. Desire is not yet awake, it is only a gloomy foreboding. In desire there is always present the object of desire, which rises up and manifests itself in a bewildered twilight." (p. 61)

In the second stage, personified by Papageno in *The Magic Flute,* desire is the awakening after the dream. "But this movement of the sensual, this earthquake, splits the desire and its object infinitely asunder for the moment. . . . The result of this separation is that desire is pulled out of its substantial rest in itself, and consequently the object no longer falls under the qualifications of substantiality, but disperses itself in a manifold." (p. 64) Whereas in the first stage desire is defined as dreaming, in the second it is seeking: Papageno discovers.

"The first stage desired the one ideally, the second stage desired the individual under the qualification of the manifold; the third stage [Don Juan] is a synthesis of these two. Desire has its absolute object in the individual, it desires the individual absolutely." (p. 68)

Now, to return to Kierkegaard's central argument, the most abstract idea was defined as sensual genius, but the highest degree of sensual genius is found in the seducer. That term, however, must be used in a special sense when applied to Don Juan.

To be a seducer requires a certain amount of reflection and consciousness, and as soon as this is present, then it is proper to speak of cunning and intrigues and crafty plans. This consciousness is lacking in Don Juan. There-

fore, he does not seduce. He desires, and this desire acts seductively. To that
extent he seduces. He enjoys the satisfaction of desire; as soon as he has
enjoyed it, he seeks a new object, and so on endlessly. . . . To be a
seducer, he needs time in advance in which to lay his plans, and time afterward
in which to become conscious of his act. A seducer, therefore, ought to be
possessed of a power Don Juan does not have—the power of eloquence. As
soon as we grant him eloquence he ceases to be musical, and the aesthetic
interest becomes an entirely different matter. . . . (p. 80)

But what is this force then by which Don Juan seduces? 'It is the power
of desire, the energy of the sensual desire. He desires in every woman the
whole of womanhood, and therein lies the sensually idealizing power with
which he at once embellishes and overcomes his prey. . . . (p. 81) He
desires sensually, he seduces with the demoniac power of sensuality, he seduces everyone. The word, the speech, are not for him, for then he becomes
a reflective individual. Thus he does not have existence at all, but hurries in
a perpetual vanishing, precisely like music, about which it is true that it is over
as soon as it has ceased to sound, and only comes into being again, when it
again sounds. (pp. 82–83)

I am not sure that Kierkegaard's arguments will completely convince anyone who was not in agreement with him at the outset, but, if
nothing else, he does make a strong case for his opinion that Don Juan
can be perfectly expressed only in music. We shall have occasion to
return to Kierkegaard's analysis of the opera after we consider its plot.[2]

Most readers of this book, I trust, have seen Mozart's *Don Giovanni,* but surely no one has seen or heard it as E. T. A. Hoffmann did.
Since his interpretation of Mozart's opera is of paramount importance
in the subsequent development of the Don Juan legend, I shall quote
Hoffmann's account of a performance he witnessed.[3]

In the andante [of the overture] I was seized by the dreadful chill of
the infernal *regno al pianto;* my mind was penetrated by the horror-inspir-

[2] For some objections to Kierkegaard's approach to *Don Giovanni,* see Chap. XIX
("Kierkegaard on Mozart and Music") in W. J. Turner, *Mozart: The Man and
his Works* (Doubleday Anchor Book, A 24, 1954), pp. 332–47. Turner's criticism
of Kierkegaard, while often quite valid, fails to take into account the Danish philosopher's point that music is best qualified to convey the *immediate* expression of the
erotic.

[3] The account is translated from Hoffmann's short story *Don Juan,* as contained
in *E.T.A. Hoffmanns sämtliche Werke* (Munich and Leipzig, 1912), I, 87–103.
I have indicated in brackets the parts of the plot omitted by Hoffmann without
which the action would not be clear to those who do not know *Don Giovanni* very
well. Translations from the Italian have likewise been added by me.

ing presentiment of terror. The triumphant fanfare in the seventh measure of the allegro seemed to me like joyful blasphemy; I saw fiery demons stretch their red-hot claws—towards the life of gay people who were dancing merrily on the thin cover of the bottomless pit. I saw clearly in my imagination the conflict between human nature and the unknown, monstrous powers that hover about man espying the moment when they can drag him to his ruin.

Finally the storm abates; the curtain rises. It is pitch-dark. Leporello, freezing and ill-humored, wrapped in his cloak, walks to and fro in front of the pavilion. *Notte e giorno faticar* [Night and day I have to slave]. . . . Suddenly Don Giovanni storms out; behind him Donna Anna, clinging to his coat. What a sight! She could be taller, more slender, and her gait more majestic; but her face! Eyes that flash love, anger, hate, despair like so many brilliant sparks emanating from one focus; eyes that burn like Greek fire through and through! Her dark hair, in braids, undulates in curly waves down her neck. Her white nightgown betrays charms dangerous to gaze upon. Her heart, gripped by the terrible event, beats violently. And now—what a voice! *Non sperar se non m'uccidi* [Hope not to escape unless you kill me]. The tones, cast out of ethereal metal, flash like lightning through the storm of the orchestra. In vain Don Giovanni tries to free himself. Does he really want to? Then why does he not push the woman back with a heavy blow and flee? Does the evil deed make him powerless or is it the inner conflict between love and hate that robs him of courage and strength?

The old papa has paid with his life for being stupid enough to attack this powerful opponent in the dark; Don Giovanni and Leporello step forward while conversing in recitative. Don Giovanni takes off his coat and now he appears gorgeously dressed in red velvet with silver embroidery. A strong, splendid figure; his face displays masculine beauty: a distinguished nose, piercing eyes, softly-shaped lips. For a second a strange muscle movement above his eyebrows gives him a satanic appearance which, without depriving him of his beauty, inspires an involuntary shudder. It seems as if he could practice the magic art of the serpent, as if women, once he has looked at them, can no longer do without him, so that, driven by a sinister power, they rush toward their own destruction.

Leporello, tall and thin, clad in a striped red and white vest, a small red coat, and white hat with red feather, bustles about him. His features are at once good-natured, knavish, lascivious, and ironically impertinent; his black eyebrows form a strange contrast with his grayish hair and beard. It is evident that the old fellow is worthy of being Don Juan's helpful accomplice. They have scaled the wall just in time.

Torches. Donna Anna and Don Ottavio appear: he a delicate, overdressed fop of twenty-one at most. Being Anna's bridegroom, he probably lives in the house, since he could be summoned so swiftly; he could have rushed to the scene to save the old man at the initial sounds of combat, but he first had to spruce up. Besides, he was none too anxious to venture out into the night.

Ma qual mai s'offre, o dei, spettacolo funeste agli occhi miei! [Oh, what a dreadful sight my eyes behold!] There is more in the horrifying, heart-rending tones of this recitative and duet than Anna's despair over Don Giovanni's terrible crime which threatens him with ruin besides resulting in her father's death. More than this wrings these sounds from her fear-stricken breast: only a ruinous and fatal inner struggle can produce them.

Elvira enters the scene. She is tall and skinny; her face shows traces of great but wilted beauty. As she scolds the treacherous Don Giovanni with *Tu nido d'inganni* [You nest of deceit], and the compassionate Leporello remarks quite aptly: *parla come un libro stampato* [she talks just like a book], I thought I heard someone close to me. . . .

[During this interruption Leporello sings his famous catalogue aria *Madamina.* Don Giovanni attempts to seduce Zerlina as they sing the duet *La ci darem la mano,* and Anna tells Ottavio she has recognized the voice of the man who killed her father. Don Giovanni is making preparations for the wedding ball he is giving for Masetto and Zerlina, whom he still desires to conquer.]

In his wild aria *Fin ch'han dal vino* Don Giovanni bares his innermost and rent being as he gives vent to his contempt for the insignificant people around him, whose only purpose is to serve his pleasures and into whose dull life he interferes with ruinous consequences.

The masks appear, their terzetto is a prayer that rises to heaven in pure, beaming rays. Now the middle curtain rises on a scene of merrymaking with the sound of glasses touched as the peasants and all kinds of masked guests move about in a gay whirl. Now the three plotters, sworn to vengeance, make their appearance. The atmosphere becomes more solemn until the opening of the dance. [Don Giovanni manages to draw Zerlina into a neighboring room. Shortly after a scream is heard.] Zerlina is saved and in the thundering finale, Don Giovanni faces his foes with drawn sword. He wrests the bridegroom's [Ottavio's] dress sword from his hand and, like mighty Roland, opens himself a path to freedom through the common rabble which tumbles before him in a confused heap.

[In the second act Don Giovanni gives a serenade under Elvira's window, but he is actually after her maid. Elvira comes out and is led away by Leporello with whom Don Giovanni has exchanged costumes. A number of imbroglios follow in the course of which Masetto, in pursuit of Don Giovanni, receives a beating from the latter, who is dressed as Leporello. This one barely escapes punishment when he is discovered by Ottavio. Both Don Giovanni and Leporello take refuge in a cemetery where the master, offended by the inscription on the Commander's tomb, has his servant invite the statue to supper.]

The finale began amid outrageous gaiety: *Già la mensa è preparata!* [The table is already set.] Don Giovanni, seated between two girls, was caressing them while one cork popped after another, releasing the effervescent spirits that had been hermetically sealed and allowing them free rein. The scene represents a small room; in the background, a large Gothic window looks out into the night. Even as Elvira entered in order to remind the traitor of his vows, one could see lightning flash across the window and hear the muffled rumbling of the approaching storm. Finally there is the mighty knock at the door. Elvira and the girls flee and, to the ghastly accompaniment of chords from the infernal world of spirits, the colossal marble statue enters; next to it Don Giovanni seems like a pygmy. The ground shakes under the giant's thunderous steps.

Through the storm, through the thunder, through the howling of demons, Don Giovanni shouts his dreadful *No* [in reply to the statue's demand of repentance]. The hour of his downfall has come. The statue disappears, the room is filled with heavy smoke in which hideous larvae take shape. Don Giovanni, who now and then can be seen among the demons, is writhing under the torments of Hell. Suddenly there is an explosion as if a thousand thunderbolts were striking. Don Giovanni and the demons have disappeared, God only knows how! Leporello lies unconscious in one corner of the room.

How salutary is now the appearance of the remaining cast as they vainly look for Don Giovanni who has been snatched away from human vengeance by infernal powers. It seems as if only now the awful circle of the hellish spirits has lost its effect. Donna Anna seemed completely changed: her face was covered with mortal pallor; her eyes had lost their brilliance, her voice quivered unevenly. But thereby she achieved a heart-rending effect in the little duet with her mawkish fiancé who wants to celebrate their wedding at once, now that Heaven has successfully relieved him of the dangerous task of vengeance. The fugal melody of the chorus brought the work to a magnificent close.

Both Hoffmann and Kierkegaard insist strongly that *Don Giovanni* can be considered as music only. "If you propose to treat the matter as something outside of music," Kierkegaard warns, "then you may, for all of me, admire the music in this opera as much as you wish, you will not have grasped its absolute significance." (p. 94)

This is not the place for a detailed analysis of the music in Mozart's opera, which is, after all, a task for the musicologist. However, *Don*

Giovanni has tempted many literary men, and some have come up with quite startling insights which had escaped the trained musicians;[4] in fact, the notes of most music commentators on this opera betray the influence of Hoffmann's interpretation.

Kierkegaard, who deals at length with the inner musical structure of Mozart's masterwork, points out that, even more than in drama, in opera everything depends on maintaining the unity of mood. If this is true, then *Don Giovanni* is the perfect opera because the hero not only provides the main interest but he is reflected in, he echoes through, all the other characters. "His passion sets the passion of all the others in motion; his passion resounds everywhere; it sounds in and sustains the earnestness of the Commandant, Elvira's anger, and Anna's hate, Ottavio's conceit, Zerlina's anxiety, Mazetto's exasperation, and Leporello's confusion." (pp. 96–97)

As an example Kierkegaard cites Elvira's first aria (*Ah, chi mi dice mai*), which she sings while Don Giovanni and Leporello stand in the background:

Elvira's aria begins. I do not know how to characterize her passion other than as love's hatred, a mingled, but still sonorous, full-toned passion. Her inmost being is stirred by turbulent emotions, she catches her breath, she grows faint, as every passionate outbreak becomes weaker; there follows a pause in the music. But her emotion shows clearly that her passion has not reached its full expression; the diaphragm of wrath must yet vibrate more intensely. But what is to call forth this agitation, this incitement? There is but one thing that can do this—Don Juan's mockery. Mozart has, therefore—would I were a Greek, for then I would say, quite divinely—made use of this pause in the music to fling in Don Juan's jeering laughter. Now passion blazes stronger, breaks more violently within her, and bursts forth in sound. Once again it repeats itself; then her emotion shakes her to the

---

[4] Among these, only Hoffmann was a trained musician, yet in his short story no technical analysis is present; however, in one section of his *Kreisleriana* ("Über einen Ausspruch Sacchinis und über den sogenannten Effekt in der Musik," pp. 417–26 in the above-named edition), Hoffmann cites the modulation of the Commander's "*Sì*" in the cemetery scene of the second act as most effective (p. 418); he also points out the orchestral accompaniment to the aria *Non mi dir, bel idol mio*, where the figure of the second violin and the viola advancing in octaves strikes him as "deeply moving." (p. 425) Musset increases our appreciation of Don Giovanni's serenade *Deh vieni alla finestra* by remarking that its tripping accompaniment constantly mocks the pompous seriousness of the banal verses. (*Namouna*, I, xiv and xv)

depths of her soul, and wrath and pain pour forth, like a lava stream down its familiar course, and with this the aria ends. (p. 99)

Kierkegaard also shows how Don Giovanni pervades the mood of the opera even when he is not on the stage, as in Leporello's catalogue aria:

Leporello gives Elvira an epic survey of his master's life, and we cannot deny that it is entirely proper that Leporello should recite it, and that Elvira should listen to him, for they are both intensely interested in the matter. As we therefore always hear Don Juan in the whole aria, so in some places we hear Elvira, who is now visibly present in the scene as a witness *instar omnium*, not because of some accidental advantage she has, but because, since the method is essentially the same, one example does for all. If Leporello were character, or a self-reflective personality, then it would be difficult to imagine such a monologue, but precisely because he is a musical figure who is submerged in Don Juan, this aria has so much meaning. He is a reproduction of Don Juan's whole life. Leporello is the epic narrator. Such a one should not be cold or indifferent toward what he tells, but still he ought to maintain an objective attitude toward it. This is not the case with Leporello. Consequently he is fascinated by the life he describes, he forgets himself in telling about Don Juan. Thus I have another example of what I mean when I say that Don Juan echoes through everything. The situation, therefore, does not lie in the conversation between Leporello and Elvira about Don Juan, but in the mood that sustains the whole, in Don Juan's invisible, spiritual presence. (p. 108)

Everybody has heaped praise on Mozart, but very few have added a kind word about Lorenzo Da Ponte, his librettist; in fact, Da Ponte has usually been ignored or mistreated by the most enthusiastic admirers of *Don Giovanni*. Hoffmann explicitly excludes the libretto from his meditations on Mozart's opera, and Kierkegaard bases his discussion on an imperfect German translation of the text.

Of course, *Don Giovanni* is a masterwork because Mozart wrote immortal music for it, but would it have been just as great a creation if an inferior libretto had been used? It is certainly more than an accident that three of Mozart's outstanding operas (*The Marriage of Figaro, Don Giovanni, Così fan tutte*) were composed to texts by Da Ponte.

The reason for the slighting of Da Ponte's libretto, it seems, is partly to be found in the error of literary critics who judge a libretto as they would a play, and forget that the mere reading of a libretto gives us a very incomplete idea of its effectiveness. The librettist must develop the action of his text along clear and simple lines, yet without imposing a specific interpretation upon the composer; the text itself must be poetic, yet again in such a way as to be capable of musical translation.[5]

Judged from this point of view, Da Ponte's libretto for Mozart's *Don Giovanni* is, if not perfect, at least excellent. It is true that Mozart's collaborator borrowed extensively,[6] but we are here not concerned with originality. What matters is that Da Ponte borrowed so intelligently that he succeeded in creating a splendid synthesis of all the previous Don Juan versions worth borrowing from, and in producing a work that is not pieced together but thoroughly unified. From Tirso he took Doña Ana, but he combined Tirso's de la Mota and Octavio into one person and dropped Don Juan's father and the unnecessary scenes of the *Burlador*. He wisely replaced Tirso's Isabela by Molière's Elvire, modeled Leporello after Sganarelle and omitted M. Dimanche, Elvire's brothers, Dom Juan's hypocritical conversion, and Sganarelle's claim of his wages from the French author's work. Zerlina and Masetto are skillful combinations of the corresponding characters in Tirso (Tisbea and Aminta; Batricio) and Molière (Charlotte, Pierrot).

Don Giovanni is described as a *dramma giocoso*, a designation which, if we are to believe W. J. Turner, is significant. "In these two great works [*Don Giovanni* and *Così fan tutte*]," he writes, "the two forms: (1) Opera Seria and (2) Opera Buffa—that is, of Tragedy and Comedy —are for the first time in the history of the opera perfectly united into one, and we may take as a sign that Mozart was aware of this new unity the fact that he described each of them as a *dramma giocoso* instead of *opera buffa*."[7]

Again the contribution of Da Ponte is ignored, yet it is his effective use of Leporello which helps bring about this perfect blend of tragic and comic elements. Not only does the servant's comical fear of inviting the statue and his remarks from under the table during the finale

---

[5] There are exceptions to this rule, as for example the collaboration of Richard Strauss and Hugo von Hofmannsthal, but these cases are rare.

[6] Especially from Bertati, who had written the libretto for Gazzaniga's opera *Il Don Giovanni, ossia il convitato di pietra* (1787). Bertati's authorship has been questioned by some critics who prefer to label the libretto as anonymous.

[7] Turner, *Mozart*, p. 321.

deepen the tragic atmosphere of these scenes but they also enable Mozart to write some of the most magnificent and complex music in the entire opera. It is remarkable that Da Ponte managed to preserve both the essential characters and scenes of the preceding Don Juan versions by showing us on stage the duel in which the Commander is killed and by restoring the insulting epitaph on the latter's tomb, which provides a strong motive for Don Giovanni's invitation—all scenes which Molière had omitted. Most important of all, Da Ponte endows the statue with the seriousness and dignity which had generally been abandoned after Tirso's play.

The one source from which one might wish Da Ponte had borrowed less is the *commedia dell'arte,* for the imbroglios in the second act interfere with the smooth flow of the action. In every other respect *Don Giovanni* presents a unified aspect,[8] the common denominator being Don Giovanni, who, although he has fewer arias than any of the other important characters, makes his presence felt in every scene of the opera.

Da Ponte's Don Giovanni possesses the courage, vitality and passion of Tirso's "caballero," the irony and wit of Molière's "grand seigneur méchant homme," and the finesse of the Italian "galantuomo."[9] These traits are well integrated into one personality, and Manuel de la Revilla pays the librettist a great compliment in saying that "Da Ponte surpasses his predecessors also in . . . a certain balance in the character of Don Juan, who appears less repulsive than in Molière and in Zamora and more refined and shaded than in Tirso."[10] The over-all impression one gains of Da Ponte's Don Giovanni, however, is not that of a romantic hero; he is a cynical realist who searches for no ideal of any sort except his own pleasure. We shall have to return to this question when discussing Hoffmann's interpretation. A curious fact might be noted in passing: neither Don Giovanni nor Molière's Dom Juan actually conquers a woman in the course of the action. Dom Juan is

[8] Such arias as Ottavio's *Dalla sua pace* and Elvira's *Mi tradì,* which interrupt the action, were added later as a concession to the demands of singers and in order to make the opera more acceptable to the Viennese public.

[9] Da Ponte was well acquainted with Casanova, who may have aided him with literary advice. Cf. René Dumesnil, *Le Don Juan de Mozart* (Paris, 1927), pp. 31 f.; also Paul Nettl, "Casanova and Don Giovanni," *Saturday Review,* XXXIX, No. 4 (January 28, 1956), pp. 44 ff.

[10] In Magnabal, *Don Juan et la critique espagnole,* p. 23.

prevented from possessing the peasant girls by the arrival of pursuers; Da Ponte's hero is frustrated in his attempt on Donna Anna by her screams,[11] and in his two attempts on Zerlina, once Donna Elvira interferes and the second time she screams for help.

Leporello bears a closer resemblance to Sganarelle than to Catalinón; he is more enterprising than the latter and even would like to leave his master and become a gentleman himself. Less moralizing than Sganarelle, he feels an unavowed pride in his master's accomplishments and occasionally even tries to imitate him, as when he pinches one of the peasant girls at the wedding. Kierkegaard feels that there is something erotic in Leporello's relationship to Don Giovanni, that there is a power by which he is captivated, against his will. All in all, however, Leporello continues to be not only the comic but the balancing element as well.

Elvira presents us with an interesting problem. Hers is the ungrateful fate of the abandoned woman who pursues her seducer, and as such she arouses both pity and mockery. Tragic as such a role may be in itself, and much to our shame, we cannot prevent an involuntary laugh at such a sight. Both Mozart and Da Ponte bring out this dual aspect of Elvira's situation in wonderful ways. Da Ponte makes her stand by during Leporello's catalogue aria and has her cruelly deceived again when she protects her companion in the second act against Ottavio's sword but discovers soon that it is Leporello disguised as his master. Even in Elvira's first aria (*Ah, chi mi dice mai*), the gay strains of the orchestra seem to mock the hysterical cries of Elvira, and the large leaps in the scale of the aria itself produce a comical effect. However, as the action progresses, Elvira takes on an increasingly imposing aspect. She first becomes the symbol of vengeance as she joins with Anna and Ottavio, but of a vengeance mixed with deep personal suffering which makes her deception during the second act far more tragic than comic.

[11] It is assumed that, following the tradition established by Tirso, he did not succeed in deceiving Donna Anna before she discovered that he was a stranger. This rather unacademic problem is somewhat complicated by Ana's exclamations in Tirso: "¡Falso! no eres el marqués,/que me has engañado" (II, 513–14: "Liar! You are not the marquis; you have deceived me") and "¿No hay quien mate este traidor,/homicida de mi honor?" (II, 518–19: "Is there no one to kill this traitor, who has soiled my honor?"). Yet these words must be attributed to Ana's excessive sense of honor, since there is no reason to doubt Don Juan's sincerity in confessing to the statue: "A tu hija no ofendí,/que vió mis engaños antes" (III, 963–64: "I did not offend your daughter, for she discovered my deceit in time").

In her final appearance, just before the entrance of the statue, she has reached the sublime state of self-abnegation.

The role of Donna Anna, already increased in importance by Zamora and Goldoni, assumes even greater significance than heretofore. (This may be due, to some extent, to the demands by singers for more arias.) Nevertheless, the librettist in no way indicates any suppressed affection on her part toward Don Giovanni. "Donna Anna represents daughterly love as Elvira symbolizes marital love. From the moment her father has expired, she is possessed by only one thought: to avenge him, to pursue his murderer and to make him expiate his terrible crime."[12] Does the music by itself indicate such a concealed feeling as Hoffmann claims to detect in it? We have no statement to that effect by either Mozart or Da Ponte, and so the reader will have to decide this question for himself by listening carefully to Anna's music, especially in the scene after her father's death. We shall have to return to this problem in the next chapter.

As for Ottavio, there can be no question that he is the conventional, sighing and considerate lover, far outshadowed by the powerful personality of Don Giovanni. Nevertheless, Ottavio is not the cowardly fop that Hoffmann makes of him. If given an opportunity, he would meet Don Giovanni in a duel (and probably be killed, true enough), but the very nature of the Don Juan subject requires that Ottavio (i.e., the *human* opponent of Don Juan) be inferior to the seducer; otherwise divine interference would become unnecessary.

Before going on to the romantic Don Juan, let us cast a brief look backward. In Spain, Tirso begins the legend with a play containing religious and moral intentions; upon entering Italy, the supernatural and religious elements of the *Burlador* are replaced by the comic scenes of the *commedia dell'arte*; in France, Molière keeps the statue as a stage effect and concentrates on the portrait of a wicked nobleman.

In general, the trend of development has been toward unity and simplification of the action. Thus Tirso's de la Mota and Octavio are usually combined into one person; the women are still ladies of rank and peasant girls, but their number has decreased; the statue, except for Da Ponte's libretto, is reduced to a stage effect. Don Juan's servant, honest and well-meaning in Spain, dominates as a comic figure in Italy,

---

[12] René Dumesnil, *Le Don Juan de Mozart* (Paris, 1927), p. 57.

becomes a still humorous but moralizing Sganarelle, and finally turns into a Leporello who participates in the adventures of his master. Don Juan himself evolves from a light-hearted Spanish madcap to a brutal Italian seducer; Molière supplies him with an education, wit, and cynicism, while Da Ponte produces a synthesis containing the best of his predecessors. The legend, twice in danger of degeneration, was saved each time, once by Molière and then by Mozart's *Don Giovanni*.

The seventeenth century was primarily concerned with the religious and moral aspects of the Don Juan legend. It tried to answer the question: *How does the hero act and what are the consequences of his actions for himself and for those affected by him?* The eighteenth century gave the seducer a new field of action—the drawing room. Taking up Molière's outline, it dealt with the question: *How does he carry out his seductions?*

The nineteenth century will pursue another problem. Not content with an observed character who, in classical fashion, is presented to us ready-made, that century will explore the question: *Why does he seduce and why can no woman hold him?* Neither the Burlador's declaration that his greatest pleasure is to deceive women, nor Dom Juan's explanation that beauty attracts him wherever he encounters it, nor Don Giovanni's assertion that he needs women more than the bread he eats and the air he breathes will satisfy the demands of the nineteenth century.

CHAPTER SEVEN

Hoffmann's Romantic Interpretation of Don Juan

> Nur der Dichter versteht den
> Dichter; nur ein romantisches Ge-
> müt kann eingehen in das Roman-
> tische.[1]
>
> E. T. A. HOFFMANN,
> *Don Juan*

ॐ

At first glance, E. T. A. Hoffmann's tale *Don Juan*[2] does not seem worthy of special attention. Viewed as a short story and compared to Hoffmann's other tales, *Don Juan* is rather disappointing. Almost nothing happens. The storyteller, a traveling enthusiast whose diary supposedly provides the material for Hoffmann's *Fantasiestücke in Callots Manier*, stops at a hotel and is ushered to the guest box of an adjoining theater by the waiter. On the bill that night is Mozart's *Don Giovanni*. The enthusiast, as we already saw in the last chapter, watches the first act with great excitement. As the curtain falls, he notices a woman who has silently entered his box—it is Donna Anna. They carry on a lively conversation in Italian during which she expresses her deep, romantic love of music. She disappears at the end of the intermission and, during the epilogue that brings the opera to a close, the enthusiast notices that Anna seems to be singing her part under great emotional stress. Annoyed by the snobbish talk at his dinner table, he finally returns to his box in the now abandoned theater. There he writes down his impressions of the opera and of the characters

---

[1] "Only a poet can understand another poet; only a romantic spirit can enter the romantic realm."

[2] *E.T.A. Hoffmanns sämtliche Werke* (Munich and Leipzig: Georg Müller, 1912), I, 87–103.

for a friend of his. At two o'clock it seems to him as if he noticed the scent of Donna Anna's perfume. The next day he learns that the singer who played the role of Donna Anna died at two o'clock sharp.

Truly, there is nothing in the story itself that can be considered revolutionary. It is a different matter when we turn to the letter the enthusiast writes to his friend: there we find a startling interpretation of Don Juan which will give a new direction to the legend. Indeed, it may be said that in its broad outlines the history of the Don Juan legend can be divided into two main parts, and the dividing line is Hoffmann's five-page letter.

The author devotes all his attention to Don Juan, Donna Anna, and the relationship between the two. To begin with, Hoffmann gives us some information about Don Juan that none of his predecessors had supplied in their versions: what he looks like, what kind of an education he has had, what made him the way he is.[3] Hoffmann heaps on Don Juan every possible advantage a man can possess and then presents him as a masterpiece of nature fallen through Satan's trickery:

You may take my word for it, Theodore, nature endowed Don Juan like her favorite darling with everything that lifts a man through closer contact with the divine above the common herd, above the mass products flung out of workshops as mere ciphers before which a digit must be placed to give them any value at all. Thus he was destined to conquer and to rule. His was a strong, magnificent body, an education radiating that spark which kindled the notion of the most sublime feelings in the soul, a profound sensibility, a mind that apprehends swiftly.

But such is the terrible consequence of man's fall that the fiend retained the power to lie in ambush for this man and to set him evil traps even while he was striving toward the most sublime, which expresses his godlike nature. This conflict between divine and demonic forces produces the concept of earthly life, just as the hard-won victory creates the concept of supernatural life.

Before Hoffmann it had been more or less assumed that Don Juan preyed on women in order to satisfy his physical desires, his vanity,

---

[3] There is only one reference to Don Juan's looks in Tirso. This can be found in the first words Tisbea addresses to Don Juan: "Mancebo excelente,/Gallardo, noble y galán." (I, 579–80: "Excellent young man, elegant, noble and handsome"). No such reference can be found in Molière or in Mozart's opera. As for his past or his motives, nothing is revealed to us in any of these works.

or merely for the pleasure of the game.[4] Hoffmann breaks with this traditional attitude and proposes a new and startling motive to explain Don Juan's habit of flitting from woman to woman: he is in quest of the ideal woman who will give him paradise on earth.

Don Juan was inspired by his demands on life, which were determined by his physical and mental constitution. An eternal, ardent longing that made his blood seethe in his veins drove him to seize greedily and restlessly all the phenomena of this earthly world in the vain hope of finding satisfaction in them!

There is probably nothing on earth that so exalts man's intimate nature as love. In its mysterious and powerful workings, love destroys and transfigures the innermost elements of existence. No wonder then that through love Don Juan hoped to still the longing that rent his heart and that the Devil waited for this moment to cast the noose around his neck. By the cunning of man's archenemy the thought entered Don Juan's mind that through love, through the enjoyment of woman, he might obtain on earth what dwells in our hearts merely as a heavenly promise, namely that infinite longing which brings us into direct contact with the supernatural.

Fleeing restlessly from one beautiful woman to a still more beautiful one, drinking in her charms with rapturous ardor to the point of destructive intoxication, always feeling deceived in his choice, always hoping to find the ideal of ultimate satisfaction, Don Juan was bound to find at last all earthly life dull and shallow.

Closely related to the ideal-seeker and a consequence of Don Juan's impossible quest is another aspect under which Hoffmann depicts his hero: the *révolté*, the man who, disappointed in his hopes, turns angrily against God and men:

Since he despised humanity, he rebelled against that phenomenon [i.e., love], which he had considered the zenith of life and which had disappointed him so cruelly. Henceforth the enjoyment of woman no longer served to satisfy his sensual desires but was turned into an opportunity to cast impious scorn on nature and the Creator. Moved by profound contempt for the ordinary view of life, to which he felt himself superior, and by bitter scorn for people who could expect to find in happy love and its subsequent bourgeois union even the slightest fulfillment of those lofty desires which hostile nature planted in our hearts, Don Juan wrought havoc especially

---

[4] A possible exception might be made for Nicolas Vogt, the first author to combine Don Juan and Faust in his play *Der Färberhof oder die Buchdruckerei in Mainz* (1809), but this phantasmagory scarcely deserves to be studied from the point of view of characterization.

on such relationships. He rebelled by boldly facing the unknown, fate-guiding being that appeared to him like a malicious monster playing a cruel game with the pitiful creatures of his mocking moods.

Now every time he seduces a beloved bride, every time he manages to destroy the happiness of lovers by a mighty, ominous blow that can never be undone, he feels he has achieved a magnificent triumph over that hostile power; and this triumph lifts him above our narrow life, above nature—above the Creator! Ever more he wants to go out of and beyond life, but this attempt only causes him to rush headlong into the abyss of Hell. His seduction of Anna and all that goes with it marks the summit of his attainment.

Hoffmann and Kierkegaard differ strongly on the importance of Donna Anna's role in Mozart's opera. Kierkegaard considers her insignificant;[5] Hoffmann assigns her the female lead. Let us look at the opera itself. Donna Anna appears on stage in Don Giovanni's presence three times, all during the first act, and only in their first scene together (when she does not know who he is) do they exchange more than mere formalities. Don Giovanni actually spends far more time with Elvira and Zerlina, but this does not destroy Hoffmann's argument, which, as he specifically emphasizes, is based on suggestions in the music only.

As Kierkegaard pointed out, Don Giovanni is present in the minds of the characters even when he is not on stage. Hoffmann was even more radical in his claim that arias directly addressed to Ottavio, such as Anna's "Crudele" in the second act, actually refer to Don Giovanni. Hoffmann also assumes that, contrary to tradition,[6] Don Giovanni has succeeded in seducing Anna before either appears on stage; equally important for later versions is his suggestion that Anna is indeed the ideal woman but that Don Giovanni has met her too late:

In her extraordinary natural endowments, Donna Anna is Don Juan's female counterpart. Just as Don Juan was originally a wonderfully strong and magnificent man, so she is a divine woman against whose pure soul the Devil has been powerless. All the tricks of Hell could ruin her only on earth. As soon as Satan had accomplished her corruption, the forces of Hell, according to the dictates of Heaven, were no longer to postpone the execution of vengeance. . . .

You have certainly noticed, dear Theodore, that I have spoken of Anna's seduction; and I shall tell you in few words, as best I can at this time

[5] *Either-Or*, I, 100. (See Note 1 to Chapter 6 above.)

[6] See Note 11 to Chapter 6 above.

of night, when thoughts and ideas emanating from the depth of my soul fly ahead of words, how I see the entire relationship between these two natures in strife (Don Juan and Donna Anna) in the music without regard to the text.

I have already expressed the opinion that Anna is set up as a counterpart to Don Juan. Suppose Anna had been destined by Heaven to make Don Juan recognize the divine nature within him through love (which Satan skillfully used to ruin him) and to rescue him from the despair of his vain striving. But it was too late; he saw her at the moment when he had reached the height of wickedness and then he could find enjoyment only in the diabolical pleasure of ruining her.

This brings us to the final trait with which Hoffmann endows Mozart's hero: the irresistible lover. If, in the past, a woman pursued Don Juan, she did so in order to obtain the fulfillment of a marriage vow or to see justice done against a perfidious lover, although in Molière's Elvire gestures can be detected that convey more than the indignation of an abandoned wife. But Hoffmann is not content with such subtle allusions: he boldly states that Don Juan has left an indelible impression on Anna which explains the anger with which she pursues her father's murderer:

She was not saved! When he fled out of the house, the deed was done. The fire of a superhuman sensuality, a blaze out of Hell, engulfed her innermost being, making all resistance vain. Only HE, only Don Juan could kindle in her that voluptuous madness with which she embraced him who was committing his sin while the overwhelming, destructive fury of infernal spirits raged within him. When he set out to escape after the accomplished deed, the thought of her ruin invaded her with tormenting pain like a hideous monster spewing a deadly poison.

Her father's death by Don Juan's hand, her engagement to the cold, unmanly, colorless Don Ottavio, whom she had once thought she loved— even that love whose flame had flared up at the moment of greatest enjoyment and is now blazing within her, aglow with annihilating hate—all this tears at her heart.

She feels that only Don Juan's destruction can bring peace to the fears of her tormented soul; but this peace spells her own earthly ruin. Therefore she incessantly exhorts her ice-cold bridegroom to vengeance; she pursues the traitor herself and regains some calm only after the infernal powers have dragged him to Hell—but she cannot give in to the bridegroom who presses impatiently for marriage: "*Lascia, o caro, un anno ancora, allo sfogo del mio cor!*" [Let my heart mourn for yet a year.] She will not survive this year; Don Ottavio will never embrace the woman who was saved by her pious soul from remaining Satan's ordained bride.

How vividly I felt all this deep within me in the heart-rending chords of the first recitative and during Anna's recital of Don Juan's nocturnal assault. Even Donna Anna's scene in the second act, the word "Crudele," which, superficially considered, refers only to Don Ottavio, expresses in secret undertones and in the most wonderful allusions that disposition of the soul which consumes all earthly happiness. What else is the meaning in the text of that strange added phrase which the poet perhaps dashed off unconsciously: *"Forse un giorno il ciel sentirà pietà di me!"* [Perhaps Heaven will yet one day take pity on me.]

Hoffmann's interpretation of Mozart's *Don Giovanni* met with considerable criticism during the nineteenth century, when it was generally felt that Mozart's music did not possess much emotional depth. The critics were especially indignant at Hoffmann's assertion that Don Giovanni succeeded in seducing, or, more accurately, in deceiving Anna. Even Ellinger, one of Hoffmann's early biographers, registers disagreement with the author's views:

Despite the influence of Hoffmann's interpretation on the future, one must say that it does not correspond to the picture which Mozart had intended to present. Even with the greatest admiration for Mozart's music, save for the second half of the last finale, one will be unable to find in the figure of Don Juan any such demonic accents as Hoffmann reads into it. One will search in vain in Mozart's work for the traces and marks of inner conflict in a nature that was originally great and noble; nor will one find indications that Don Juan's wild lust of seduction originates from a conscious revolt against the divinity and from a presumptuous defiance of God. Hoffmann's explanation of Donna Anna is no less a direct contradiction of Mozart's avowed intentions. One cannot speak of a seduction of Donna Anna, and even less of an overwhelming attraction which Don Juan's personality exerted upon Donna Anna and which pushes her irresistibly toward him.[7]

Mozart's biographer Jahn is no less vehement in his rejection of Hoffmann's interpretation:

Da Ponte's text, which repeatedly emphasizes Donna Anna's affection for Don Ottavio, as well as the idealism of the music contradict Hoffmann's unfortunate thought that Donna Anna has been dishonored by Don Giovanni. It is a sad error to claim that her awareness of shame and of an inner

[7] Georg Ellinger, *E.T.A. Hoffmann: Sein Leben und seine Werke* (Hamburg and Leipzig, 1894), pp. 83 f.

conflict results in continued lying and hypocrisy with her bridegroom . . . rather than that her behavior is motivated by high morality, noble pride, and the grief of a daughter over her ignominiously assassinated father. Hoffmann's position on the two principal characters and their relationship, frequently repeated by others, is completely erroneous. . . . Both figures are as far removed from the time, the nature, the music of Mozart as the whole romantic subtlety which decorates common sensuality with the inner conflict and the contempt for the world of so-called great souls.

Whoever considers it possible that she [Donna Anna] says to Don Ottavio in the moment of the most passionate excitement with touching tenderness, "*Tu sei, perdon, mio bene,*" and has him swear to take revenge while she secretly feels contempt for him and loves Don Giovanni, must attribute to her a premeditated hypocrisy which deprives her of all tragic dignity.[8]

In spite of these harsh and not unjustified criticisms, Hoffmann's concept of Don Juan is so powerful and presented with such passionate insistence that it has gradually asserted itself over more conservative interpretations of *Don Giovanni.* By 1920, Harich states in his biography of Hoffmann: "The best thing a modern director could do for a definitive performance of *Don Giovanni* would be to immerse himself in Hoffmann's poetic re-creation."[9] It may, indeed, be safely said that no one who has read Hoffmann's short story can ever view Mozart's *Don Giovanni* without being to some degree affected by Hoffmann's interpretation, regardless of whether he rationally agrees with it or not.

It would, of course, be incorrect to state that this interpretation came to Hoffmann out of nowhere. On the contrary, there is no lack of antecedents pointing to Hoffmann's conception of Don Juan. Molière already had sketched an idealist of sorts in his wicked nobleman—a man who is forever attracted anew by beauty. But Molière's Dom Juan is too much of a realist to believe that he will ever find absolute beauty—at least not before fatigue will overtake him. Nor is Hoffmann's view of the relationship between Don Giovanni and Donna Anna without precedent. The first comparison that comes to mind is Chimène's love for the Cid, who has killed her father. Even in some of the previous Don Juan versions not all of his victims had despised

[8] Otto Jahn, *W. A. Mozart* (Leipzig, 1891), II, 432 and *passim.*
[9] Walther Harich, *E. T. A. Hoffmann: Das Leben eines Künstlers* (Berlin, 1920), I, 181.

him: Molière's Elvire continues to show affection for him even though he has abandoned her; and Córdoba y Maldonado's Doña Ana does not entirely reject Don Juan after he has killed her father.

Nevertheless, it cannot be said that Hoffmann continued an established trend. In each of the cases just cited, a previous relationship existed between Don Juan and the woman: Chimène loved Rodrigue, Elvire was Dom Juan's wife, and Maldonado's Ana had been courted by Don Juan. But Hoffmann's Don Juan, like a Greek god in human shape, appears from nowhere, seizes his prey, and the harm is done, forever.

One can also cite Chateaubriand's René as an earlier example of an irresistible lover, and there is certainly more than an accidental resemblance between Hoffmann's Don Juan and René. Both are "fatal men," but Hoffmann's hero does not at all share René's ennui, melancholy, and desire for solitude; in fact, in their behavior the two differ almost completely.

Perhaps we come closer to finding an ancestor for Hoffmann's Don Juan if we turn to Byron's heroes, not to his Don Juan but to Manfred, Lara, or the Giaour; but Hoffmann's short story was completed in September, 1812,[10] and prior to that date the only Byronic hero that could be compared to Hoffmann's Don Juan was Childe Harold. Since only the first two cantos of *Childe Harold's Pilgrimage* had been published by then (in March, 1812), it would be difficult to prove that Byron's portrait of the sated and melancholy tourist inspired Hoffmann's concept of Don Juan.

If Hoffmann was influenced by the trends of his time in shaping his Don Juan, it was in the demonic aspects with which he endows his hero. This fascination with the figure of Satan can be remarked in many authors during the romantic era, a development which Mario Praz traces from Marino's *Strage degli Innocenti* through Milton's Satan to an eventual climax in Byron's Giaour, Corsair, and Lara.[11] But again the comparison falls somewhat short of the mark, for Hoffmann's Don Juan, although rebelling against God, is not necessarily an ally of Satan. He rebels, so to speak, on his own, in his own way, and for his own reasons. In fact, it was Satan who ruined him; once he realizes

[10] *Ibid.*, I, 181. According to Harich, the work was completed on September 24, 1812.

[11] Mario Praz, *The Romantic Agony*, transl. from the Italian by Angus Davidson (London, 1933), Chapter II.

this, he might just as readily rebel against Satan, without therefore making his peace with God. Hoffmann's Don Juan is a disappointed ideal-seeker who has turned against those who, he feels, have deceived him—God and society; the former by kindling an unattainable desire in him, the latter by being unable to fulfill it. It would be equally inaccurate to speak of sadism in Hoffmann's Don Juan, for he harms his victims not with the calculated, sensuous delight in cruelty that distinguishes Sade's characters but rather with the impetuous anger of a man who realizes that he has been ruined and wants to drag others with him to perdition.

It is not from reading other authors (had he actually read Sade in 1812, for example?) or from "ideas that were in the air" but from within himself that Hoffmann drew his revolutionary interpretation of Mozart's *Don Giovanni*. It took three qualities to produce this view which no outside sources can account for: Hoffmann's fantastic imagination, his attitude toward music in general, and his personal situation at the time he wrote *Don Juan*.

Hoffmann's fame as a writer of fantastic tales has overshadowed his activities as a musician and a music critic. His compositions include a symphony, operas, chamber and vocal works, and incidental music for plays; he was employed as orchestra conductor in various towns; he wrote a large amount of music criticism; moreover, at the time he worked on *Don Juan* he had but recently completed a section of his *Kreisleriana* and was engaged in writing several reviews of Beethoven's instrumental works.

Music, Hoffmann felt, lifts us above everyday life into a different world altogether. In his review of Beethoven's Fifth Symphony he writes: "Music is the most romantic of the arts—I am tempted to say: the only purely romantic one. . . . Music opens an unknown realm to us, a world that has nothing in common with the exterior world of the senses around us, one in which we leave behind all feelings that can be expressed in order to abandon ourselves to that which is inexpressible."[12]

To be a good composer for Hoffmann means to be romantic, and he does not hesitate to give that epithet to Haydn, Mozart, and Beethoven. "The instrumental works of these three masters exhale a common romantic spirit. . . . Haydn interprets romantically the human aspect

[12] Quoted in Harich, *E. T. A. Hoffmann*, I, 126–27.

of human life. . . . Mozart lays claim to the superhuman, the miraculous that lives in the depth of our souls. Beethoven induces feelings of horror, fear, fright, pain and awakens that infinite longing which is the essence of romanticism. Beethoven is a purely romantic (and hence truly musical) composer."[13]

A composer of operas himself, Hoffmann greatly admired Mozart and especially his *Don Giovanni*. He had written many articles of opera criticism containing a number of advanced ideas which he did not always bear in mind in writing his *Don Juan*. "Opera," according to Hoffmann, "must appear as one unit in action, words, and music. . . . No dramatic poem needs clarity of action so much as opera; even with the clearest singing one still understands the words with more difficulty than under ordinary circumstances; and then the music leads the listener easily into different regions."[14] Nor was Hoffmann's unusual interpretation of Mozart's music confined to *Don Giovanni* alone: "Into his diary he enters the certainly incorrect opinion that the coloratura aria of Arbace in Mozart's *Idomeneo* is not intended to be taken seriously, but that it is merely to be considered as a satire on the singing of castrati; 'he only meant to be ironical, but many people just don't notice it.' "[15]

It took more than these musical ideas to bring about Hoffmann's interpretation of Don Juan. The story was written in Bamberg where Hoffmann had been forced to increase his meager income by giving music lessons and had fallen madly in love with one of his students, Julia Marc, who was twenty years younger than he. Since Julia moved in an entirely different social sphere, no serious relationship could develop between them. (Hoffmann was married, besides.) The situation came to a climax when Julia's mother selected a most unworthy husband for her. During a party, under the influence of alcohol, Hoffmann insulted both Julia's mother and bridegroom but apologized afterwards. This happened less than three weeks before *Don Juan* was completed. How could as impressionable a man as Hoffmann watch *Don Giovanni* under these circumstances without identifying his own emotions with those of the principal characters in Mozart's opera?

---

[13] Quoted *ibid.*, p. 127.

[14] Quoted in Erwin Kroll, *E. T. A. Hoffmanns musikalische Anschauungen* (Königsberg, 1909), p. 98.

[15] Ellinger, *E. T. A. Hoffmann*, p. 34.

According to Kunz's report, Hoffmann did not deny that for his Don Juan he had thought of Holbein, who had played the title role on the stage in Bamberg, and for his Donna Anna he had thought of his beloved Julia Marc. . . . Once we substitute, however, Julia for Anna, then the suggestion arises to see in Hoffmann's romantic Don Juan the poet himself, and, finally, in Don Ottavio, Julia's bridegroom Groepel; and I believe indeed that Hoffmann involuntarily saw the work of another artist in the light of his own love affair in Bamberg.[16]

In attempting to evaluate Hoffmann's contribution to the Don Juan legend, it must be borne in mind that his short story is not a new version but rather an interpretation of a previous version, that of Mozart and Da Ponte. Up to this point every author who had advanced a new view on Don Juan had supported it by means of a play, but Hoffmann merely presents a new interpretation—the execution of it is left to others. Hoffmann's followers will particularly exploit those aspects of his interpretation which are new in the legend: the ideal-seeker, the *révolté*, the irresistible lover. But the portrayal of these new features will require a less limited medium than the drama; Hoffmann's Don Juan cannot express himself in action—he must talk and explain himself, since the motives responsible for his actions are at times more important than the actions themselves. Hence Hoffmann's followers will call the short story or even the novel to their aid.

In spite of its revolutionary impact, Hoffmann's new conception does not necessarily break with the traditional elements of the Don Juan plot or even with the essential features of the hero himself. He continues to go from woman to woman and to kill the Commander as his predecessors had done. All that has changed is the attitude with which his actions are viewed. This new Don Juan no longer simply avows his vice or merely offers an apology of inconstancy—he presents us with a motive for his actions which, once accepted, will change the entire attitude which until then had been adopted toward him. If we agree that Don Juan is not just a young, carefree madcap in search of women to deceive, or a cynical and witty nobleman intent on living according to his pleasure, but that he flees feverishly from one woman to the next in order to find at last satisfaction in the ideal woman who will give

[16] Hans Dahmen, *E. T. A. Hoffmanns Weltanschauung* (Marburg, 1929), p. 71.

him paradise on earth—then we have no right to condemn his behavior or send him to Hell. In that case we shall either watch his punishment with regret or else try to save him.

Hoffmann's conception of Don Juan is certainly subjective and open to criticism, but it opened a new phase and new possibilities in the legend, which seemed to have reached its peak in Mozart's opera. Those writing under Hoffmann's influence will concentrate their attention primarily on three characters: Don Juan, Donna Anna or however they will name his ideal woman, and Ottavio, who will usually be depicted as an unworthy or insignificant man. The statue and the servant, who had represented divine justice and the warning voice of common sense respectively, will be relegated to inferior positions or will be entirely left out. Thus the second part of the traditional plot (the punishment of Don Juan by the statue) will decrease as the first part (Don Juan's amorous adventures) increases in importance. In the development of this trend the triumvirate of male opposition (Ottavio, the statue, and the servant) will sink lower and lower while Don Juan will be raised to dazzling heights.

CHAPTER EIGHT

The Romantic Don Juan

Mein Todfeind ist in meine Faust gegeben;
Doch dies auch langweilt, wie das ganze Leben.[1]

LENAU,
Don Juan

Hoffmann's interpretation of Don Juan was like a fresh breath of air in the evolution of the Don Juan subject, and this for two reasons: it opened the way to new treatments of the hero and the story, and it was in basic accord with the new attitudes of the young romantics.

Like many other revolutionary movements, romanticism, in its early stages, represented largely a negative reaction to accepted values and principles of conduct. This "reevaluation of all values" found its expression in protagonists who were bandits, prostitutes, rebels, and other types disapproved of by good, bourgeois society.

The resurgence of interest in Don Juan in the early nineteenth century can be easily explained, since Hoffmann's hero ideally personifies the aspirations and prejudices of the young romantics: he has been condemned by Church and state alike; he devotes his life to the single-minded pursuit of an ideal; he, more than Hernani or Antony, is the irresistible lover; and, most of all, he opposes to the self-satisfied bourgeois ideal of marriage and family the insecure life of passionate adventures accompanied by ever-new experiences and emotions.

Since romantic authors were inclined to identify themselves with Don Juan, the scope of the subject became still larger by the addition of personal experiences.[2] Thus a great variety of new material entered

[1] "Here my mortal foe is at my mercy; but this too, like all of life, bores me."
[2] Prior to Hoffmann, authors on the Don Juan subject had occasionally drawn on living models for their portraits of the hero, but they rarely, if ever, had incorporated their private experiences as the main aspect of their characterization. A notable exception is Goldoni's *Don Giovanni Tenorio*, which was inspired by a

into the Don Juan subject; nevertheless, the influence of Hoffmann can be detected in almost all romantic versions. The most frequently found treatments derive from one or more aspects of Hoffmann's interpretation: (1) the *révolté*, usually used for social criticism or satire; (2) the ideal-seeker, his quest, his sufferings; (3) the portrait of the irresistible lover, the *homme fatal*; (4) the new role of Donna Anna, who will be turned into a romantic heroine.

I

Moved by profound contempt for the ordinary view of life . . . and by bitter scorn for people . . . he rebelled by boldly facing that unknown, fate-guiding being. (HOFFMANN, *Don Juan*)

There seems to be little resemblance at first sight between the hero of Lord Byron's unfinished epic poem *Don Juan* (1818–23) and Hoffmann's description of the *révolté*; in fact, Byron's Don Juan has so little in common with any of his predecessors that, were it not for his name, he would probably not be thought of as belonging to the Don Juan legend.[3] The same can be said for the plot. Gone are all the traditional events except the shipwreck and, if we want to stretch a point, the encounter between lover and husband (I, clxxxiii–clxxxvi). Gone likewise are the traditional characters: the servant, Anna, Elvira, the Commander, etc.[4]

Since Byron's intentions were primarily satirical, a detailed character

---

personal adventure (see Chapter 5 above). This work, however, is inferior to most of Goldoni's other plays, and the very injection of personal feelings detracts from its effectiveness, primarily because these feelings are undigested and not lifted above mere private vengeance.

[3] It is difficult to understand why Gendarme de Bévotte, in *La Légende de Don Juan: Son évolution dans la littérature des origines au romantisme* (Paris, 1906), devotes eighty pages to Byron as compared with eight pages for Hoffmann.

[4] According to Elizabeth French Boyd, *Byron's Don Juan: A Critical Study* (New Brunswick, 1945), pp. 35–37, Byron had frequently seen the pantomime based on Shadwell's *The Libertine*, first produced by Garrick and revised by Delpini, with music by Gluck. He probably had also seen Mozart's *Don Giovanni* and seen or read Goldoni's *Don Giovanni Tenorio*, but there is no evidence that he knew Molière's *Festin de Pierre* or Hoffmann's *Don Juan*. As for Miss Boyd's speculation that Byron may have seen Tirso's *Burlador* in Spain in 1809, there is little evidence to support it. One might be tempted to wonder whether Byron would have created a different kind of Don Juan if he had known the works of his predecessors. Would he have turned Don Juan into a more typical Byronic hero like Conrad, Lara, or Mazeppa?

analysis of his hero would be out of place; yet, contrary to other protagonists of satire (Candide, for example), the character of Byron's Don Juan undergoes a certain development which undoubtedly would have been still more striking if Byron had finished his poem. What distinguishes Byron's hero most from previous Don Juans is that it is never he who does the seducing: he is either seduced by a more experienced woman or else he falls into a young maiden's arms in a spontaneous embrace, equally desired by both of them and engaged in without forethought or prior maneuvering.

His initiation into love at the age of sixteen by Julia shows him as a seduced adolescent whose good looks were stronger than the married woman's hypocritical determination that "love, then, but love within its proper limits" was to mark their relationship.

His relationship with Haidée, "Nature's bride," demonstrates that natural and spontaneous love which Byron wanted to oppose to the insistence on propriety and cant that he so despised in his own country.

With Gulbeyaz, Don Juan assumes a defensive role. She, the Sultan's favorite who secretly has the pretty youth bought off the slave block, orders him to make love to her. Don Juan refuses, not necessarily because his pride is hurt but because the memory of Haidée is still fresh in his mind, and Byron obviously pokes fun at his hero's inexperience in this scene.

By the time he comes to the Russian court, Don Juan has learned to put his good looks to best advantage. Catherine, despite her "womanhood in its meridian," has no difficulty in enticing the now more experienced young man, but theirs is no longer a natural relationship:

> Her majesty look'd down, the youth look'd up—
> And so they fell in love;—she with his face,
> His grace, his God-knows-what . . .
> He, on the other hand, if not in love,
> Fell into that no less imperious passion,
> Self-love.   (ix, lxvii, lxviii)

Finally, in London, we have before us an accomplished ladies' man who knows how to deal effectively with the more or less veiled attacks on his independence by women of all ranks and ages:

> But Juan had a sort of winning way,
> A proud humility, if such there be,
> Which show'd such deference to what females say,
> As if each charming word were a decree.
> His tact, too, temper'd him from grave to gay,

> And taught him when to be reserved or free:
> He had the art of drawing people out,
> Without their seeing what he was about.
>
> (xv, lxxxii)

The poem breaks off with Don Juan surrounded by three women: Lady Adeline, a high-society lady who is drifting into a more than matchmaking interest in Don Juan; Aurora Raby, the trim and proper antithesis of Haidée; and "her frolic Grace," the Duchess Fitz-Fulke.

Byron was determined to punish his hero for having become unnatural, but he had not made up his mind how he would end Don Juan's career. On February 16, 1821, he wrote to his editor, Murray: "I meant to take him the tour of Europe, with proper mixture of siege, battle and adventure, and to make him finish like Anacharsis Cloots in the French Revolution [i.e., guillotined]. . . . I meant to have made him a *Cavalier Servente* in Italy, and a cause for divorce in England, and a sentimental 'Werther-faced man' in Germany. . . . But I had not quite fixed whether to make him end in Hell, or in an unhappy marriage, not knowing which would be the severest. The Spanish tradition says Hell; but it is probably only an Allegory of the other state."

It is obviously not Don Juan who represents the *révolté*. This role is assumed by Byron himself, who in long and numerous digressions expresses his own revolt by criticizing and satirizing social attitudes that are either stuffy (as in Spain) or hypocritically prudish (as in England).

It should be added that Byron's Don Juan is not a conventional *homme fatal*, either; instead he offers an alternative to the combination of satanic handsomeness and impetuous passion with which Hoffmann had endowed his hero. Byron's Don Juan represents a new type of irresistible lover: one who is so nice-looking, so naturally attractive that his main concern is not seduction but, on the contrary, protecting himself against being seduced by women he does not love. Nor is Byron's hero unfaithful. This young man, "a generous creature,/As warm in heart as feminine in feature," does not leave a woman he likes "unless compell'd by fate, or wave, or wind, / Or near relations, who are much the same." (viii, liii–liv)

By taking the utmost liberty with hero and subject, Byron opened the way to what amounts to license. Henceforth Don Juan becomes a name that an author may freely bestow on any hero, just so long as he has some adventures with women—and even this will not always be necessary. In the hands of a writer like Byron such lack of respect for tradition did not impede the production of a masterwork; in less talented hands the results will not always be equally gratifying.

II

By the cunning of the archenemy, the thought entered Don Juan's mind that through love, through the enjoyment of woman, he might obtain on earth what dwells in our hearts merely as a heavenly promise.
(HOFFMANN, *Don Juan*)

The most radical feature in Hoffmann's interpretation of Don Juan is no doubt the author's claim that his hero's actions are motivated not by sensuous desires but by the search for an ideal. The medieval theme of the quest had been rediscovered by romantic authors who were repelled by the classical ideals of the *honnête homme* or the *philosophe*. Therefore a new model was introduced: the Poet in pursuit of an ideal. One of the first to use this theme was the German poet Novalis, whose image of the "blue flower"[5] became symbolic of this aspect of romanticism. For Don Juan the obvious quest seemed that of the ideal woman. As Gautier puts it, the romantic Don Juan is "Adam expelled from Paradise who remembers Eve, before the fall—Eve, the symbol of beauty and gracefulness."[6]

Alfred de Musset's poem *Namouna* (1832) cannot really be considered a translation of Hoffmann's ideal-seeker into a Don Juan version—it is rather a lyrical commentary on, and expansion of, Hoffmann's interpretation. The style is Byron's (even if Musset defends himself against this charge[7]), the basic idea is Hoffmann's, but the execution is pure Musset—that combination of light-hearted surface and somber, melancholy undertone which characterizes his works.

[5] In his novel *Heinrich von Ofterdingen* (published in 1802).

[6] Théophile Gautier, "Italiens: *Don Giovanni*," *Histoire de l'art dramatique en France depuis vingt-cinq ans*, IV, 37.

[7]   You tell me to my face that Byron is
          My model, and know not that Pulci is.
          Read all Italians and behold him steal.
          To no one aught belongs, but all to all. (ii, viii and ix)

The translations from *Namouna* throughout this chapter are by Marie Agatha Clarke, *The Complete Writings of Alfred de Musset*, Vol. I (New York, 1905). Since these translations are rather free, the original French will be quoted in the following footnotes.

The plot of *Namouna* is insignificant. It tells of Hassan, a young Frenchman turned Moslem, who, in order to overcome his excessive tenderness for women, has two girls brought to him every month who do not understand French and whom he sends away at the end of the month. Finally Namouna, a Spanish girl, enchants him so much that he gives her money to return home; but the girl manages to be resold to him in disguise. All this is told with constant witty digressions which make up the greater part of the poem.

The second of the three cantos is almost completely devoted to Musset's musings about Don Juan. There are two kinds of *roué*. The first type is handsome like Satan, heartless and cold as a viper, corrupting without pleasure, and loving only himself but nevertheless loved by women. This, according to Musset, is Lovelace. As for the French *roué*, the author expresses his contempt for Molière's Dom Juan, who asks merely for good wine[8] and whom Musset places beneath Valmont.

But there is another type of lover:

> Thoughtful as love, handsome as genius is; . . .
> Just twenty, his young heart has felt the kiss
> Of love—fruit of the tree of life abloom.
> Must he, like Christ, while loving, suffer doom?
> So young and handsome 'neath a sky of fame,
> At twenty rich as miser with his hoard,
> With heart of hope to win a splendid name,
> Beloved by all, an open-hearted lord,
> Candid and fresh, his young heart like a flower,
> Where'er bestowed, is maiden's richest dower.
> Four daughters of a prince repeat his name;
> And if for mistress he desired a queen,
> Three palaces or more he could then claim. . . .[9]

---

[8] Musset, one of the few French romantics who appreciated Molière (cf. *Une Soirée perdue*), is here quite unfair to the great comedy writer, for he ignores Dom Juan's long recitative in Act I, Scene i.

[9]
> Pensif comme l'amour, beau comme le génie;
> Il vient d'avoir vingt ans, son cœur vient de s'ouvrir;
> Rameau tremblant encor de l'arbre de la vie,
> Tombé, comme le Christ, pour aimer et souffrir. (II, xxv)
> Le voilà, jeune et beau, sous le ciel de la France,
> Déjà riche à vingt ans comme un enfouisseur;
> Portant sur la nature un cœur plein d'espérance,
> Aimant, aimé de tous, ouvert comme une fleur;

However, this personage offers some puzzling paradoxes: he is young, handsome, rich, well-liked—and yet he spends his time in cheap taverns or sleeps outdoors when pursuing women. A first hypothesis might be that this man is in revolt against his society which has hurt him. But Musset denies this:

> No one but sees how deep in sin he sank.
> His genius known, his famous words they con;
> But wait, the fellow bears a name—Don Juan.[10]

Musset's Don Juan, although killing fathers in cold blood, is highly sentimental in his love affairs. Every one of his three thousand [*sic*] women has cost him tears; he has been in love with each of them as they with him. Then why did he leave them all? Because he is on a quest:

> Expecting ever some fresh sun to gem
> New lives when weary nights your love outgrew,
> At evening saying, "Now, perchance, 'twill beam"—
> Old man, awaiting, watching for day's gleam.
> Thy earliest wish, a dream, a shadowy face,
> And digging through a human hecatomb,
> Despairing priest! nor find thy goddess' home.[11]

Just what was Don Juan seeking? Musset poses the question and supplies his own answer:

> Si candide et si frais que l'ange d'innocence
> Baiserait sur son front la beauté de son cœur. (II, xxviii)
> Quatre filles de prince ont demandé sa main.
> Sachez que s'il voulait la reine pour maîtresse,
> Et trois palais de plus, il les aurait demain. . . . (II, xxxi)

10   Ce qu'il a fait de mal, personne ne l'ignore;
> On connaît son génie, on l'admire, on l'honore.—
> Seulement, voyez-vous, cet homme, c'est don Juan. (II, xxxvii)

11   Toi! croyant toujours voir sur tes amours nouvelles
> Se lever le soleil de tes nuits éternelles,
> Te disant chaque soir: "Peut-être le voici,"
> Et l'attendant toujours, et vieillissant ainsi! (II, xliii)
> Prenant pour fiancée un rêve, une ombre vaine,
> Et fouillant dans le cœur d'une hécatombe humaine,
> Prêtre désespéré, pour y chercher ton Dieu. (II, xliv)

Where then, they ask, that woman all unknown,
Who only could have checked his courser's vein?
She whom he called, who came not, lurked alone?
Where had he found, when lost, and why complain? . . .
Was there not one, a nobler, finer far
Among the beauties, who in certain way
Possessed some feature of his shadowy star?
They all resembled, but 'twas never she;
Don Juan looked on. "She's like"—away was he![12]

Still, undaunted and hopeful, Don Juan continues on his way, taking and leaving women until he comes to the end of his road.

One day there came to you a dreadful guest,
And as you grasped his cold, extended hand,
You fell exhausted at your ample feast,
And straightway sought old Charon's grisly strand.
No longer will you raise your brimming cup,
And drink to beauty, for your game is up.[13]

As in many of his other works, in *Namouna* Musset expresses the conflict in his double role as a lover, a conflict that is probably best illustrated in *Les Caprices de Marianne* (1833), where Musset depicts himself in two characters—Célio, the sighing, tender lover with a heart too full of his love to dare approach his beloved, and Octave, the cold, cynical but successful lover. But while these conflicting traits are depicted separately in *Les Caprices de Marianne* and while they

[12]   "Quelle est donc, disent-ils, cette femme inconnue,
Qui seule eût mis la main au frein de son coursier?
Qu'il appelait toujours et qui n'est pas venue?
Où l'avait-il trouvée? où l'avait-il perdue? (II, xlvi)
N'en était-il pas une, ou plus noble, ou plus belle,
Parmi tant de beautés, qui, de loin ou de près,
De son vague idéal eût du moins quelques traits?
Que ne la gardait-il! qu'on nous dise laquelle."
Toutes lui ressemblaient,—ce n'était jamais elle;
Toutes lui ressemblaient, don Juan, et tu marchais! (II, xlvii)

[13]   Et le jour que parut le convive de pierre,
Tu vins à sa rencontre, et lui tendis la main;
Tu tombas foudroyé sur ton dernier festin:
Symbole merveilleux de l'homme sur la terre,
Cherchant de ta main gauche à soulever ton verre,
Abandonnant ta droite à celle du Destin! (II, liv)

are apparently chronologically more or less separated in Hassan, it is in his portrait of Don Juan that Musset achieves a synthesis of these incongruous aspects of his own personality. This accounts both for the appeal of the hero and for the contradictions which such a combination is bound to bring with it.

Whether or not one agrees with Gendarme de Bévotte that "it is in Musset that the romantic conception of Donjuanism attained its most profound expression,"[14] the second canto of *Namouna* contains an evocation of the ideal-seeker that has become the model for that type of Don Juan.

Once the portrait of the ideal-seeker was drawn, the next step was to confront him with the ideal woman. This dramatic scheme has proved to be very attractive, but the resulting versions have, on the whole, been rather disappointing. Not only are these works dramatically inferior, but this very approach to the Don Juan problem tends to diminish the stature of the hero. An ideal-seeker who finds fulfillment probably did not have a very high ideal in the first place.

In all cases Don Juan meets his ideal woman too late. The main contribution to the legend by the authors involved lies probably in their explanations why the habitual seducer cannot find happiness. It is either because his debaucheries have deprived him of any sense of discrimination among women, as in R. Hörnigk's tragedy *Don Juan* (1850);[15] or else, "burnt like Cain by an invisible flame," he is no longer capable of love, as Villiers de l'Isle-Adam demonstrates in his poem *Hermosa* (1859).

The most probing analysis of a Don Juan who finds the ideal woman is contained in Hans Bethge's tragicomedy *Don Juan* (1910). The author shows Don Juan caught in the conflict between his role of an inconstant seducer and his desire to be faithful to the one woman he cannot forget. Both factors are equally strong in him and the result is a painful indecision which is finally resolved when the woman kills Don Juan and then follows him into death with her child.

---

[14] Gendarme de Bévotte, *La Légende de Don Juan* (Paris, 1911), II, 17.

[15] The same theme can be found in Henry Roujon's novel *Miremonde* (1895). An easier way out was chosen by Loriot-Lecaudey and Charles de Bussy in their dramatic poem *Don Juan au cloître* (1898), in which the hero, about to escape from a monastery with his ideal woman, who had followed him there disguised as a man, is killed by the monks.

III

Nature endowed Don Juan with everything that lifts a man above the common herd. Thus he was destined to conquer and to rule.
(HOFFMANN, *Don Juan*)

The romantics were fascinated by the *homme fatal*. From Chateaubriand's René to Dumas père's Antony this type appears again and again in novels and plays: a somber yet passionate man, pursued by fate, who irresistibly attracts women on whom, in turn, he leaves a fatal mark.

Hoffmann had turned Don Juan into that kind of character. This transformation necessitated corresponding changes in his motivation and behavior. He no longer has to play the deception game of the Burlador, who lacks this mysterious attractiveness; nor does he have to bother with peasant girls: why waste his time with an Aminta, a Charlotte, or a Zerlina when he only has to choose among duchesses, countesses, and famous beauties?

The role of the irresistible lover facilitates Don Juan's task considerably. He is now assured of success before he even sets out to make a conquest. While this relieves the hero of possible frustration, the story is likely to lose much of its tension, for the point of interest is no longer a contest between a seducer and a resisting woman but rather questions such as: How long will she be able to resist him? What means of seduction, if any, will he employ? Unless the irresistible lover is also an ideal-seeker, his motives will not always be clearly stated nor need they be. He is irresistible—why should he not seduce women?

Nikolaus Lenau's dramatic poem *Don Juan* (1844) shows the irresistible lover in action. The work was written just before the poet became insane but, aside from a possible looseness in the sequence of scenes, it shows no traces of mental disorder; in fact, *Don Juan* contains some of the most lyrical passages Lenau ever penned. To some extent, the hero seems to reflect the restlessness and the amorous temperament of his author. Lenau, tired of Europe, had left for America in 1832, but a year later he was back, disillusioned; he had also been close to marriage at various times, but a fatal indecision had kept him from taking the final step. Largely responsible for this was the tyrannical influence exerted on him by Sophie Löwenthal, the wife of a friend. Sophie, while granting him no favors, was loath to give up the exclusive adoration of her poet. The resulting emotional strain certainly played a part in his eventual breakdown.

Lenau's great poems mirror the fluctuations of his philosophical thought. *Faust* (1833–36) was written under the influence of his reading Spinoza; in *Savonarola* (1836–37) he turned to orthodox faith; *Die Albigensier* (1838–42) bears the imprint of Hegel; in *Don Juan* the poet returned to Spinozist and neo-Platonic ideas.

Thus he proposes a different motive to explain why his hero seduces woman after woman. Lenau's Don Juan feels he is the blind instrument of a superior spirit. "At times," he muses, "I am overcome by a strange feeling, as if the blood in my veins had emanated from a higher sphere, as if a spirit gone astray had become a part of me." Gradually he realizes the nature of this spirit that drives him on and on. It is Lust, the goddess of creation.

In Lenau's *Don Juan* lust is manifested in a boundless appetite for women. He is the Faust of love,[16] who desires the enjoyment of every beauty present or past:

If only, like a gust of pleasure, I could traverse that magic circle, immeasurable in size, of female beauty with its manifold charms—and then die, clinging to the lips of the last one! If only I could fly through space to wherever a beauty blooms, kneel down to each and, were it only for a moment, conquer her! With time itself I live in strife. When I behold a maiden beautiful but young, I curse my cruel fate that caused us to be born at different times: I feel as if I were an impotent old man until she has matured. And when I see a stately matron pass of whom old people still say with delight, "Once she was charming and wore the crown of beauty," then I wish I could return to olden times. I fain would melt together time and space.[17]

[16] Lenau had previously written a *Faust* (1836). Two other writers wrote a *Faust* before producing a *Don Juan*: Karl von Holtei, 1829 and 1832; Braun von Braunthal, 1835 and 1842.

[17] These verses of Lenau's dramatic poem, along with two other passages (the one beginning with "Ich fliehe Überdruss und Lustermattung . . ." and "Es war ein schöner Sturm, der mich getrieben . . . ," the latter translated below in this chapter) are written on the flyleaf of the score of Richard Strauss' tone poem *Don Juan* (Op. 20). Although musical commentators have claimed to recognize scenes from Mozart's *Don Giovanni* in Strauss' composition, the composer, in his instructions to a conductor, asked that no thematic analysis be inserted in the program notes except the verses he had selected from Lenau.

Possessed by this spirit, Don Juan finds no resistance from and feels no pity for the women he covets and over whom he passes like a storm, often leaving a broken life or even death behind him. His violence is that of a beast of prey:

I have clawed many a woman and dragged her to the couch of lust, yet never felt a prick of conscience when from my bed she fell into the grave; for in one hour she was generously paid for all the dull happiness, the insipid pleasures I destroyed.

As Pan in pursuit of nymphs, so Don Juan goes after women, and when he comes across asceticism his spirit feels offended. Therefore he introduces twelve prostitutes disguised as pages into a monastery and takes delight in the resulting orgy, which ends when the Prior sets fire to the place. One by one women pass by in brief but not monotonous episodes, for Don Juan knows how to entice each by different means. Only one, Anna, seems to inspire him with real love. But he moves on until, after a successful attempt on Isabella (as in Tirso), he kills her bridegroom and invites the statue of a governor whom he had previously defeated in a duel.

Now Don Juan's inevitable fate is drawing near in the shape of the only enemies he fears: fatigue, age, satiety, dulling of the senses. Even a splendid feast with several beautiful prostitutes cannot arouse him.

A beautiful storm it was that drove me. It has now spent itself and left calmness in its wake. An air of death has covered all my wishes, all my hopes. Perhaps a bolt of lightning from heights that I disdained has struck and killed my amorous energy; and suddenly my world was filled with desolate gloom. Or else, perhaps, the fuel has burnt, and chill and bleak now gapes the empty hearth.

Don Juan wants to live no more; yet he will not take his own life, for that would offend his goddess. He therefore hopes that an enemy will appear to put an end to his joyless existence. Ironically, however, this enemy turns out to be not the statue but the governor's son, the weak and inexperienced Don Pedro, who is surrounded by Don Juan's victims and their children. Don Juan soon wins a decisive advantage over his challenger, but he does not strike. "Here my mortal foe is at my mercy, but this too, like all of life, bores me." He throws his sword away and Don Pedro deals him a deadly blow.

Several keen insights stand out in Lenau's portrayal of Don Juan:

above all, that satiety and boredom are the fatal enemies to which he must eventually succumb, especially since he is incapable of changing his way of life and of adjusting to oncoming age. Don Juan's season is spring and early summer—there can be no autumn or winter for him. The fact that the statue does not appear is another brilliant stroke, for it symbolizes that Don Juan's punishment does not come from without—it is within him. Lenau himself points this out: "My Don Juan is no hot-blooded man eternally pursuing women. It is the longing in him to find a woman who is to him incarnate womanhood, and to enjoy in the one all the women on earth, whom he cannot as individuals possess. Because he does not find her, although he reels from one to another, at last Disgust seizes him, and this Disgust is the Devil that fetches him."[18]

There is much resemblance between the indifference of Lenau's Don Juan toward his victims and the disdain displayed by Charles Baudelaire's hero in the sonnet *Don Juan aux enfers* (1846), who looks unmoved and fixedly at the vessel's track as he descends the Styx amongst the cries of the women he has deceived.

But as in other aspects of the legend, here too the tendency appears to "go one better." By the time Julius Hart writes his tragedy *Don Juan Tenorio* (1881), the hero no longer even has to make an effort to seduce his victims. Donna Blanca, with whom we find him at the opening of the play, exclaims: "You are just too handsome; when you look at us, who can resist you? You are a magician." And he so fascinates Donna Anna that she will commit acts under his spell which, once she realizes what she has done, will drive her to insanity.

Thaddäus Rittner, in his drama *Unterwegs* (1909), goes still one step further. His Don Juan is a baron who has recently raped the proud daughter of his neighbor. His victim attempts to kill him but falls under his spell. Tiring of her soon, the baron turns to his secretary's wife, whom he enlightens thus: "I wanted to point out to you that, properly speaking, every woman remains misunderstood so long as she does not encounter me or someone like me." He only has to get rid of his earlier victim, who by now is begging for his affection, before devoting himself to his new love. Unfortunately, the baron's secretary does not approve of this latest affair and stabs his master. Left alone

[18] Quoted in Henry T. Finck, *Richard Strauss: The Man and his Work* (Boston, 1917), p. 166.

with the baron's dead body, the secretary's wife kisses him and exclaims joyfully, "He has returned my kiss."

IV

Only HE, *only Don Juan could kindle in her that voluptuous madness with which she embraced him.* (HOFFMANN, *Don Juan*)

As Don Juan became a romantic, so did Donna Anna. Although Córdoba y Maldonado had indicated some inclination for Don Juan in the heart of the Commander's daughter, and even if Mozart's music can be interpreted as conveying similar feelings in Donna Anna, prior to romanticism it was impossible that this woman should give in to the pleas of the man who had killed her father. Before that could happen, Donna Anna had to be turned into a weak romantic heroine, like Adèle in Dumas père's *Antony* or Doña Sol in Victor Hugo's *Hernani*. Only a woman who is completely under the ban of fascination emanating from an *homme fatal* can forget her filial duty to such an extent.

Alexander Pushkin, in his dramatic poem *The Stone Guest* (1830),[19] introduces some variations on Hoffmann's theme which make Anna's love for Don Juan more plausible: the Commander was not her father but her husband, whom she had married by her mother's command; and, although Don Juan killed the Commander in a duel (why, we are not told; was it over another woman?), Anna and he have never seen each other until they meet in the cemetery, where Don Juan and Leporello have taken refuge upon returning from exile and where Anna comes to pray at her husband's tomb. Scene 2 shifts to the house of Laura, one of Don Juan's former mistresses, who still longs for his return. Finding Don Carlos with her, Don Juan calmly kills him and makes love to her without removing the corpse from the room. Scene 3 takes us back to the cemetery. Don Juan, disguised as a monk, gains Anna's confidence and then avows that he is a nobleman and passionately in love with her. Moved by his declaration, Anna grants him a rendezvous at her home the next day. In a burst of excessive joy Don Juan bids Leporello invite the Commander's statue to Anna's home. In the final scene, in Anna's room, Don Juan prepares her by degrees for the revelation of his real identity. When he finally does so, she finds she cannot hate him; upon his urging, she grants him another

---

[19] The text used is contained in *The Works of Alexander Pushkin* (New York, 1936), pp. 438–63. The translation is by A. F. B. Clark.

rendezvous and a kiss. At that moment the statue enters, takes Don Juan's hand, and the hero expires with Anna's name on his lips.

Pushkin's dramatic poem leaves us with an unanswered question: Would Don Juan have been faithful to Anna if he had lived, or would he have left her like all the other women he has loved? Don Juan's words seem to be a sincere confession of love found at last; in fact, in this scene he foreshadow's Zorrilla's Don Juan Tenorio:

DON JUAN: I've long been adept in lechery;
            But since I saw you first all that has changed;
            It seems to me, that I've been born anew!
            For, loving you, virtue herself I love—
            And humbly, for the first time in my life,
            Before her now I bend my trembling knees.

ANNA: Yes, Don Juan is eloquent—I know!
            I've heard them say: he is a sly seducer,
            A very fiend. How many wretched women
            Have you destroyed?

DON JUAN: Not one of them till now
            Was I in love with.

Yet there are indications in the play that cast some doubt on the duration of these vows. Not only has Don Juan, "since he saw her first," paid a more than social visit to Laura, but early in the work he recalls a somewhat similar situation with Inez, who has died meanwhile:

DON JUAN: . . . But her eyes,
            Her eyes alone, her glance too . . . such a glance
            I never since have met. And then her voice
            Was soft and weak, as though she were not well. . . .
            Her husband was a rough and heartless blackguard—
            I realized too late . . . Alas, poor Inez! . . .

LEPORELLO: What of it? On her heels came others.
DON JUAN: True!
LEPORELLO: And if we live there will be others still.
DON JUAN: E'en so.

Clarence A. Manning suggests a helpful explanation by pointing to resemblances between Don Juan and similar characters in Pushkin's works. "We must consider Don Juan," he writes, "not as a gay deceiver deliberately ruining the women who allure him but a young man who is sincere at the moment he speaks, however changeable may be his feelings."[20]

Eventually even the Commander began to sympathize with his own killer. In Adolf Widmann's play *Don Juan de Maraña* (1858) Donna Anna not only marries Don Juan after he has killed her uncle, the governor Ulloa, but she also pleads with his former mistress Isabella not to reveal the identity of the killer, for Don Juan has accepted the offer of a mysterious knight to take the blame for the murder. And when the statue appears, it asks Don Juan to forgive its injustice! Don Juan too has been changed by Anna's love: his desire is to establish peace and good will everywhere.

The Donna Anna of Julius Hart's tragedy *Don Juan Tenorio* (1881) goes still further. Although she is temporarily torn by scruples after Don Juan has killed her father, he even succeeds in inducing her to poison her bridegroom Octavio.

This chapter affords a mere glimpse of the fertility of Hoffmann's conception, for his influence can be detected in one form or another in the majority of Don Juan versions produced since the 1830's. Hoffmann, by offering a character sketch rather than a full-fledged version, threw out a challenge that has met with overwhelming response. Time and again novelists, dramatists, poets have attempted to force Hoffmann's conception into the strait jacket of a definitive version—yet it is apparent that none has succeeded; none has even come close to realizing it completely. Hoffmann's interpretation has been as appealing to authors as Don Juan to women. Each author has been convinced that he could succeed where so many others have failed; but when faced with the task of translating Hoffmann's views into a Don Juan version he found himself before an almost insoluble riddle.

Whenever Don Juan veers from his single-minded chase after women, a series of perplexing problems present themselves. These may be examined in the light of the two main features in Hoffmann's interpretation:

(1) The *révolté*. This is actually the less exploited feature of

[20] Clarence A. Manning, "Russian Versions of Don Juan," *PMLA*, XXXVIII (1923), 482–83.

the two. So long as Don Juan merely rebels against the laws governing the relations between the sexes (as does the Burlador), his character is still clearly defined; but when he adds to this a rebellion against family and religion (as does Molière's hero), and against society and therefore laws in general (as does Hoffmann's hero), he must become either an outlaw or a reformer. In either case his burden has multiplied and women become merely one among many preoccupations in his life—in one case he is a Robin Hood with a zest for conquering females in his spare time; in the other, a Peter the Great surrounded by admiring mistresses.

(2) The irresistible lover in search of the ideal woman or of a more generalized ideal. Most of those who limited Don Juan's ideal to women could not resist the temptation of having him meet his ideal. As we have seen, this often led to the elimination of his most essential trait—his inconstancy. So long as Don Juan stuck to his business of seducing women, his ideal was at least theoretically within his reach, but in burdening him with a more inclusive ideal Hoffmann's followers set him a task beyond his power. Pursuing women, as he must to deserve his name (even if he were pursuing the ideal one), is not a very effective way of solving political, social, and economic problems, nor is it likely to lead to the discovery of an ambitious but vague ideal. There is one more drawback to the Don Juan with a vague ideal: one cannot help suspecting at times that he is proclaiming his ideal in order to throw a protective cover over his misdeeds.

The revolution which Hoffmann and his followers carried into the Don Juan legend becomes even more apparent when we look back to the Burlador. What has become of this gay, lively madcap, of this "force of nature"? With their subjective approach the romantic authors have turned this force inward until action has been replaced by words. So much of his energy has been lost in the process of introspection that boredom and indecision, unthinkable in the active Burlador, have come over him and defeated him.

꩜

CHAPTER NINE

Don Juan and Faust

DON JUAN: Wozu übermenschlich
Wenn du ein Mensch bleibst?

FAUST: Wozu Mensch
Wenn du nach übermenschlichem nicht strebst? [1]

GRABBE,
Don Juan und Faust

꩜

At the outset of this study Don Juan, Don Quixote, Faust, and Hamlet were cited as four of the greatest literary figures ever conceived. Of these four, Faust and Don Juan enjoyed immense popularity during the nineteenth century and inspired many artistic efforts. Most ambitious among these were the attempts by several writers to incorporate both Don Juan and Faust into a single work.

Actually, Don Juan had been pushed into the direction of Faust by Hoffmann and his successors, as they endowed their hero with an ideal which tended to become ever more inclusive. A man who consciously seeks the ideal woman must necessarily have intellectual qualities, and his quest for an absolute suggests certain similarities with Faust's. Conversely, Faust had created his deepest impression on the romantics in the Gretchen episode, which, whatever the attending circumstances, involves a seduction and thereby recalls Don Juan.

Thus, on the surface, the two legends seemed to have some important aspects in common; to these might be added the appearance of supernatural personages and a duel with the father or brother of the seduced woman. But the greatest temptation to join these two literary giants in one work can be found in a number of rather facile antitheses which oppose the Spanish grandee to the German magician as examples

---

[1] DON JUAN: Why be superman if you remain human?
  FAUST: Why be human if you do not strive to be superhuman?

of contrasting attitudes and ways of life: Don Juan, born in the South, created by a Catholic philosophy, gay, enjoying life, striving for the absolute in voluptuous pleasure; Faust, the Northerner, a product of Protestantism, grave, meditative, striving for the absolute in knowledge and experience in the largest sense; both of them attempting to transgress the limits imposed upon human existence, one seeking forbidden knowledge, the other forbidden pleasures, both contemptuous of human laws and avid for new power and conquests.

The works embodying the Don Juan and Faust legends usually contain one or several of these four devices: (1) fusing the two heroes into one; (2) having them meet as enemies or in a common effort; (3) making direct comparisons of the heroes' philosophies; (4) incorporating elements of one legend into the other.

I

One of the most ambitious and grandiose theatrical schemes ever conceived is Nicolas Vogt's unfinished play *Der Färberhof oder die Buchdruckerei in Mainz* (1809). Vogt's plan for fusing the arts went even beyond the ideas which Richard Wagner was to conceive later in the century. The author is not content to combine two of the most fertile legends of all times in order to create what should be the finest achievement in dramatic art; he also has recourse to the music of Haydn and Mozart, adds ballet sequences and tableaux of Oriental splendor for stage effects, and draws on Raphael, Michelangelo, and other Renaissance painters for specific scenes.

If the execution of this project had been in any way proportionate to its conception, Vogt's tragedy-opera-ballet extravaganza might have become a great creation. Unfortunately, the dramatic skill of the author was greatly inferior to his imaginative power, and the result of his effort is as confused a phantasmagory as can be imagined.

Vogt accomplishes the fusion of the two heroes in a somewhat mechanical way by endowing Faust with Don Juan's attractiveness, while later on when Faust and Wagner reappear as Don Juan and Leporello, Mephistopheles remains at Don Juan's service. So long as the hero turns to science for the satisfaction of his desires, he is Faust; when he moves to Castile and devotes himself to sensuous pleasures, he becomes Don Juan.

Elements drawn from both legends are freely used by the author: fatal duels with the fathers of offended maidens, the pact with Mephis-

topheles, the invitation of the dead man's statue, the Zerlina episode
from Mozart's *Don Giovanni*, etc. Once Don Juan appears in Castile,
however, Vogt pulls out the stops altogether. There the hero courts
the Infanta Elvira (to the strains of Don Giovanni's serenade), defeats
the Moors with Mephistopheles' aid, and, after being arrested by the
Grand Inquisitor for black magic, has the evil spirit help him defeat the
Castilians in turn. In the last scene we see Don Juan as emir of a
Saracen state, replete with Oriental parades to the music from Mozart's
Abduction from the Seraglio. But the arrival of the statue puts an
end to this colorful celebration. As Don Juan is dragged off to Hell,
the archangel Michael appears bearing the cross while a group of
angels sing the last chorus of Haydn's *Creation*.

The most interesting of Vogt's abortive attempts seems to be his
use of *tableaux vivants* reminiscent of theatrical practices during the
Roman decadence. The author calls on a painting by Teniers (probably
his *Temptation of Saint Anthony*) to create a tableau in which, at the
arrival of the cross-bearing Grand Inquisitor, the dancing girls change
into mice; or again, at the opening of the third act, as Don Juan dreams
in his cell that his bride and his guardian angel are with him, the stage
represents tableaux drawn from Guercino's *Saint Petronilla* and
Raphael's *Annunciation*. Vogt was obviously ahead of his time in
being the first to combine Don Juan and Faust, and in his ideas on the
fusion of the arts, but his play makes it only too clear that being the
first does not always mean being the best.

II

Christian Dietrich Grabbe's drama *Don Juan und Faust* (1829)
is undoubtedly the most interesting work among those which combine
the two legends. Grabbe's dramatic scheme, although not always orderly, is nonetheless extremely ambitious, for in this drama the two
giants meet face to face in the struggle over the possession of Donna
Anna.

Grabbe's work is very uneven: flashes of genius are obscured by
passages of pompous verbosity, but on the whole the author succeeds
admirably in delineating the two heroes in their individual passions.

Don Juan is depicted as a dashing Spanish nobleman whose motto
"King and Glory, Fatherland and Love" relates him to other *Sturm
und Drang* heroes. Having determined to gain Anna's love at any
price, he stages a sword fight with Leporello in front of the governor's

mansion. While Anna's father and her bridegroom Octavio pursue Leporello, Don Juan unsuccessfully tries to approach Anna. He then claims that his opponent was Faust.

A comparison of the two protagonists shows that Don Juan strives without caring about an ultimate goal: "Don't speak to me of goals," he exclaims, "even if I strive for one. Damn the very thought of it. Any goal means death. Happy the man who strives forever, glorious the one who could always thirst." (I, i)

Faust, on the contrary, states that he must have an ultimate goal: "I sought the sight of God, and here I am facing the gates of Hell. But I still can march forward, stumble on, even if the road goes through flaming fire. A goal! I must have a goal before me. If there is a path to Heaven, it surely leads through Hell—at least for me." (I, ii)

In any work dealing with Faust an initial monologue is expected. Grabbe, although essentially writing a variation of Goethe's version, manages to introduce distinct notes of his own when he describes the striving of his Faust in rather physical terms. "I wandered on and on," the hero muses, "until the sun stayed far behind me . . . and now, behold, there is the goal: an abyss into which the streams of thought and feelings crash, foaming—never to return." (I, ii)

Faust is seeking permanence in a world in which "we create out of ruins." "Only Don Juan," he adds, "can flit about amidst the lava of destruction and pluck millions of flowers without thinking that they are many but ephemeral. One may find diversion but not security or calmness where the one flower that does not wilt is absent." (I, ii)

Goethe's Faust has often been criticized because, when he has the opportunity to question Mephistopheles about the problems which have driven him nearly to suicide, he agrees to fly off to Auerbach's Cellar for a gay drinking bout with men who have very little to teach him. Grabbe's hero is not so easily taken in by Mephistopheles' tricks. Although the latter invites him to fall in love with Donna Anna, Faust indignantly rejects this offer: "Do you think I dragged you from that stagnant swamp of yours only to confine myself to a girl's world, to play with pins instead of tearing at the locks that guard the secrets of the universe? . . . Let us be off. . . . Envelop me! Down into Hell, then back to the stars above! If there is firm ground below, my feet shall tread on it; if there is a view above, my eyes shall feast on it." (I, ii)

This promising beginning does not continue long. Faust sees

Donna Anna in Mephistopheles' magic mirror and becomes Don Juan's rival in spite of his earlier declaration. While the Spaniard kills both Octavio and the governor in duel, Faust makes off with Anna to a magic castle on top of Mont Blanc. But there he is unable to capture the heart of Anna, who has meanwhile fallen in love with Don Juan. When the latter arrives with Leporello at the castle, Faust has a wind blow them away to the cemetery where the governor is buried. There Don Juan, angered by the inscription on the tomb, invites the statue to supper. Meanwhile Faust has been unable to gain Anna's love, and in a fit of anger he resorts once more to his magic power, this time to cause her death. But once he realizes what he has done, Faust is overcome by sorrow and soon dies. Mephistopheles takes his soul and that of Don Juan too, when the latter refuses to heed the statue's warning to repent.

Although Grabbe does not choose between his two heroes, the gallant Don Juan leaves a more pleasing impression than Faust, whose arrogance and lack of feeling make him at times repulsive. The symbolic significance of the drama is utterly pessimistic: "Man is matter and spirit: of these two elements, one engenders only sensuality and egoism; the other, vanity and impotence. All of life oscillates between these two poles, equally removed from the truth. If man follows Faust, he accomplishes nothing, he is a tormented sufferer, a victim of his dream; if he imitates Don Juan, he falls into brutality and materialism. There is but one victor on earth: Satan."[2]

III

Those writers who compare Don Juan and Faust either express their preference for the Spaniard, or else each hero in these versions wishes he had lived like the other.

Eugène Robin, in his dramatic poem *Livia* (1836), has Faust and Don Juan discuss their respective ways of life. Faust is finally forced to agree that the gay Don Juan has made a better choice than he, who is sad because of his inability to attain the knowledge he desires. Don Juan chides him for turning away from love and life; then he disappears, leaving Faust to his fate, which is, however, averted by the pure love of a self-sacrificing woman.

The Brazilian poet Paulo Menotti del Picchia likewise limits his comparison to the love life of Don Juan and Faust. The poem *A angustia de D. João* (1928) shows Faust as being inferior to Don Juan

[2] Gendarme de Bévotte, *La Légende de Don Juan*, II, 83.

in so far as women are concerned, since his excursion into love was
limited to Gretchen, whereas Don Juan exhausted a great number of
possibilities. Even if Don Juan failed, he had acted in the hope of
attaining an ideal so subtle that even he cannot define it, something
so vast that it cannot be contained in a woman's body.. His anguish is
caused by the fear that no woman can incarnate his dream.

In Théophile Gautier's poem *La Comédie de la mort* (1838),
Faust and Don Juan each views his own life with regret and envies the
other. Faust, having found nothing, wishes he had enjoyed life more.
"A single kiss from your rosy lips, so fresh and small, fair Marguerite,
is worth more than all that," he concludes.

Don Juan recounts his search for the ideal woman, one who would
be a combination of Cleopatra and the Virgin. But then he complains
that "to love is to be ignorant, to live is to know."

Almost one hundred years later, Max Jacob disagreed with Gautier. In Jacob's "Poème dans un goût qui n'est pas le mien" (from
Cornet à dés, 1923), Don Juan and Faust have tried to change their
ways of living. But they soon return to their former lives, even though
they are disgusted with them. Each of the two is vainly trying to recapture the thrill of his first success, and so Don Juan continues to seek
this emotion in love and Faust returns to science, even though his
methods are outmoded.

IV

In several works the wager in Goethe's "Prologue in Heaven" is
applied to the career of Don Juan.

Aleksei K. Tolstoi's dramatic poem *Don Juan* (1860), dedicated
to the memory of Mozart and Hoffmann, begins with such a prologue,
in which Satan and a celestial choir contend for Don Juan's soul. While
Hoffmann merely indicated that Satan had ruined Don Juan by making him believe he could find paradise on earth, Tolstoi's evil spirit
predicts the hero's future: "When he desires, burned by my flame, to
find happiness in the arms of love, the vision of perfection will dis-
appear and the woman will appear before him as she is. He will rage.
Let him ever seek with eternal thirst a new ideal in the arms of every
girl! So with flaming zeal, with stubbornness on his brow, with despair
in his heart, with passion in his eyes, let Juan seek Heaven on earth and
in each triumph prepare himself a new woe."

This explains, at least in part, why Don Juan gives a public serenade under the window of the town whore on the very evening his engagement to Anna is announced. After the usual adventures, in the course of which Don Juan kills Anna's father and his rival Octavio, he realizes that he loves Anna. But by then Anna has died and the woman he sees is her ghost. The Commander's statue warns him to repent. In despair, Don Juan curses life and Satan is ready to take him, but the celestial choir interposes itself. The poem closes with Don Juan, about to die in a monastery, asking to be buried near Anna and the Commander. The choir of monks asks God for his pardon.

A similar but more complicated wager is made in the prologue of Waldemar Bonsel's dramatic poem *Don Juan* (1914). After a grandiose opening, Satan accuses God of appealing only to the weak. "You will lose the first," the Demon claims, "who truly makes the Earth his own." Satan then proceeds to propose the wager in this spirit and in very clear terms: "Let me have power to imbue one man with all the capacities for earthly pleasure that exist but singly in the best of men. If you can draw this man unto yourself, then, verily, your creation will be complete."

In a somewhat surprising spirit of fairness, Satan promises to stay within the limits God has imposed on man, and he adds the specification that Don Juan is to carry within himself all the great problems of mankind, but that he is to be unaware of the wager. And to this challenge God replies: "In this man I shall risk my heart."

A promising beginning, once again. We expect another Faust who will unite in him all that mankind has struggled with and striven for. Alas, our hopes are disappointed. In small, disjointed sections Don Juan mysteriously appears and conquers, "a Satan crowned by God," as one of his victims calls him. Young maidens, a duchess, a nun—whoever they be, they fall, without a struggle and without complaint, but great revelations there are none. It is Maria (the name is no doubt symbolic) who is the first woman before whom he bows his head and, although he leaves her side and despite Satan's threats, he returns to this woman. It had been Satan's will that he was never to linger near or return to a woman, but love (Goethe's "ewig Weibliche") has restored Don Juan to God.

It is always difficult to judge the fairness of any wager in which God is one of the parties. The author usually equivocates between the legalistic view—which, first of all, would have to grant that at least in theory God could lose his bet—and the moral view, which is concerned with showing somehow that even Satan cannot help but play his part in God's scheme—a noble thought but deadly as theater if it dominates completely. Even Goethe's *Faust* suffers from this tendency of sitting between two chairs. In Bonsel's poem, in any case, God must have bet in full knowledge of the outcome (a not quite fair bet, in human terms), or else we would have to accuse Him of "risking his heart" on poor odds.

None of the attempts to treat Faust and Don Juan in a single work has benefited either figure; their resemblances, if any, are superficial. Fundamentally, the two heroes are quite dissimilar:

Don Juan is the natural man, thriving on pleasure, master of the instant who never asks more of the present moment than it can give him. He is incapable of regret, of remorse and almost of thought. One could not think of him as melancholy. . . . Don Juan, at the height of his career, can only be handsome, brilliant, happy, completely devoted to the pleasures of the senses, suffering from his limitations at times—but open to all pleasures, and incapable of satiety and disgust, of any sort of metaphysical self-poisoning. . . . A melancholy Don Juan is a romantic misconstruction.

Faust is just the opposite. In him thought and reflection dominate, but not instinct. He feeds on problems and not on enjoyments. He carries within him the duality of a bad conscience which poisons all his pleasures. He wants both to live and to surprise the secret of life, to feel and to know, to act and to judge. Once one has entered into the labyrinth of problems, one ceases to be an instinctive and happy being. Ravaged by reflections, Faust must be accessible to remorse. In his mind he carries a judgment about himself but also about nature and God. He believes or feels himself to be responsible, even though he denies it. He can, therefore, at certain moments, contemplate suicide. . . . One cannot imagine Don Juan cursing life to which he adheres with all his powerful animalism. One does not think of him, whose only destiny is to "live," as calling for death.[3]

Whenever Don Juan and Faust are placed in opposition or united in one person, both of them lose, for they are not the sort of personalities that complement each other—there simply is not room enough for both of them in one work. In the final analysis it is only the Gretchen episode which draws them together, but it must be remembered that

[3] Geneviève Bianquis, *Faust à travers quatre siècles* (Paris, 1935), pp. 326 f.

for Faust women constituted only one of many attempts to find a solution to his problem, and he concentrates on one or two. In view of Hoffmann's interpretation it might be claimed that Don Juan, too, has an
ideal; yet this ideal is either limited to women or else so vague that,
intellectually speaking, he is dwarfed by the depth and maturity of
Faust. On the other hand, as a seducer Faust is no rival for Don Juan;
his behavior with Gretchen is clumsy, sentimental and remorseful,
betraying the old philosopher who has so little confidence in his personal charms that he places his trust in magic and precious gifts. Finally, the task of melting such giants as Don Juan and Faust into one
character would require a genius of Rabelaisian proportions. Of those
who have tried to achieve this feat, most have obviously failed; only
Grabbe's drama is not without merit.[4]

[4] Traces of the Faust legend can be detected in a number of other Don Juan
versions, for example in a drama by Braun von Braunthal (1842) and a tragedy by
Hörnigk (1850), both entitled *Don Juan*, in both of which the hero enlists the aid
of Satan or Mephistopheles. However, in this chapter we have limited ourselves to
those works in which the author made a conscious effort to fuse the two legends.

CHAPTER TEN

Miguel Mañara: The Converted Don Juan

Aquí yacen los huesos y cenizas del peor
hombre que ha habido en el mundo.[1]
Inscription on the tomb of Miguel Mañara

So far as is known, the legend of Don Juan Tenorio is not based
on the life of any particular individual; at least, all claims to that effect
lack creditable evidence to support them. Then why does one find
repeated references to "the real Don Juan"? This epithet has, somewhat inaccurately, been used to designate a historical personage whose
existence is beyond doubt and whose life and legend came to be inti-
mately associated with the Don Juan subject. His name was Miguel
Mañara and he was born in Seville in 1626. Since he was only four
years old when *El Burlador de Sevilla* was first published, he cannot
very well have been Tirso de Molina's model for Don Juan Tenorio,
as some sources imply. Nevertheless, Mañara's life and the legend
that later grew around it offered certain analogies to the Don Juan
story which eventually led to efforts to associate or combine the two
legends.

There is ample documentation on Mañara's life. We know where
he lived, where he is buried; there is even a painting of him by Juan
de Valdés Leal; yet the material at our disposal has to be approached
with caution, because in some parts history and legend have become so
closely intertwined that it is not always possible to separate the two.
Unfortunately, most of what is known about Mañara is derived from
testimony by witnesses who wished to effect his canonization. While
their sincerity need not be doubted, they probably sinned as much by
omission as by overzealousness. Biographers of Mañara, for their

---

[1] "Here lie the bones and ashes of the worst man that ever lived."

part, have done little to help us draw a sharp dividing line between fact and fiction.[2]

Juan de Cárdenas' biography, which appeared only one year after Mañara's death, glosses over his youth by mentioning simply that it was "very stormy." This very reluctance to elucidate leads one to suspect that Mañara was moved by more than mere pious exaggeration when he wrote in his last will: "I, Miguel Mañara, ashes and dust, miserable sinner, have served Babylon and the Demon, its prince, with all kinds of abominations, haughtiness, adulteries, blasphemies, scandals, and robberies. My sins, my infamies are innumerable; only the intelligence of God can bear them, only his mercy pardon them."

What were these terrible sins of which Mañara accuses himself? Nothing definite is known about them, but legend and the imagination of authors have filled in the gap. After sifting out doubtful and obviously legendary information about Mañara's life, it is possible to piece together the following biography:

Miguel Mañara Vincentelo de Leca was born in Seville in 1626.[3]

---

[2] The following sources may be consulted on Mañara's life: Juan de Cárdenas, *Breve relacion de la muerte, de la vida y virtudes de Miguel Mañara* (Seville, 1680); Colonna di Cesari Rocca, "Don Juan (Miguel Mañara), sa famille, sa légende, sa vie d'après des témoignages contemporains," *Mercure de France*, CXIX (1917), 193–220; Paul Olivier, "La Canonisation de Don Juan," *Revue de France*, I (March 15, 1921), 214–22; Michel Lorenzi de Bradi, *Don Juan, la légende et l'histoire* (Paris, 1930); Esther van Loo, *Le Vrai Don Juan: Don Miguel de Mañara* (Paris, 1950). The two last-mentioned are the most complete studies on the subject, but neither makes a clear distinction between historical and legendary material. The canonization records at the Bibliothèque Nationale (taken from the Vatican by Napoleon) should have been examined more critically, and Madame Van Loo's assertion that events might be any less legendary because they were related by descendants of Mañara is open to serious doubt. The claim of both authors that Mañara's dissolute life was caused by a desire to outdo the Burlador also remains unsubstantiated.

[3] In a small pamphlet given to visitors by the Santa Caridad in Seville, the dates cited do not agree with those generally given by the biographers of Mañara. According to the pamphlet, Mañara was born not in 1626 but on March 3, 1627; he married not at the age of thirty but in 1648 (which would leave relatively little time for his "stormy youth"); his wife died in 1662; his admission into the Santa Caridad is dated December 10, 1662, and his death is said to have occurred on May 9, 1679. There seems to be a serious contradiction, however, so far as the date of marriage is concerned, with Mañara's own *Discurso de la verdad* (p. xxiii), where he states: "And I who am writing this, I confess with grief in my soul and tears in my eyes that *for more than thirty years* [italics mine] I abandoned the holy

His father, Don Tomaso Mañara, and mother, Geronima Anfriano, were both descendants from a turbulent race of Corsican adventurers and soldiers of fortune. His mother gave him a strict and religious education to arm him against vice, but the passionate nature of young Miguel soon caused him to enter upon a disorderly path of life. At the age of thirty, he married Girolima Carillo de Mendoza, but, after a few years of happiness, his wife died. He took her coffin with him into the wildest section of Andalusia, where, almost out of his mind, he prayed for her resuscitation. After confessing to a monk, he regained his composure somewhat and returned to Seville, where he entered a monastery. Fearing, however, that an inactive life would not save him from the tortures of Hell, he decided to devote himself to caring for the poor. He therefore had the Church of Charity (Iglesia de la Caridad) rebuilt and a hospital constructed next to it.

Thereafter he led a saintly life. Not only did he spend fifty thousand ducats on the needy, but he also devoted himself completely to the sick and the poor; he kissed their hands, washed their feet, and arranged marriages for poor and virtuous orphans. Not content with this, he wore a hair-shirt, slept on a coffin smaller than his body, ate only meagerly, and ordered the cook of the monastery to slap him every morning. When he felt death approaching, Mañara inflicted further humiliation upon himself by requesting to be buried under the threshold of the church; only in the inscription which he devised for his tomb is there a last glimmer of pride beneath his apparent self-abasement: "Aquí yacen los huesos y cenizas del peor hombre que ha habido en el mundo—Here lie the bones and ashes of the worst man who ever lived." He died on May 9, 1679.

One year after his death, letters containing the testimony of twenty witnesses were sent to Rome in order to obtain his canonization; his process was taken up in 1749 and once more in 1770, this time with thirty-five new testimonials. On May 13, 1778, the Commission of Rites recognized his cause and the Pope ratified its decision. Since that day Mañara has carried the title of "Venerable," the first step toward

---

mountain of Jesus Christ, and in my madness, in my blindness, I served Babylon and its vices. . . ." The pamphlet also repeats the claim previously made that after his death Mañara's body remained in perfect state for seven months. Incidentally, one of the ironies of history is that Mañara should have become a popular dramatic hero, for in a letter written after his conversion he most strongly condemns theatrical performances.

canonization. Up to now, though, his process has not been renewed, probably because of the expense involved; moreover, canonization requires four indisputable miracles, whereas only three have been cited in favor of Mañara: that of a certain Johannes Meléndez, a poor paralytic who, after having been cared for by Mañara, suddenly got up and danced the seguidilla; a sudden and inexplicable multiplication of grains planted by him; and the quick conversion of twenty-four English Protestants.

Legend has filled in the gaps in our knowledge about Mañara's life, primarily with respect to his "very stormy" youth and the causes which led to his conversion. We are told that he was nicknamed the "Burlador de Sevilla" and that one day he was surprised in the room of a girl by her angry father, whereupon blood flowed. He is said to have fled to Italy, Germany, and Flanders, where he fought with the Spanish army. Having returned to Spain thanks to the efforts of his family, a number of miraculous events are said to have happened to him. Thus, it is said, one day, under the influence of wine, he asked a man on the other side of the river for a light, whereupon a hand extended across the river and presented him with a burning cigar from which Mañara lit his own without batting an eyelash. Furthermore, he engaged in bullfights without getting hurt. He left a house just as it collapsed behind him. While recuperating from an illness, he drew up a catalogue of his conquests, listing the wives and mistresses of a pope, of an emperor, and of princes and lesser nobles as well as women of low birth. When it was remarked that God was missing in his list of cuckolds, Mañara remembered Teresita, who had since entered a convent but whose passion was reawakened by his advances. During a dinner Mañara threw his catalogue on the table and a fist fight was barely averted.

There is no agreement on the particular event which led to his conversion. His companion Don Alfonso Pérez de Velasca recounts that one day while they were riding together, they heard lugubrious songs and, upon reaching the street corner, beheld the skull of a converted Jewish prostitute who had requested that it be exhibited there in retribution for her sins. Suddenly Mañara received a blow in the neck which caused him to lose consciousness; upon recovering he heard a voice saying, "Bring on the coffin; he is dead," but could see no one; yet this event saved his life, for three insulted guests of the catalogue dinner had waited all night in order to assassinate him. Another report tells of his learning that a shipment of ham, destined for him, had been retained by the customs. Angered, he rushed out to punish the guilty officials, but, halfway there, he stopped, reflected and returned home. He had gained the consent of Teresita to escape with him, but, shocked by all the miracles which had happened to him, he wrote to her that he would enter a monastery, whereupon she exclaimed in despair, "He never loved me."

Witnesses tell of additional miraculous events. The priest Hippolyte Casafonda relates how one day Mañara watched a funeral procession and asked who was being buried; the answer was, "Don Miguel de Mañara." He laughed and asked others in the procession; the answer was always the same. Finally he fainted and had to be carried home unconscious. Another day he was following a woman who reminded him of his deceased wife. Unable to catch up with her, he called after her: "Heartless creature, will you not look at me?" She turned around: the beautiful body of the woman was crowned by a skull!

An examination of the Mañara legend brings various influences to light. Thus the account of the knight who witnesses his own funeral can already be found in Antonio de Torquemada's *Jardín de flores curiosas* (Salamanca, 1570) and was later used by Lope de Vega in *El vaso de elección.* Traces of the Don Juan legend are obvious in the killing of the seduced girl's father and in the catalogue scenes.

A comparison of the two legends shows that they have one important feature in common—the amorous exploits of the two heroes. In their subsequent development they differ radically: whereas Don Juan invites the statue to supper and eventually dies from its handshake, Mañara marries and, after the death of his wife, is led by miraculous incidents to take up a pious life until he dies in an odor of saintliness.

An element of confusion was introduced into several later treatments of the Mañara legend whose authors changed Miguel Mañara's name to Don Juan Mañara, Don Juan de Mañara, or Don Juan de Maraña by metathesis; but in all cases it is Mañara's conversion which clearly distinguishes the Mañara legend from the legend of Don Juan Tenorio.

Although the Mañara legend had probably achieved considerable popularity in Seville and possibly in other Spanish towns, it was practically unknown to the rest of Europe until 1834, when Prosper Mérimée used it as the basis for his short novel *Les Ames du purgatoire.*

Mérimée generally adheres to the outlines of Mañara's life but takes the liberty of filling in where factual information is lacking. He was also the first to join the two legends firmly by introducing features from the Don Juan story into that of Miguel Mañara and by changing Mañara's Christian name to Juan.

In Mérimée's novella, Don Juan de Maraña, brought up to be pious by his mother and to be brave by his father, is sent to the University of Salamanca, where he makes the acquaintance of the sinister Garcia. After following two beautiful sisters, Fausta and Teresa, from a church to their home, they give them a serenade to which the sisters respond. One night, however, their courting is disturbed by the arrival of a competitor whom Don Juan kills in the ensuing duel; but in his hasty escape he leaves his sword behind. Later that night Teresa comes to his room to return the sword and from then on the two men gain free access to the sisters' apartment. Tiring of them soon, Garcia suggests an exchange, to which Don Juan agrees after some hesitation. He presents a letter to Fausta in which Garcia assigns her to him. Fausta becomes enraged, screams, and holds on to his coat as he tries to flee. Her father rushes in. His shot misses Don Juan and kills Fausta; Don Juan kills the father and escapes.

The two friends flee to Flanders, where they enlist in the army; after a battle their mortally wounded Spanish captain gives Don Juan money to have a Mass celebrated for his soul, but Garcia gambles the money away. Overcome by visions of his captain's face in pain, Don Juan gives a priest his own money to have a Mass said for him. Garcia is killed and dies unrepentant; Modesto, a sullen soldier who suddenly disappears, is suspected of having killed him.

Upon learning that his parents have died, Don Juan returns to Seville to take over his inheritance; his house becomes a center of libertinism. One day, while ill, he draws up a list of his conquests, but a friend remarks that God is missing in the list of betrayed husbands. Determined to fill this gap, Don Juan enters a church and attracts the attention of a nun—it is Teresa, who is deeply troubled by the encounter. She agrees to escape with him. The night before the appointed day is a terrible one for Don Juan; he is frightened by a painting of souls in Purgatory which are suffering terrible tortures, yet he does not repent of his past life. While preparing for the elopement, he watches a funeral procession; to his inquiry of who is being buried, he receives the answer, "Don Juan de Maraña." He follows the procession into a church, where he learns that it consists of souls released from Purgatory by his mother's prayers in order to celebrate a last Mass for him. He has a vision of Garcia and the captain who are advancing toward him, shouting "Now he is ours." A terrible serpent comes from behind, ready to jump upon him. He loses consciousness and, upon recovering, he decides to enter a monastery. After having his money distributed among the poor, for Masses for the souls in Purgatory, and for the construction of a chapel and a hospital, he writes letters of his conversion to his friends and to Teresa, who soon dies, saying "He never loved me."

Maraña takes his vows as Brother Ambroise and thereafter "he was the example for that devout community as he had formerly been the model of the libertines of his age." Modesto, the soldier who had killed Garcia and who in reality is Teresa's brother, comes to challenge him, but Don Juan refuses to fight until Modesto slaps him. He kills his opponent and then, filled with remorse, he orders the cook of the monastery to slap him on both cheeks every morning. He continues his penitence for several years and dies after having ordered the aforementioned inscription for his tomb.

Although *Les Ames du purgatoire* is not one of Mérimée's major works, it reveals his excellence both as a storyteller and as a psychologist. He realized clearly that it would not do to handle the first part of Maraña's life exactly as if it were Don Juan's and then suddenly bring about the hero's conversion by miraculous events. Mérimée is therefore careful to lay the seeds for Maraña's eventual conversion in the first pages of the story where he describes his mother's efforts to instill religious sentiments in her son by impressing him with a painting of souls in Purgatory. Nor does Don Juan immediately turn to sensuous pleasures upon entering the University of Salamanca; on the contrary, he is prepared to take his studies seriously until Garcia and his own passionate nature lead him astray. But even in the midst of his debaucheries, Don Juan commits pious acts such as providing a Mass for his deceased captain. His conversion is therefore not due to horrifying events alone; these are rather the culminating effects upon a religious disposition that has never completely left Don Juan. What lends additional weight to the verisimilitude of the hero is that he devotes himself completely to the life he leads at any time, a trait that is in harmony with his passionate character. Mérimée, although making no special point of it, implies that there are subtle affinities between a

life of sensuous thrills and even the most austere religious devotion.
This makes Maraña's conversion far more convincing than mere miraculous events could have done.

The crucial point in any treatment of the Mañara legend is the
means by which the hero's conversion is brought about. Just as in the
Don Juan story, the two parts of the Mañara plot must be firmly linked
in order to bring about structural unity.

Dumas the Elder, in his miracle play *Don Juan de Marana ou la
Chute d'un ange* (1836), was far too much concerned with stage effects
to give any thought to structure. There is a good and a bad angel;
there is a descent by Don Juan's half-brother into the tomb of their
father in order to obtain the dead man's signature on a last will (and he
obtains it); there is the statue of a dead woman that seizes Don Juan
by the hair (and causes his conversion); there is a grand finale in which
the ghost of a man who had gambled away his mistress to Don Juan
enters and kills him while the bad angel calls for vengeance, the good
angel for mercy, and the angel of judgment for justice.[4] All this and
more. No wonder that Don Juan is converted by nothing more than a
frightening experience. Recovering from a vision of his victims, Don
Juan declines the good angel's love (she has signed away a thousand
years of bliss for one day with him) with these words: "I am no longer
your bridegroom, no longer Don Juan, your husband. I am Brother
Juan the Trappist. Remember, Sister Martha, that we must die."

It is not surprising to find a preposterous plot in the huge production of Dumas *père*; it is difficult to understand, however, how the
author of *Antony* could have failed to see the possibilities which Don
Juan offered him to create a splendid *homme fatal* instead of the un-
memorable hero of this miracle play.[5]

---

[4] This denouement was later changed to one in which, during the duel between
Don Juan and Sandoval, the former's female victims appear and one by one refuse
to pardon him. Finally Martha (i.e., the angel who has taken her place) comes
forward and forgives him. Don Juan repents and dies with the hope of being pardoned.

[5] For a parody of Dumas's play, see Roberge, *Don Juan de Marance, ou la Chute
d'un ange*, "drame ... raconté par Robert Macaire et Bertrand ..." (1836). Imitations and translations of Dumas's play have been frequent. In Arnold Bennett's
play *Don Juan de Marana* (about 1913), the author devised a new ending: Don
José, who has come to kill Don Juan, agrees to desist, provided that a pure woman
will redeem him with her life. Marta offers herself, and Don Juan becomes a monk.

The Mañara legend was quickly seized upon by writers who had been dissatisfied with the stern moral attitude of Tirso de Molina. To them the punishment of Don Juan seemed too severe. Why, they asked, should God want to send a young madcap like Don Juan to Hell rather than illuminate him by His mercy?

One of the most vehement advocates of this opinion was Désiré Laverdant who first wrote a two-volume study to justify his views[6] and then a drama with a title that leaves no doubt regarding the fate of his hero: *Don Juan converti* (1864). In order to realize this conversion, Laverdant calls Columbus to his aid. Don Juan, who has finally fallen in love with Anna, is persuaded by Columbus to join him on his voyage to the New World and, when they sight land, the sinner falls to his knees and confesses his belief in God.

Edmond Haraucourt does not go so far afield as Laverdant. In his drama *Don Juan de Mañara* (1898) the hero is converted after a vision of his own funeral. Prior to that, Don Juan had caused the death of his future sister-in-law by breaking into her room the night before his wedding. While trying to escape, he had also killed her father. Haraucourt attempts to make Don Juan's conversion appear more plausible by indicating that the hero was religious in his youth, but Gendarme de Bévotte is certainly over-sympathetic in claiming that "the reasons which lead him toward faith arise from within, not from without."[7] The gradual transformation of the hero which such a change would require is lacking in this drama. Just before his vision Don Juan has abducted his former fiancée from a convent, and his conversion may therefore be ascribed to satiety or fear of death.

That the Mañara legend can be treated effectively within its historical framework is demonstrated by O. V. de Lubicz-Milosz's mystery play *Miguel Mañara* (1912). The author, a Lithuanian who wrote in French, has in recent times gained considerable recognition as a profound religious poet. Aside from occasional bombast, this play is one of the most appealing Mañara productions of this century. Milosz, like Haraucourt, shows us a satiated hero, one who has exhausted all the sensuous pleasures a man can experience: "Satan," he says in the first scene, "has withdrawn from me and I am chewing the

---

[6] *Les Renaissances de Don Juan* (Paris, 1864).

[7] Gendarme de Bévotte, *La Légende de Don Juan*, II, 170.

bitter herbs from the rock of boredom. I served Venus with unbounded enthusiasm at first, then with malice and disgust. Today I would twist her neck with a yawn." Miguel's disgust is limited to amorous adventures and to the world as he sees it around him. His desire is to experience something greater than heretofore. Disgust with the old, as Milosz shows, is a mere first step in the direction of a new view of life; if it is the direct cause of a conversion, this will be one of inglorious defeat. Its function should rather be to dispose the soul to new impressions. Mañara's empty heart is filled by the naïve but very womanly love of Girolama Carillo de Mendoza. Her purity impresses itself so deeply upon him that, after her premature death, he is almost inevitably drawn to the religious life.

In his wife and in religion Mañara finds the revelation he had never suspected: that God is love. It was love, the love of a pure, unaffected woman, that caused Miguel to change his way of living. The abbot to whom he confesses after Girolama's death likewise corrects his idea that penitence means self-punishment: "Penitence is not pain. It is love." Love too is what cures the cripple Johannes Melendez:

DON MIGUEL: You have suffered much at the hands of men, my Brother Johannes. And what name do you give God in your thoughts? Do you call Him Pain, or Justice, or Vengeance?

JOHANNES: I give Him the name you just exclaimed a short while ago.

DON MIGUEL: And that name is?

JOHANNES: Love.

"Throw away your crutches," says Don Miguel, and Johannes is cured.

Several works draw on episodes of the Mañara legend for short stories or poems.[8] Of these, José de Espronceda's dramatic poem *El estudiante de Salamanca* (1840) is the most remarkable. The author, one of the foremost Spanish romantic poets, turns to the Don Juan legend both for his concept of the hero and for the ending.

Don Felix de Montemar, a student at the University of Salamanca, has seduced Elvira, who has died as a result of it. Her brother,

---

[8] Among others Louis How, *The Other Don Juan* (poem, 1932). Franco Alfano's opera *L'Ombra di Don Giovanni* (1914), later revised as *Don Juan de Mañara* (1941), depicts an imaginary return of Mañara to the home of his ancestors in Italy.

who attempts to avenge her, is killed by him. Walking in the street,
Felix's eye is caught by a woman. He follows her. Without looking
back, the woman warns him that he is offending God. Felix answers
like a true Tenorio, who only lives in and for the present moment:

> Life is life: when it ends, pleasure too ends with it. Why should we
> burden ourselves with uncertainties? For me there is never a tomorrow or
> a yesterday. . . . If I die tomorrow, whether it be for better or worse, what
> does it matter to me what people may say? I am enjoying the present, I reap
> now and, if he wants to, let the Devil take me when I die.

Even though he has a vision of a double funeral, his own and that
of Elvira's brother, he continues his pursuit of the unknown woman
but cannot catch up with her. As she is about to enter a house, her voice
warns him to desist or else he will die of it. Felix enters the house after
her—the woman is the skeleton of Elvira. While she seeks his lips,
voices tell him that she is his wife. Horrified, he tries to avoid her
touch, but she does not set him free and he dies in her clutches as the
Devil comes for him.

Although the Mañara legend abounds in events to which the hero's
conversion may be credited, a few writers preferred to devise new ones.
As a matter of fact, the first version of a converted Don Juan had
nothing to do with the Mañara plot and appeared two months before
Mérimée's *Les Ames du purgatoire* was published. Blaze de Bury's
dramatic poem *Le Souper chez le Commandeur* (June 1, 1834) was
no doubt written with serious and edifying intensions, but its effect
is not always that intended by the author. Don Juan appears at the
Commander's tomb where he finds all the dead members of the Commander's family united. They are startled by the appearance of Donna
Anna, who has just died and has been condemned to ten thousand years
of Purgatory unless her urn is filled with tears. We are not told how
big the urn is, but this task obviously requires the conversion of a hardened sinner. Don Juan, unanimously elected to play the tearful part,
refuses at first. Finally, however, he is so much overwhelmed by
Anna's beauty that he curses Satan, prays to the Virgin, and weeps out
his conversion and Anna's salvation.

Gregorio Martínez Sierra's play *Don Juan de España* (1921)
seems intended as an illustration of Leporello's catalogue aria. The
variety of women Don Juan attempts to seduce is practically unequaled

in any other version: a society lady in Italy, a young bride in Flanders, three Frenchwomen during a celebration in Paris, a fifteen-year-old girl in an Aragonese tavern (who resists him because he had seduced her mother), and finally a gypsy girl in Seville who saves his life by receiving a blow destined for him. Awed by so much love, Don Juan exclaims, "I am yours, Constancilla!" but a voice echoes: "Yes, you are mine!" It is the voice of a veiled lady who has pursued him throughout his career. She is Death. Don Juan follows her, screaming for confession. After his conversion he is mortally wounded when he attempts to stop a fight between beggars. Clara, a mysterious lady, receives his final confession, absolves him, and offers her own soul in return for Don Juan's salvation.

Joaquín Dicenta, in order to convert the hero of his play *La conversión de Mañara* (1905), has the aging Mañara encounter his own son in the person whom Doña Inés has chosen to defend her against him. Mañara breaks his sword, gives his blessings to the marriage of the young couple, and withdraws to a life of meditation.

Numerous attempts have been made to bring about a popular synthesis of the Don Juan and Mañara legends. Obviously, these two subjects can be more easily combined than the Don Juan and Faust themes, since Don Juan's adventures can conveniently fill the gap in our knowledge about Mañara's youth.

Albert T'Serstevens states that his novel *La Légende de Don Juan* (1923) is an attempt "to unite in one personage the principal aspects of the Tenorio and Mañara legends." What the author does, however, is to divide the two subjects mechanically by relating the Don Juan legend first (with considerable fantasy) and then letting Tenorio return to earth as Don Juan Mañara. The latter is converted by the Wandering Jew and dies a saint.

Joseph Delteil's novel *Don Juan* (1930) seeks to exploit the more sensational aspects of both legends. The result is a disharmonious mixture of popular mysticism and earthy sensuousness that borders on bad taste. The association of these two passions can very easily be justified, but Don Juan does seem to overdo matters when, in order to kill the *odor di femina*, he digs his hands into excrements. The mystic theme is sounded in a mock marriage between Don Juan and the Commander's daughter Thérèse while they are children, a ceremony which assumes greater significance by Don Juan's placing a ring on the finger of a statue of the Virgin. It is the Virgin who calls him to her after Thérèse has died.

In Delteil's novel, as in that of T'Serstevens, the statue receives ill treatment. In the latter work, the representative of divine justice weeps as Don Juan thunders "Be silent, wretch!" and in Delteil's the statue becomes tipsy in the company of pretty women and then informs Don Juan that women merely use him (Don Juan) as an instrument and that he has syphilis. This indeed is a new and realistic punishment, but it shows how far the religious element in the Don Juan legend has deteriorated.

In Mirko Jelusich's novel "Don Juan: The Seven Deadly Sins,"[9] written in Croatian, the author has Don Juan and Mañara meet. At first Don Juan wants to kill Mañara because he feels this man knows more about him than anyone else; but he soon realizes that his judgment has been too hasty. In the ending Jelusich combines the two legends in the most logical manner possible: Don Juan is not punished by the statue. "You are so unhappy," the voice says, "that I cannot punish you. Live." Don Juan seizes the statue's hand, loses consciousness, and, upon recovering, runs to a monastery where he is received by the forgiving statue of the Virgin.

Jean Suberville adds another dimension to his drama *La Passion de Don Juan* (1932) by making Don Juan's salvation the object of a struggle between John of the Cross and the demon Asmodeus. The author has his hero converted by the love of Girolama, and then he introduces a new twist: Don Luis, whose wife Don Juan had seduced, takes revenge by shooting Girolama. Luis reappears in the monastery to which Don Juan has retired and confesses his deed, but with a great effort Don Juan masters the temptation of anger and forgives his enemy.

We have seen how the Mañara legend burst into popularity in the 1830's, crossing paths with the Don Juan legend, even threatening for a time to eclipse it, and finally continuing on its own path, carrying

---

[9] This novel has been available to me only in a German version, entitled *Don Juan: die sieben Todsünden*, published in 1936. According to Singer's *Bibliography*, it was originally written in Croatian, but I find a *Don Juan* (1931) by Jelusich listed in Wilhelm Kosch, *Deutsches Literatur-Lexikon* (Bern, 1953), vol. II.

along, in turn, elements of the legend which it had invaded. The appeal of the Mañara legend is unmistakable: it offers a quasi-historical background, a hero capable of development, a big *scène à faire* (his conversion), and a decidedly happier ending than that of the traditional Don Juan story. Beyond this (and in contrast to the Hoffmannesque concept) the Mañara denouement is built on a solid moral basis: Mañara's penitence is the only possible justification for permitting Don Juan to die not only unpunished but with the virtual certainty of salvation, for only by sacrificing himself for the benefit of his fellow men can he make amends for the wreckage his selfish passion has wrought.

It is quite understandable that the Mañara legend has enjoyed special favor among Catholic writers who, desiring to bring the sinner back into the fold, preferred the Mañara denouement to that of the punishing statue. But in attempting to execute this project, the author is beset by numerous problems. In choosing his plot, he must decide whether he wants to treat the story of Mañara historically, in which case he will write a mere dramatized biography, or whether he is to draw his material from the legend. In shaping his hero, the author is not dealing with an essentially unchanging character (like the Burlador, for example) but with one who, in the relatively narrow compass of a novel or a drama, has to be turned from one extreme into another. It is not enough to present a hero who plays the part of the Burlador and then is suddenly converted by a miraculous event; to do that, the faltering author has to call on God's grace for help (a most difficult matter on the stage) or else resort to such infantile metamorphoses as Dumas's "I am no longer your bridegroom, no longer Don Juan, your husband. I am Brother Juan the Trappist." Nor is it a satisfactory solution to effect Mañara's conversion by an accumulation of miraculous events, for in that case we gain the impression that the egoistic hero has been frightened into taking that step. To harmonize the two disparate parts of the Mañara story, the author might do better if he laid the foundations for his conversion in Miguel's character, developed them during the action, and then, if need be, let a supernatural event give him the final impetus. Of all those who have treated the Mañara legend, only Mérimée and Milosz have come close to achieving that kind of characterization.

While, on the whole, the Mañara legend has not proved to be so elastic and hence amenable to variations as the Don Juan legend, it is safe to state that the definitive Mañara version is yet to be written, for at present the possibilities contained in the subject are still far from exhausted. In the absence of a definitive treatment by a first-rate writer, the Mañara legend will probably continue to appeal to religious-minded authors whose faith is often greater than their artistry. Whatever the future may hold in store for the Mañara legend, this much seems certain: unless its psychological basis is more thoroughly explored, the legend is likely to degenerate into a mere story of amorous adventures, ghosts, spirits, and stage effects.

CHAPTER ELEVEN

Zorrilla: The Saved Don Juan

Lo que justicias ni obispos
No pudieron hacer
Con cárceles y sermones,
Lo pudo con su candidez.[1]

ZORRILLA,
Don Juan Tenorio,
Part One, IV, ix

Every year, early in November, on All-Souls' Day, a drama is performed all over Spain and Latin America: *Don Juan Tenorio* by José Zorrilla y Moral. In 1880, thirty-six years after its production, the author strongly condemned his work.[2] It was composed hastily, he stated; the meter used is bad; the "sofa" verses are out of place in the action; Don Juan is a worthless braggart. He was proud only of having created Doña Inés. Be that as it may, Zorrilla's fame rests primarily on this work, which can properly be considered the national drama of Spain.

Surely, such popularity must be based on more than accident and caprice. And yet, few dramatic works have met with more severe and continuous criticism; only in recent times has critical fury abated somewhat, so as to permit a more balanced judgment of *Don Juan Tenorio*.

In the development of the Don Juan legend Zorrilla's drama occupies a position analogous to the works of Molière and Mozart.

---

[1] "What neither justice nor bishops could do with prisons and sermons she accomplished with her purity."

[2] In *Recuerdos del tiempo viejo* (Barcelona, 1880–82), Part I, pp. 162–80, Zorrilla denies any personal resentment, but it is a tragic fact that he had sold the rights to *Don Juan Tenorio* for the insignificant sum of 4,200 reales before the Spanish copyright law was passed. By 1880 the play had attained great popularity and the author, penniless, had to beg alms from theatrical producers and the state.

On the one hand, *Don Juan Tenorio* modernizes both hero and action; on the other hand, it is a synthesis of the interpretations and trends which had evolved during the preceding years of the nineteenth century—an irresistible lover, an ideal woman, a religious and mystical atmosphere, and, finally, the logical culmination of Don Juan's rehabilitation: the saving of the hero through the intercession of a pure woman.

The action takes place in Seville, around 1545, during the carnival season. Don Juan has returned to Seville in order to meet Don Luis Mejía, with whom he had made a bet as to which of the two could commit more misdeeds in one year. Don Juan recites his adventures in Rome, Naples, and Spain, which he summarizes thus: "Wherever I went, I offended reason, I mocked virtue, made fun of justice and misled women. And I went down to cabins and up to palaces and scaled the walls of convents and left everywhere bitter memories." (Part One, I, xii)

Don Luis too has left chaos behind him in Flanders and in Paris, but he now intends to change, for he is going to marry Doña Ana. The two competitors compare lists: Don Luis has killed twenty-three men and betrayed fifty-six women; Don Juan has killed thirty-two men and betrayed seventy-two women, thus winning the bet. However, Don Luis points out that a nun is missing among his conquests, and Don Juan promises to add one to his list, along with the woman whom a friend of his is about to marry. He asks for only six days to fulfill his promise: "One to make them fall in love, another to succeed with them, one more to abandon them, two to find a new one, and one hour to forget them." (Part One, I, xii)

Don Juan's father and the Commander Gonzalo de Ulloa, whose daughter Inés Don Juan is to marry, have witnessed this scene. When the Commander tells him furiously that he will not consent to let him marry Inés, Don Juan laughs and responds that he will take her himself. His father's remonstrances do not affect him, either. Upon their departure, both Don Juan and Don Luis are arrested: each had arranged to have the other imprisoned. Both men escape. Don Luis hurries to his fiancée's home to protect her, but he is taken prisoner by the men of Don Juan, who gains access to Ana's room by bribing her maid.

Gonzalo de Ulloa has decided to have his daughter take the veil, but Don Juan has bribed her chaperon Brígida to take his letter to her.

Inés, much troubled by his assurances of love, faints when Don Juan boldly enters her cell. He picks her up and carries her away to his house. Upon regaining consciousness, she wants to leave the house at once; Don Juan enters and gains her love but is, in turn, deeply stirred by her innocence. Their moment of happiness is disturbed by Don Luis, who, although his life belongs to Don Juan by virtue of their wager, challenges him to a duel. He is followed by the raging Commander. Don Juan falls on his knees before the old man and begs him for the hand of Doña Inés. Don Gonzalo remains unmoved by this plea; when Don Juan exclaims that he is causing him to lose his hope for salvation, the angry Commander replies: "And what concern of mine is your salvation, Don Juan?" (Part One, iv, ix) Overcome with anger when Don Luis calls him a coward, Don Juan kills both men. His servant Ciutti warns him of the approaching police and he escapes.

The second part of the drama opens with Don Juan's return to Seville after an absence of five years. In accordance with the last will of his father, his palace has been turned into a cemetery for all the victims of his son. Don Juan sinks down at the tomb of Inés and gives vent to his grief. Her spirit appears and tells him that God has ordered her to wait for him and that she will be condemned or saved with him. When the spirit disappears, Don Juan believes it all to have been a hallucination, but Inés' statue is missing from her tomb. His hands are still shaking when two of his former companions pass by. Irritated by their teasing, he invites them to dine with him, and, in order to prove that he is not afraid, he invites the statue of the Commander too.

At the dinner they hear the approach of steps. Don Juan, who thinks it is a practical joke of his friends, calls for the guest to come in. Don Gonzalo's statue enters through the wall and, while the others faint, announces to Don Juan that it has come to prove that there exists an eternity beyond man's life, that he is to die the next day, and that God has given him time to set his conscience in order. To convince himself, Don Juan shoots at the statue, which disappears through the wall the way it had entered. The spirit of Inés appears and warns him to heed the statue's words. Don Juan, still believing that the apparitions were a hoax, awakens his friends, who swear they had nothing to do with it and, in turn, accuse him of having played a joke on them. An argument ensues in the course of which Don Juan challenges his friends to a duel.

In the next scene Don Juan returns to the cemetery, regretting that he has killed his friends. He calls the Commander, whose tomb opens, showing a table set with snakes, bones, and fire. All the tombs open up except that of Inés. The Commander's statue declares that Don Juan's time is up. Don Juan is finally convinced that there is a world beyond:

DON JUAN: Unjust God! Now that I have no time to repent you make your power known to me!
STATUE: One moment of contrition brings salvation to a soul, and this moment is given to you, too.
DON JUAN: Blot out thirty cursed years of crimes and misdeeds in one moment? Impossible! (Part Two, III, ii)

He hears a funeral go by and learns that he is dead—it is *he* who has been killed in the duel. The Commander's statue asks for his hand and then declares in a voice of thunder that he will be dragged to Hell. But Don Juan struggles and, raising his free hand to Heaven, exclaims: "Almighty God, I believe in you; have pity on me, my Lord!" (Part Two, III, ii) Thereupon Inés' tomb opens and she takes his free hand. Both of them are saved: "It is a mystery which transcends the comprehension of the living; and only in a purer life the just will understand that love saved Don Juan at the foot of the grave." (Part Two, III, iii)

There are several features in Zorrilla's drama which a dry analysis cannot describe; for example, the strange mixture of reality and fantasy during the second part, where stage effects blend happily with a tense plot situation as Don Juan, somewhat like Everyman, finds no one willing to take his side until Inés seizes his hand raised toward Heaven in a last plea.

What matters still more is Zorrilla's poetic brilliance. In this connection it should be noted that the Spanish-speaking countries, unlike much of the rest of Europe, never denounced romanticism vehemently. In Spain, romanticism was not a protest against previous literary traditions but rather a continuation of what constitutes a very basic emotional inclination in the Spanish character. Hence Zorrilla's poetry is as appealing to the modern spectator as to the author's contemporaries. Almost every Spaniard knows by heart the famous "sofa" verses in which Don Juan declares his love to Doña Inés. They invoke the breeze, the flowers, and the serene waters of the Guadalquivir, which can be seen from the window. There is conventional love rhetoric in these verses, but they also convey a sensuous and languorous mood so as to unite sentiment and scene most admirably.

A story cannot continue to appeal unless its plot and hero are brought into harmony with changing conditions. Zorrilla did much toward that end, for he continued the tradition at the same time as he synthesized contemporary trends; besides, he added his own contribution.

Don Juan Tenorio contains the basic traits of Tirso's Burlador. He is a ruthless seducer; he is brave; he is a nobleman who cares only for his own pleasures. He does not, like the Hoffmannesque hero, seek an ideal woman; but when he encounters that ideal, he is, in the manner of Mañara, so overcome by her innocence and beauty that he will bend his proud knees. Like the Burlador, Don Juan Tenorio does not analyze himself—he acts, and there is something genuine and refreshing in his impulsiveness that had been absent from Don Juan versions for a long time.

Zorrilla modernized the Don Juan subject in other ways too, yet without destroying its basic elements. There is, for example, the difficult problem of motivating Don Juan's actions, particularly his fickleness. The ideal-seeker, as we have noticed previously, does not make for good theater. Zorrilla's solution may not be profound but it is effective: the bet between Don Juan and Don Luis. It is quite plausible that a proud and vain young Spaniard should be urged on to a great number of adventures and seductions by the challenge of a wager. If this spur is added to a passionate temperament, the number of conquests (which is, incidentally, considerably below the one cited by Leporello) may well reach seventy-two.

Another crucial problem is the invitation of the statue. Here too Zorrilla modifies and modernizes. A nineteenth-century Don Juan cannot be expected to hold the same beliefs as his predecessor in the seventeenth: the Burlador could be a libertine and yet believe in the existence of God; Don Juan Tenorio is bound to add religious skepticism to moral license. Zorrilla capitalizes on this change of conditions to alter the tenor of Don Juan's invitation and hence the whole moral basis of the drama. The words Don Juan employs are significant. He invites the statue of Don Gonzalo "so that I may learn from you whether there is a world beyond this one and another life in which, to speak the truth, I never have believed." (Part Two, I, vi) The central theme of Zorrilla's play is therefore not concerned with the problem of overconfidence in God's mercy but with a libertine's challenge to the other world to manifest itself; therefore the statue's function is not so much to avenge as to prove the existence of a beyond. This factor justifies, to some extent at least, the eventual salvation of Don Juan.

Zorrilla's drama has been the subject of much criticism, some of which is unjustified. For example, we read in the *Encyclopaedia Britannica*: "The play is in fact little more than an adaptation of the elder Dumas's *Don Juan de Marana*, which, in its turn, derives chiefly from Mérimée's novel *Les Ames du purgatoire*."[3] A mere comparison of the plots of the three works mentioned above will suffice to prove that this statement is completely unfounded; Zorrilla's drama is, on the contrary, highly original.[4] Its only models are, primarily, Tirso's *Burlador* and, to a lesser extent, the Mañara legend from which the gap in Don Juan's list and the vision of his own funeral are borrowed. Several critics have claimed to see Dumas's influence in the person of Don Luis, whom they believe to be derived from Don Sandoval of Dumas. While this is not impossible, an examination of the role of Don Luis indicates an at least equally close relationship to de la Mota of the *Burlador*. The only resemblance between Don Luis and Sandoval is that both point out to Don Juan that a nun is

---

[3] Article "Don Juan," in the 1957 edition.

[4] This criticism may have been based on Thomas Fitz-Gerald's article, "Some Notes on the Sources of Zorrilla's *Don Juan Tenorio*," *Hispania*, V (1922), 1–7, which denies Zorrilla's claim that he only knew Tirso's *Burlador* and a recasting of it by Solís (which has never been found), and which insists that the influence of Dumas in Zorrilla's play is undeniable.

Fitz-Gerald's thesis has been strongly supported by J. A. Thompson, *Alexandre Dumas Père and Spanish Romantic Drama* (Baton Rouge, 1938), pp. 160–74, who cites thirteen cases of resemblances between the two plays.

It was not until 1945 that new light was cast on the problem. J. K. Leslie, "Towards the Vindication of Zorrilla: the Dumas-Zorrilla Question again," *Hispanic Review*, XIII (1945), 288–93, points out that many of the resemblances cited by Thompson are neither in the first edition of Dumas's *Don Juan de Marana ou la Chute d'un ange* (1836) nor in the Spanish translations by J.-M. Ll[ivé] (1838) and García Gutiérrez (1839); in fact, they do not appear until the Lévy frères edition of Dumas's play in 1864. Since Dumas visited Spain in 1846, he may have become acquainted with Zorrilla's play, so that it may very well have been Dumas who imitated Zorrilla, and not vice versa.

missing in his list; but this feature had already been contained in the Mañara legend, which probably was Zorrilla's source for this. If we compare Don Luis and de la Mota, however, more similarities appear: both have led a dissolute life, both are about to change their way of living and for the same reason, namely, Doña Ana; both also tell Don Juan of their intentions. Thus, since Zorrilla needed a rival for Don Juan on account of the bet, he may have raised de la Mota to this position.

More serious than the foregoing criticisms is that of Spanish critics, most of whom are very severe on Zorrilla. Manuel de la Revilla calls Zorrilla's hero "the least in conformity with the legendary type, the falsest and perhaps the least well conceived of all."[5] This accusation is certainly unfair; it fails to take into account the need for change and modernization that has been stressed above. There are, indeed, changes in Don Juan's behavior and methods of seduction, but that is certainly to be expected in view of both the religious skepticism and the refinement of seductive methods that the eighteenth century had devised.

Don Juan is not a believer like the Burlador and, while not an outspoken atheist, he certainly harbors strong doubts regarding the existence of anything that cannot be checked by normal rules of evidence. But even an enlightened Don Juan is still a Spaniard, raised in an atmosphere in which the supernatural element occupies an important place. Although his reason may deny the existence of such forces, he cannot fully make up his mind until he has seen undeniable evidence one way or the other. Therefore he challenges the world beyond to reveal itself. In his encounter with these forces he does not equal the magnificent Burlador, but his actions are determined by his attitude. The modern mind refuses to accept miraculous events as such and will try desperately to find a reasonable explanation for them. This accounts for Don Juan's belief that the appearances of the Commander's statue and of Inés' spirit are a practical joke on the part of his friends. He holds on to this conviction until the evidence to the contrary becomes so overwhelming that it crushes him.

Don Juan's ways of approaching women have changed too. He no longer uses coarse deceit; he has acquired some of Lovelace's refinements: he writes passionate love letters, he uses go-betweens such as Brígida, he bribes chambermaids, he is ready to use force, if neces-

<hr />

[5] In Magnabal, *Don Juan et la critique espagnole*, p. 27.

sary. Yet this same man falls so completely in love with as inexperienced a woman as Inés that he will fall on his knees before the angry
Commander and even submit to his insults for a while. This has been
strongly criticized by Spanish critics, especially Jacinto Grau,[6] as unworthy of a Don Juan.

The change that takes place in Zorrilla's hero is, indeed, a swift
and startling one: he is transformed from a hardened evil-doer into
a gentle and submissive lover. The only explanation for this is that
Inés constitutes for him the *coup de foudre* which accomplishes the
impossible. Kneeling before a furious father is certainly not typical
of Don Juan; but only by recalling what this act of abasement means
for a proud Spanish caballero can we appreciate how profoundly Don
Juan has been impressed by Inés. This scene is, in my judgment, a
sublime one, because it lets us see the impetuous Spanish Don Juan
who is subject to sudden changes that need not be slowly prepared or
long sought for.[7]

Other criticisms of Zorrilla's hero are more difficult to refute. Why,
for example, does Don Juan Tenorio shoot Don Gonzalo without giving him an opportunity to defend himself? Only the imminent arrival
of the police, which does not leave time for a duel with two men, can
explain this action. It must also be admitted that Don Juan refuses
repeatedly to assume responsibility for what he has done and shifts
the blame onto others. Thus he makes Heaven responsible for his
future actions when his last hope of keeping Inés is destroyed;
or, again, he blames his two friends for the duel and their presumed
death.

The drama itself suffers from several weaknesses. For one, Don
Juan's servant. Zorrilla revealed that Ciutti was modeled after an
Italian servant he once had had,[8] but this does not prevent Ciutti from
being insignificant and colorless. The play could only have gained by

---

[6] In his Introduction to *Don Juan en el drama* (Buenos Aires, 1944).

[7] I am here primarily speaking in terms of effective theater, but even with that
limitation it may be felt that this contradicts my previous objection to the sudden,
unmotivated conversions in Mañara versions. However, it is far more likely for a
sensuous libertine to be suddenly changed by really falling in love with a woman
than to be unexpectedly converted by miraculous events. That is why I particularly
praised Milosz's play *Miguel Mañara* for combining these two aspects.

[8] Zorrilla, *Recuerdos del tiempo viejo*, I, 165.

a different choice. The author also tends to abuse the effects of super-natural forces: Inés' spirit turns up a bit more frequently than even a miracle play warrants.

But the most important defect of Zorrilla's drama can be found in its moral and religious significance. Two principal meanings can be drawn from it: (1) the existence of a world beyond which reveals itself upon being challenged; (2) the salvation of a sinner through the love of a pure woman. Taken by themselves, these features are not necessarily objectionable; nor is the author the first Spanish writer who saved Don Juan: Zamora's hero had died with the hope of being pardoned. But the manner in which Don Juan is saved by Zorrilla has justly been criticized:

Don Juan is saved by virtue of his repentance after death (a heresy from the theological point of view) and thanks to a loving and generous woman who offers herself to God as a sacrifice and who takes it upon herself to make Don Juan's fate her own—a heroic agreement on her part, an iniquitous one on the part of God, immoral, absurd and impious in every way. This drama contains a fine justice indeed! The victims of Don Juan groan in Hell or in Purgatory, because they were not even given time to repent. Doña Inés, innocent and pure, suffers her expiation and risks eternal damnation out of love for him; the Commander, outraged in his honor and basely assassinated, has to renounce the avenging mission with which Heaven has invested him, and return to Hell . . . without having obtained vengeance or justice and after having witnessed the salvation of his assassin. Don Luis Mejía, offended personally and through his future wife, burns in Hell; while the one who, in order to win an infamous bet, had recourse to deceit and treachery, rises happily and triumphantly to Heaven. And the object of so many favors, thanks to the love of Doña Inés, is not merely singled out for repeated and salutary advice, which he disdains, but, furthermore, after having been killed by the hand of a friend whom he challenged without reason, a fantastic scene is prepared for him in order to make him repent (as if it were not already too late) and to make him gain his salvation. If such were the case, who would not want to be a second Don Juan?[9]

In fact, Zorrilla's denouement completely reverses Tirso's religious and moral purposes; it fully justifies the Burlador's "Qué largo me lo fiáis" even beyond his fondest hopes. "The punishment of Don Juan has a profound significance: it means that the individual cannot

[9] Manuel de la Revilla, in Magnabal, *Don Juan et la critique espagnole*, p. 30.

devise his moral conduct and his ideals by himself, that the truth is contained in a common rule imposed by a superior will."[10] The Mañara legend, it is true, does not punish the hero, either; but his conversion entails penitence and sacrifices by means of which he atones for his past sins. The Don Juan of Zorrilla, however, is getting something for nothing. However impressive his abasement before the Commander may appear on the stage, however sincere his love for Inés may be— these factors are far from sufficient to justify saving a man who at the very least has killed thirty-four men and deceived seventy-three women. One cannot help wondering whether even "in a purer life the just will understand" why so much favor should be bestowed upon such a criminal.

These weaknesses notwithstanding, the fact remains that Zorrilla's *Don Juan Tenorio* has been for many years by far the most frequently performed of all existing Don Juan plays; in Spain and Latin America it has pushed Tirso's *Burlador* almost completely off the stage. In order to understand this, it is necessary to recall the difference between reading and seeing a play: in a performance our critical faculties are impeded by the swiftness of the action and by the spectacle itself. Our various psychological and moral objections should not make us forget that *Don Juan Tenorio* is an excellent play, packed with action and suspense and featuring a modern hero. Another important factor can be found in the much-criticized denouement of the play. In his emotional sympathy with Don Juan, the spectator would probably leave a performance of the *Burlador* highly edified but depressed; on the other hand, the saving of Don Juan Tenorio has all the attractive aspects of a happy ending. To this might be added Madariaga's somewhat facetious remark which attributes the popularity of Zorrilla's *Don Juan Tenorio* to the hero's being saved by a woman, because the Spaniards are accustomed to having their women do everything for them.[11]

Today Zorrilla's play is no longer subject to critical controversy. Its own merits and never-ending popular appeal have ranked *Don Juan Tenorio* among the great theatrical works of modern times, perhaps less universal in appeal than others, but nearly unequaled on the Spanish stage. By this time too the question of originality no longer excites anybody (if it ever did) but the literary specialists. The simple

[10] Gendarme de Bévotte, *La Légende de Don Juan*, II, 12.

[11] Salvador de Madariaga, *Don Juan y la Don Juanía* (Buenos Aires, 1950).

fact is that *Don Juan Tenorio* has been and remains a great success.[12] Is this due to custom or to continuous appeal? Is this play kept in the repertory the way Christmas songs are revived once a year, or is there something deeper behind its popularity? No doubt the custom of performing Zorrilla's drama on All-Souls' Day is of considerable importance in keeping *Don Juan Tenorio* alive, but it is certain that it evokes deep reactions in the Spanish-speaking spectator.

Zorrilla not only modernized and brought together prevailing trends of the Don Juan subject; he also presents some of the most effective portrayals of women in the history of the legend in Inés and in Brígida, her sly and cunning chaperon.

With Zorrilla's *Don Juan Tenorio* we have reached the climax of Don Juan's rehabilitation, a development that had begun with Hoffmann's short story some thirty years before. But Don Juan's glorification did not meet with universal approval. After the applause came the howls of protest.

[12] Numerous adaptations of Zorrilla's *Don Juan Tenorio* have been made. Among these are Antonio Careta y Vidal's *El audaz Don Juan Tenorio* (1897) and *Les Amours de Don Juan*, by Edmond Lepelletier and Clément Rochel; the most recent adaptation is *Don Juan* (1953), by Ronald Duncan. Mention might also be made of *Don Luis Mejía* (1925), by Eduardo Marquina and A. Hernández Catá, which relates the adventures of Don Juan's rival.

In his tragedy *Der Sturz* (1948), Christian Schneller begins with Part Two of Zorrilla's plot. This work contains a remarkable final scene in which Don Juan boldly advances toward the ghost of Inés. Just as he extends his arms to embrace her, lightning strikes him down.

CHAPTER TWELVE

The Anti-Romantic Reaction

Oh! qu'ils t'ont mal compris, ceux
qui ont vu dans ta destinée l'em-
blème d'une lutte glorieuse et per-
sévérante contre la réalité! . . .
Ils ne savent pas que Dieu punit en
toi l'egoïsme et la vanité.[1]

GEORGE SAND,
Lélia

Mankind has devised as many, if not more, ways of deprecating as of praising people. "Character assassination" is a relatively recent term coined to describe one of the more vulgar manifestations of this ancient art, which runs the gamut from subtle allusions to sledge-hammer attacks. Don Juan, for his part, has been subjected to every conceivable kind of criticism: gentle chiding, pin-prick deflation, screaming hate, cold irony that strips away any pretense, medical and psychological examination that leaves one undressed, praise that turns to blame—he has been spared none of these.

Don Juan, it should be recalled, had been an object of criticism for practically all the seventeenth- and eighteenth-century authors who had treated the legend. Perhaps it would be more accurate to say that he had been held up as an example of unsavory behavior. These writers tried to demonstrate through Don Juan a vice of one kind or another, usually libertinism of thought and behavior, and to show the consequences such a vice entails. There is no intention of repeating here the frequent, and quite inaccurate, assertion that the characters portrayed in these works represent a general vice only and lack individuality.

---

[1] "Oh! how you have been misunderstood by those who have seen in your destiny the emblem of a glorious and persistent struggle against reality! . . . They do not know that God punishes in you egoism and vanity."

Even a cursory perusal of the Don Juan versions of Tirso de Molina and Molière would suffice to disprove this opinion. I would, however, maintain that this kind of attack, although often angry and indignant, was necessarily limited by artistic considerations. If a serious vice was to be attacked, the author very likely would have to endow Don Juan with a certain grandeur, for otherwise the celestial punishment could not be justified; besides, the hero had to be attractive to show that vice often operates under an appealing exterior. Whatever the case, the author could not permit himself to belittle Don Juan, because his work would probably suffer proportionately.

This situation was completely changed by the romantic glorification of Don Juan. Henceforth the critic's task became at least a two-fold one: it was no longer sufficient to portray Don Juan as evil—the romantic position had to be attacked as well. Thus what had begun as a frontal criticism now frequently was turned into a counterattack to chase the opponent from captured terrain. This amounted, of course, to reaction rather than action, and to all the negative aspects that accompany such an attitude. The result often tended to be a lowering of artistic standards, for what was produced under these circumstances resembled at times propaganda more closely than literature. Gone also was the balance in character description, for it no longer mattered to present the hero in his complexity of attractiveness and evil but rather to prove one position to be right and the other wrong. Hence an essay would often do the trick as adequately as a play or a novel.

The first important protests against the romantic rehabilitation of Don Juan appeared in the very midst of that movement, and it came from writers who were not entirely out of sympathy with the ideas of their contemporaries: Stendhal and George Sand.

Stendhal's remarks about Don Juan are contained in Chapter LIX of De l'Amour (1822), entitled "Werther et Don Juan." However ambivalent Stendhal's attitude toward his romantic colleagues may have been, he did write his pro-romantic pamphlet Racine et Shakespeare in 1823, and his heroes not only express a profound admiration for Napoleon but also dream of amorous conquests. Why, given these inclinations, did Stendhal not come to what seemed an inevitable conclusion: that Don Juan is the Napoleon of love, a perfect illustration, it would seem, of that sense of adventure and unreflecting courage to which the great novelist gave the name of espagnolisme?

A brief examination of Stendhal's principal heroes, who reflect his own amorous experiences, will perhaps partly explain this apparent contradiction. Lucien Leuwen, Fabrice del Dongo, and Julien Sorel are not Don Juans. First of all, their love adventures are limited, for all practical purposes, to two women. They usually love one of these passionately (Mme de Chasteller, Clélia Conti, Mme de Rênal), while the other, more intellectual and sophisticated, either takes the initiative (Mathilde de la Mole, the Duchess Sanseverina) or is forced upon them (Mme Grandet). With the first type, the men turn into sighing lovers who commit all sorts of gauche acts (Lucien's falling off his horse in front of his beloved's window, for example). If they succeed with the second (and if Fabrice does not with his aunt, it is certainly not her fault), it is because someone has prepared their conquests (his father in the case of Lucien, the advice and letters of the Russian prince in Julien's case). Julien Sorel's comportment with women does not quite fit this pattern, but after an initial coolness, he too becomes very deeply involved with Mme de Rênal; as for his eventual conquest of Mathilde, he succeeds not because of his skill as a seducer but rather in spite of his bungling. Stendhal's own amorous temperament, as reflected in his heroes and his autobiographical notes, seems thus much more akin to Werther, who, as he realized with keen understanding, is the opposite of the skilled seducer. These are some of the comparisons he establishes between the two:

The reason I believe Werther to be happier is that Don Juan reduces love to an ordinary affair. Instead of letting his desires take the place of reality (as Werther does), he has desires that are only partially satisfied by cold reality. . . . Instead of giving himself over to the enchanting day-dreams of crystallization, he thinks about the success of his maneuvers like a general and, in short, kills love instead of enjoying it more than anyone else, as is commonly believed. . . .

Don Juan disavows all the duties that tie him to the rest of mankind. In the great market place of life he is a dishonest merchant who always takes but never pays. . . . We must forgive him; he is so much in love with himself that he reaches the point where he can no longer realize the harm he is doing and where he conceives of himself as the only one in the universe capable of experiencing pleasure or pain. . . .

Werther's manner of loving is like the feeling of a schoolboy who writes a tragedy; only a thousand times more so. It is a new goal in life to which everything contributes and which changes the aspect of everything around him. Passionate love unfolds before a man's eyes all of nature with its sublime settings, as if it had been invented only yesterday. He is amazed that he has never seen this strange spectacle before. Everything is new, everything is alive, everything exhales the most passionate interest. A lover sees the woman he loves at the boundary of the horizon of every landscape he passes and, while marching a hundred leagues in order to catch a glimpse of her for an instant, every tree, every rock speaks to him of her in a different way and tells him something new. Instead of being satisfied by the splendor of this magic spectacle, Don Juan requires that his surroundings . . . be made spicy for him by some new intrigue.

George Sand's attack on the romantic Don Juan was also inspired by personal preoccupations. The authoress had already had several unfortunate love experiences and was to have additional ones later on. The chapter "Don Juan" in George Sand's novel *Lélia* (1833) was written after her break with Jules Sandeau and her unsuccessful effort to find consolation in Prosper Mérimée. Her criticisms of Don Juan echo the feelings of a woman disappointed in men, but there is more than that in what she says: it is the first time that a woman expresses her side of the story, a view long overdue if we consider the importance of women in the Don Juan plot.

In her remarks on Don Juan, George Sand deals with the following question: Should not a woman try to love a libertine in order to lead him back on the right path?

Women imagine they are angels who have received the divine mission and the power to save all the Don Juans; but like the angel of the legend, they do not convert them—they damn themselves with them. . . . A curse on you, Don Juan! You have been taken to represent grandeur, but you are only folly. . . .

Insolent fop! Whence did you take the outrageous prerogatives to which you have devoted your life? Where and when did God say to you: "Here is the earth, it is yours, you will be lord and king over all families. All the women you favor are destined to your bed; all eyes at which you may deign to smile will fill with tears and implore your mercy. . ."? You did not grant anyone the right to say: "Don Juan is a coward, for he takes advantage of weakness, he betrays defenseless women." No, you did not retreat in the face of danger. If an avenger took up arms for the victims of your debaucheries, it did not disturb you a bit if you left another corpse in your wake and you did not fear you might stumble while placing your foot triumphantly on his dead body. . . .

What did you expect, Don Juan, what did you expect from those weeping women? Was it happiness you sought in their embrace? . . . Did you believe that one day frenzy would wrest a blasphemous promise from the lips of your victim and she would exclaim: "I love you because I suffer, I love you because you are enjoying pleasure without sharing it. I love you because I feel in your transport which is abating, in your arms which open to abandon me, that you will soon tire of me and forget me . . ."? If only for an instant you believed a woman can give the man she loves something besides her beauty, her love, and her confidence, then you were but a fool. . . .

Oh! how you have been misunderstood by those who have seen in your destiny the emblem of a glorious and persistent struggle against reality! . . . They do not know, fools that they are, that your lamentations were blasphemies and that your death is a just punishment. They do not know that God punishes in you egoism and vanity, that He has smitten you with despair in order to avenge the victims whose voices rose up against you.

But you have no right to complain; your punishment is only a reprisal. You were not reasonable, Don Juan, if you did not know the fatal ending of all the tragedies you had played. You had not properly studied the models who had preceded you in the career you wanted to take up anew. You did not know, did you, that a criminal, in order to lay claim to grandeur, in order to aspire to ruling the world, must live each day in conscious anticipation of the punishment he merits? Then perhaps he can boast of courage, for he is not unaware of the end that is in store for him. But if you believed you could escape celestial vengeance, then, Don Juan, you were but a coward! (Book II, Chap. lxii)

A still more vitriolic attack on Don Juan was devised about the middle of the nineteenth century by authors who depicted the once dashing ladies' man in advanced age. What happens, they speculated, if the hero does not die at the height of his career but lives on to an age when his physical charm and vigor have left him?

Gustave Levavasseur opened this line of attack with his one-act drama *Don Juan barbon* (1848), which shows a pitiful old Don Juan incapable of standing up against his own disciple Don Sanche, who seduces Don Juan's wife and daughter and then kills the old man in a duel.

Jules Viard, in his drama *La Vieillesse de Don Juan* (1853), continues where Molière's play had left off. Don Juan is eventually returned to earth, thanks to the intercession of the beggar. There his mistress deceives him and he is unsuccessful in his attempt to seduce M. Dimanche's daughter Claudine, who is engaged to his own son Jacques. After receiving a beating from the latter, the old Don Juan returns home to implore Elvire's pardon, but both his wife and son reject him. For the first time in his career Don Juan thinks of religion, and Sganarelle chuckles: "Now he is mine; he is in my hands, I'll convert him."

The theme of the old Don Juan rebuffed continues with many variations.[2] A typical degeneration plot in the manner of Balzac[3] can be found in Henri Bataille's play *L'Homme à la rose* (1920). An aging Don Juan, preferring to write his memoirs, lets a young disciple take his place at a rendezvous, but the lady's husband surprises the couple and kills the young man. Don Juan drops his memoirs on the dead body, thus making people believe that it is he who has been killed. He then enjoys watching the grief of the women at his supposed burial. After that, Don Juan's star declines rapidly. He is first slapped by a young girl who calls him an old man; when revealing his identity, he finds that no one will believe he is Don Juan.[4] After a vision of death

---

[2] These variations may take the form of a preferred rival, as in Eliacim Jourdain's one-act drama *Don Juan* (1857), where the hero takes poison when Isabella agrees to marry him only in order to save her lover from being killed by him in a duel. Or else the old seducer meets with outright refusal, as in Camille Debans's novel *La Vieillesse de Don Juan* (1905), in which the hero dies of apoplexy upon being rejected by his daughter-in-law. A similar fate is suffered by the protagonist of Maurice Baring's "diminutive drama" *Don Juan's Failure* (1911). There he is slapped by a young coquettish girl, who has been amused by his old-fashioned declarations; but when he tries to kiss her, she reminds him that he is older than her father. In Alberto Insúa's novel *El alma y el cuerpo de Don Juan* (1915), the hero is a great-grandfather whose mistress deceives him with his grandson. One day, at a fair, he is so much moved by the love-making he observes that he stoops down to kiss a female shape lying in the grass. The girl screams and a young man stabs him. A frenzied crowd mutilates his body and then burns it.

[3] Balzac, who described numerous Don Juanesque heroes (Baron Hulot, Maxime de Treilles, Marsay, etc.), only wrote one fantastic short story about a Don Juan, *L'Elixir de longue vie* (1830). It relates how Don Juan Belvidero keeps a life-restoring ointment for himself instead of applying it to his father's body after the latter's death. After years of dissolute living, Don Juan marries a pious woman and insists on a strict religious education for their son. When he feels his end approaching, he orders the young man to apply the magic elixir to his body after his death. The son obeys but, frightened by the head that has become alive, he drops the bottle. Don Juan is buried with his head alive. The priest wants to have him canonized for a partial resurrection, but Don Juan's head jumps at him and devours him.

[4] A similar difficulty is experienced by the hero of Charles Desbonnet's play *Une Nuit de Don Juan* (1937): he exchanges clothing with his servant and in that outfit cannot even seduce an ugly servant—she does not even find him handsome.

and his past victims, he is willing to settle for any woman. At last he grudgingly agrees to pay a prostitute.

Whenever Don Juan is portrayed in advanced age, the intended effect, if it is to make him appear ridiculous,[5] may easily backfire, for there is often something tragic about an elderly Don Juan in whom a last flicker of passion reveals former splendor underneath human wreckage. The age of Don Juan lasts from ripe youth until the height of manhood; Tirso and his successors were wise in ending Don Juan's career before he had outlived his role. What happens to him after that may be of psychological and sociological interest, but such probing is usually a betrayal of the artistic intent of the legend. It is like inquiring what happens to athletes after they retire from their sport. Laughing at a fat, bald-headed ex-football star when he receives a scroll during a half-time ceremony will never erase his accomplishments on the field.

Those writers who reacted against Hoffmann's ideal-seeker tended to take a more tolerant approach. While conservative thinkers and biologists warned of the danger Don Juan represents to society and the race in general,[6] numerous authors felt that he was not lost beyond recall—he was only pursuing the wrong ideal. The first thing he must realize, they argued, is that his ideal is a dream, a figment of his imagi-

---

[5] Not all versions featuring an aged Don Juan were necessarily unsympathetic toward the hero. C. J. L. Almquist, in his play *Ramido Marinesco* (1845), presents an old seducer who has turned into a rueful monk and wants his former mistress to curse him. Their son dies when kissing a picture painted with poison by Don Juan. The mother does curse him but only indirectly, since she curses the monk and not her lover.

Other elderly Don Juans are either tempted again after retirement from the field, as are the heroes of Juan Ignacio Luca de Tena's play *Las canas de Don Juan* (1925), Robert Browning's poem *Fifine at the Fair* (1871–72), and the middle-aged hero in Carlos Sabat Ercasty's dramatic poem *El demonio de Don Juan* (1934); or else they play tricks like giving three young girls identical jewelry and making each one believe *hers* is genuine (Per Hallström's short story *Don Juan's Rubies*, 1898). Don Juan even assumes the role of Cupid in Alessandro Varaldo's short play *Don Giovanni si pente* (1922), in which the protagonist gives his own carriage to two young and inexperienced lovers after he had mistakenly believed the girl might be his daughter.

[6] See A. Rauber, *Die Don-Juan Sage im Lichte biologischer Forschungen* (Leipzig, 1899), and Ramiro de Maeztu, *Don Quijote, Don Juan y la Celestina* (Madrid, 1926).

nation, which he must give up.[7] To bring Don Juan down to earth, these writers proposed concrete ideals which would make a respectable citizen of the ideal-seeking seducer: marriage,[8] fatherhood,[9] involvement in social and political affairs,[10] and dedication to science.[11]

As might be expected, the attempt to turn Don Juan into a bourgeois did not meet with much success; in fact, it was practically laughed out of existence by the audience that attended the première of Jean Mounet-Sully and Pierre Barbier's play *La Vieillesse de Don Juan* (1906), in which the hero finally realizes that "the infinite is the child."

At times the condemnation of Don Juan is expressed or implied by showing how ruthlessly he acts and what havoc he creates around him in order to satisfy his desires.

In Karl von Holtei's dramatic fantasy *Don Juan* (1834) the hero is a reigning prince whose tyrannical acts lead to a conspiracy against him. The work is unplayable, but some of the lines are worth quoting; for example, Don Juan's self-explanation, which might well fit into Albert Camus's recent play *Caligula*:

Mine is what pleases me. I care not about custom or law; I'll crush everything, human or divine, made sacrosanct by superstition, stupidity, or time. As long as I have breath in me, I have but one goal: unlimited power over women. Mine shall be every female I desire. And if tomorrow throne, might, and realm come crashing down, I shall burn brightly in my own flames.

Don Juan begins by raping Anna, who is to marry Octavio; then, to show that man is free to act as he pleases, he kills a hermit, who turns out to be his own father. He has a former friend executed for participating in a revolt and continues his misdeeds by taking the nuns

[7] This view was symbolically expressed by Emile Bruni in his short story *Les Deux Nuits de Don Juan* (1907), where Don Juan dreams of a woman in whom he sees his ideal. A second figure, the woman's father, appears and becomes identified with Don Juan himself—his ideal is the product of his imagination.

[8] J.-E. Fidao-Justiniani's novel *Le Mariage de Don Juan* (1909).

[9] Alfred Friedmann's drama *Don Juans letztes Abenteuer* (1881); Paul Heyse's tragedy *Don Juans Ende* (1883); Jean Mounet-Sully and Pierre Barbier's play *La Vieillesse de Don Juan* (1906).

[10] Theodor Creizenach's poem *Don Juan* (1836); Estéban Echeverría's poem *El ángel caído* (1844–46); Jean Aicard's dramatic poem *Don Juan 89* (1889).

[11] Giovanni A. Cesareo's fragment of a poem *Don Juan* (1883).

out of a convent and turning them over to a procuress. Anna finally reappears and kills herself before his eyes despite his pleading and declarations of love. Tired of living and faced with satiety, Don Juan puts an end to his existence.[12]

It is usually from within a group that its most formidable opponents arise, and from such a source Don Juan was to receive a heavy blow. Edmond Rostand has often been called a late romantic, but by the time he wrote his dramatic poem *La Dernière Nuit de Don Juan* (published in 1921 but written before World War I), the author of *Cyrano de Bergerac* had considerably modified his views.

Rostand's point is that the romantic Don Juan is a puppet created and adored by his creators, but just the same a puppet that can be torn to pieces like Olympia in E. T. A. Hoffmann's famous tale. Therefore the Devil is disguised as a puppet player when he visits Don Juan, who has been permitted to return to earth for ten years. In the second act the Devil assumes the function of his own advocate. First he questions Don Juan on the meaning of the phrase "to possess a woman." When Don Juan replies that it is to know women, to hold their souls naked, the Devil turns the pieces of Don Juan's torn-up list into the ghosts of his victims and asks him to identify them; but Don Juan guesses wrong each time. The women tell him how they had pretended to be whatever he wanted them to be. Don Juan now changes "possess" to mean "dominate."

GHOST: You looked at me when I had chosen you. . . .
DON JUAN: But I seduced you!
GHOST: When we decided it for you! . . .
THE DEVIL: "Oh, how I seduced the magnet," the iron said to itself. (II, i)

But Don Juan does not give up that easily. He claims now that he

---

[12] Other condemnations of Don Juan show him as equally ruthless. In Carsten Hauch's tragedy *Don Juan* (about 1836), Arthur de Gobineau's dramatic poem *Les Adieux de Don Juan* (1844), Ernest Dutouquet's poem *Une Aventure de Don Juan* (1864), and Henri de Régnier's play *Les Scrupules de Sganarelle* (1908) Don Juan destroys the happiness of a couple by first seducing the bride and then killing the groom.

Guerra Junqueiro goes furthest in his attack on Don Juan in his poem *A morte de D. João* (1874) where the protagonist is turned into the symbol of moral corruption and social evil. The author punishes Don Juan by reducing him to a syphilitic old man who starves to death in an alley.

pleased the women. When questioned by the Devil, they ascribe it to his perfume, his tobacco, or other unimportant features—"for women have Don Juan as men have prostitutes." Don Juan protests that, if they took him, he left them, which causes the Devil to remark: "I believe you read too much what is written about you." Don Juan's claim that he made women suffer is likewise rejected, for the tears were merely part of the program along with candy and flowers. Now Don Juan calls on his last trump card: he was seeking the ideal woman whom he could not find. Thereupon a white ghost appears; she is the blank which Don Juan left in his list, because he had forgotten her name. He pursues her in vain among the ghosts.

DON JUAN: Why do you make me pursue your voice from woman to woman?

WHITE GHOST: To teach you that with a little love you could have found me in each of them!

DON JUAN: You existed only in one of them!

WHITE GHOST: And I was waiting for you in them all!

THE DEVIL: Then you searched in order not to find?

DON JUAN: That is possible! For, if I had found her, I would have died of boredom. (II, i)

In despair, Don Juan calls for Molière's beggar to confirm his claim of having been the first to use the term "humanity." But the beggar wants to return the gold piece Don Juan had given him "for the love of humanity."

DON JUAN: But I want to explain to you . . . Liberty—

BEGGAR: It is too great a worry which suddenly occupies you.

DON JUAN: The People—

BEGGAR: No, Don Juan, no higher than the skirt!

DON JUAN: But the future—

THE DEVIL (to the Beggar): Ah! ah! so the debauchees end up as apostles.

BEGGAR: I am going to strangle you for daring to soil the words which nourish our hope. (II, ii)

Don Juan is now ready to give up.

GHOST: Ah! there was nevertheless more to it than that. He is hiding his supreme excuse out of pride.

DON JUAN: No excuses!

GHOST: He could not get along with himself: those who do not like themselves need the love of others. (II, ii)

Fittingly enough, Don Juan is condemned to be a puppet and re-appears as such, singing "the famous Burlador."

Rostand's annihilation of Don Juan seemed to mark the extreme limit of criticism, but worse was yet to come. At least the author had let the hero wear his clothes and fineries, his victims had paid him a compliment or two, and the Devil himself had been his interrogator. All this implied some sort of past splendor—exaggerated perhaps, mis-interpreted if you will, but exciting nonetheless.

The most destructive criticism of Don Juan was pronounced neither by angry conservatives nor by disillusioned romantics or by brilliant essayists but by scientists, physicians, and psychologists. They put Don Juan on the examining table or on the comfortable couch, undressed his body and his soul, and put him down as a case study of abnormal physiology or psychology.

Whatever previous writers had found wrong with Don Juan, none had doubted his sexual prowess, for how else could he possibly have so many amorous adventures? The first, so far as I know, who coupled amorous fame with at least temporary impotence was Crébillon fils in that much maligned book *Le Sopha*.[13] Nearly two centuries later, Gregorio Marañón opened the line of those who looked at Don Juan from the medical and pathological point of view.[14] Following are a few of his observations which accentuate the lack of manliness in Don Juan. Marañón finds, in fact, many feminine traits in the hero:

> If we want to know him fully, we have to undress and dissect him down to the deepest biological roots and the most remote times when he did not yet dream that he might some day become a hero. (p. 31)

> Don Juan, seen from close by and without literary or philosophical preju-dices, is a low-class ruffian without intelligence or interest. His adventures consist of unfair acts and frequently downright dirty tricks. Yet basically he is not responsible, because his actions are determined by the imperious commands of organic conditions over which he has no control. (p. 32)

[13] In the episode of Mazulhim and Zéphis (Chap. 10) and again in that of Mazulhim and Zulica (Chap. 11).

[14] The quotations are translated from "Notas para la biología de Don Juan," in *Cinco ensayos sobre Don Juan* (Santiago de Chile, 1957), pp. 27–51; same article, *Revista de Occidente*, III (1924), 15–53. Other articles by the same author on the Don Juan subject include: "Biología de Don Juan," *El Universal Ilustrado* (1924); "Les Origines de la légende de Don Juan," *Revue Hebdoma-daire*, 48th year (January 21, 1939), pp. 263–87; and *Don Juan; ensayos sobre el orígen de su leyenda* (Buenos Aires–Mexico City, 1940).

Marañón dwells on two primary features of Don Juan which point toward femininity: his habit of lying and his delicate physiognomy.

He almost never speaks the truth. And lying is also a predominantly feminine trait, because in the human species the lie, whose moral aspects have been greatly exaggerated, is, biologically speaking, a defense mechanism of the weak. . . . All children lie because they are weak, and women do so frequently because they are less strong than men. Despite his bravado, Don Juan . . . almost never executes his amorous enterprises openly but usually takes advantage of feminine relations and gossip. Yet he not only lies in his actions but also, and quite shamelessly, in relating his exploits—something that men of typically virile make-up never do. (pp. 44–45)

According to Marañón, the real he-man is a stocky, hirsute, and unpleasant-looking type with curly hair that turns gray precociously, a tendency to be cross-eyed, and prognathism of the lower jaw.

Let us merely say that this last trait, one of the most typical of the authentic hypergenital temperament, is almost always absent in the physiognomy of the Don Juans. Some time ago I pointed out that Casanova . . . had a receding chin and a gigantic figure, both fatal details in judging the intimate veracity of his amorous adventures. (p. 47)

H.-R. Lenormand, in his play *L'Homme et ses fantômes* (1924), goes even further than Marañón in calling Don Juan a homosexual who is unwilling to admit it.[15]

In Don Juan the body is male and the soul female. . . . His body craves the woman and his soul the man. He seeks in the woman the phantom of the man. That is why each of his victories is a profound defeat. That is why he flees from women, raging because he finds that they own a treasure he will never possess. He avenges himself on them for his inability to be happy. . . . Don Juan is not a sick man. He is . . . a hesitation of nature. (III, xiii)

The final blow to Don Juan's romantic glory was delivered by psychologists who classified him as a definite type of abnormal behavior and then filed him away as an interesting case. I shall quote briefly from three representative psychologists: a Freudian, an Adlerian, and a specialist in nervous diseases.

In *Die Don-Juan Gestalt* (1924) Otto Rank, who has dealt with

---

[15] A somewhat similar opinion is expressed by Miguel de Unamuno in his play *El hermano Juan o El mundo es teatro* (1934), where the author arrives at the conclusion that Don Juan is neutral.

Don Juan in several of his writings,[16] points out the possibility of in-
terpreting the hero's fickleness as being caused by an Oedipus complex:
"The many women who must be replaced represent for him the *one*
irreplaceable mother; while the deceived, betrayed, and attacked opponents, who are finally killed, represent the *one* invincible deadly
enemy: the father." (p. 11)

F. Oliver Brachfeld, an Adlerian, ascribes Don Juan's behavior
with women to feelings of inferiority:

The timid Amiel and the bold Don Juan both suffer from the same trouble—
an insecure ego which cannot find its feminine counterpart. . . . The necessity for finding this counterpart is imposed on all of us by the fact that in
our species sexuality bifurcates into two complementary currents and thus
forms the *couple*, which is the fundamental human unit. The Don Juan
differs from the timid man only in that he over-compensates his initial weakness. He was timid himself at the start. He tries to compensate for his terrible feeling of incompleteness by the excess and variety of his conquests.[17]

Gonzalo R. Lafora, a specialist in nervous and mental diseases,
finds that Don Juan exhibits typical symptoms of hysteria, some of
which are: the tendency to tell lies, exaggeration, egocentrism, a disproportionate irritability resulting in violent psychological reactions
to insignificant events; a rigid sense of etiquette; and the excessive
predominance of the affective, emotional, and sexual over the intellectual and cerebral forces. With his psychological experience, Lafora
tries to answer one of the questions the romantics had struggled with:
What is the secret ill that makes him so inconstant, so discontent that
he goes from woman to woman? Two theories are suggested:

The first is based on the permanent effect which the initial sexual
experience may have on a person's amatory desires. According to this
theory, "Don Juan received his initiation into the mysteries of love
through some wonderful experience in his early youth at the hands,
let us suppose, of a loved mistress who understood them well, but who
passed away leaving him with a never-fulfilled longing for a love that
might equal hers."[18]

---

[16] Among others, in *Seelenglaube und Psychologie* (Vienna, 1932), and *Don
Juan: une étude sur le double*, transl. from the German by S. Lautmann (Paris,
1932).

[17] F. Oliver Brachfeld, *Inferiority Feeling in the Individual and the Group*,
transl. from the French by Marjorie Gabain (New York, 1951), p. 212.

[18] Gonzalo R. Lafora, *Don Juan and Other Psychological Studies*, transl. by
Janet H. Perry (London, 1930), p. 54.

The second theory is derived from the view of Don Juan as a hysterical subject—changeable in everything and never satisfied. This psychological state, according to Lafora, "makes people continually seek to exchange old emotions for new [ones]. They are like children who want a plaything very badly until they get it, and take it to bed with them in order to see it on opening their eyes the first thing in the morning; after which the toy lies about the house broken and despised, replaced by another better or worse that has attracted the little one's attention another day."[19]

Lafora's comparison is a striking one. We can see a series of broken lives all around Don Juan's bed; yet, if the psychologists had had the last word, the toy breaker would soon have joined his toys, taken apart and reduced to tiny proportions himself under the unmerciful analysis of his examiners.

To be sure, the psychologists have given us some important and interesting insights into Don Juan's possible motivations, but, since they reduce Don Juan to a case study, a strict application of their findings to literary works would necessarily result in inferior productions. Minor authors tried to utilize the new information gained by describing Don Juan's career from birth to death, but the more conscious artists followed the view which, perhaps inadvertently, had slipped into one of the psychological studies quoted above: "Every man has in him a Don Juan *in spe*, who may or may not reach maturity; it will depend upon how much courage is there and what opportunities life supplies in each particular case."[20] It remains up to the writers to supply these opportunities and to make us sense that part of Don Juan's personality which escapes psychological analysis: that irreducible quality which is largely responsible for Don Juan's success both in his adventures and in his literary career.

[19] *Ibid.*, pp. 55–56.
[20] Brachfeld, *Inferiority Feeling*, p. 213.

CHAPTER THIRTEEN

Don Juan at the Turn of the Century

La séduction, si elle n'est pas un art,
n'est qu'une violence.[1]

ARMAND HAYEM,
Le Don Juanisme

Criticism rarely hurts Don Juan. In the early stages of his career he had been severely attacked and punished; if anything, this ill treatment, and especially the form which his punishment took, only contributed to his fame. In modern times Don Juan realized the advantages of publicity, and he was quite right in considering scathing criticism as an excellent way of calling himself to the attention of the women he wished to conquer, for nothing will serve to arouse a woman's curiosity more thoroughly than a bad reputation. Those who wanted adventure would know where to find him, those who felt tempted to reform him were welcome to try.

What makes Don Juan eternally young is that he reflects faithfully the changing modes of, and attitudes toward, the relations between the sexes. As the moral climate changed, Don Juan was once more called upon to serve as an illustration of the times. In considering his new role, one point has perhaps not been sufficiently emphasized: namely, that there is a close resemblance between the elegant lover of the *fin de siècle* and the *roué* of the eighteenth century.

The late nineteenth century manner of conquering women was eventually dubbed "Donjuanism"; yet its origins can be traced back at least to Molière's Dom Juan, who "takes less pleasure in making women fall than in seeing how they fall."[2] But whereas in Molière's libertine the intellectual and aesthetic enjoyment of the game may

---

[1] "When seduction is not an art, it is mere violence."
[2] Chap. 4, n. 1 above.

rank as high as physical pleasure, with the turn-of-the-century Don Juan one gains the impression of watching a first-rate chess player who could checkmate his partner at will but prolongs the match until he simply can no longer avoid the fatal move.

The search for the immediate ancestor of this cat-and-mouse type of seducer leads us once more to Kierkegaard. We have already noted his intense interest in Mozart's *Don Giovanni*. The same volume (*Either-Or*) contains a section entitled "The Diary of a Seducer."

Johannes, the seducer, possesses a weapon Don Juan never had—patience. He studies each case carefully, maps his plans, and carries them out with complete mastery of himself and of the situation. Like the romantic Don Juan, he too wants to enjoy women as fully as possible, but he has studied them and knows what he can expect of each.

The trick, as regards an impression [he writes in his diary], consists in being as sensitive as possible, both in knowing what impression one makes upon the girl, and what impression each girl makes upon one. In this way one can be in love with many girls at once, because one loves each girl differently. To love only one is too little; to love all of them is a surfeit; to know one's self and to love as many as possible, to let one's soul conceal all the power of love in itself, so that each girl gets her own proper nourishment, while the consciousness embraces the whole—that is enjoyment, that is really living.[3]

The victim Johannes has chosen is Cordelia, a seventeen-year-old girl, to whom he pays no special attention for the time being. But his aim is already entered into the diary: "When one can so arrange it that a girl's only desire is to give herself freely, when she feels that her whole happiness depends on this, when she almost begs to make this free submission, then there is first true enjoyment, but this always requires spiritual influence."[4]

For the conquest of Cordelia, Johannes chooses a method that seems surprising at first: he will not play the role of the sighing lover or even the interesting man of the world. Instead he decides to be prosaic in his behavior with her, for he already foresees her eventual reactions:

First her femininity is neutralized by prosaic reason and ridicule, not directly but indirectly, and at the same time by an absolutely colorless intellectuality. She almost loses her sense of the feminine, but in this condition she cannot stand by herself; she throws herself into my arms, not as if I were a lover,

---

[3] Kierkegaard, *Either-Or* (Princeton, 1949), I, 300.
[4] *Ibid.*, I, 283.

no, I am still quite neutral. Then her femininity awakens; one arouses her to the highest pitch; one allows her to offend against this or that accepted moral standard; she vents her rage upon it; her femininity reaches almost supernatural heights; she belongs to me with the force of a world-passion.[5]

Johannes uses a timid young man who is in love with Cordelia as a straw man, while he himself plays the inveterate bachelor who lends a helping hand. But gradually he comes out of his passive role and begins to play on Cordelia's emotions. One day he casually mentions that he is in love with a young girl and then suddenly proposes to Cordelia. Her aunt agrees to their engagement, yet he still displays no particular passion except in rather flowery and almost didactic love letters. He is now ready for the final phase of the affair:

So far I should call her passion a naïve passion. When the change comes, and I begin to draw back in earnest, then she will really muster all her resources in order to captivate me. She has no way to accomplish this except by means of the erotic, but this will now appear on a very different scale. . . . She fights for her own sake because she knows that I possess the erotic; she fights for her own sake in order to overcome me. She develops in herself a higher form of the erotic. What I taught her to suspect by inflaming her, my coldness now teaches her to understand, but in such a way that she believes she discovered it herself. Through this she will try to take me by surprise; she will believe that her boldness has outstripped me, and that she has thereby caught me. Then her passion becomes determinate, energetic, conclusive, logical; her kiss total, her embrace firm.—In me she seeks her freedom, the more firmly I encompass her, the better she finds it. The engagement is broken. When this happens, then she needs a little rest, so that this wild tumult may not bring out something unseemly. Then her passion gathers itself again, and she is mine.[6]

Johannes carries out his program as planned. Cordelia breaks the engagement, he possesses her as he had anticipated—and then abandons her.

By the 1880's the type of seducer sketched by Kierkegaard some fifty years earlier had become fashionable. The Don Juan of the late nineteenth century shows the traces of Lovelace, Valmont, Byron, and Musset: he is well educated, witty, and attractive; but he is also impeccably dressed and his mustache is beyond reproach. Many defini-

[5] *Ibid.*, I, 286–87. Translation slightly altered.
[6] *Ibid.*, I, 342–43.

tions of what came to be known as "Donjuanism" were attempted and they do not necessarily agree on all points; among these, A. Hayem's essay on the subject, *Le Don Juanisme* (1886), seems to come closest to embodying the main features of this type of seducer:

Donjuanism is a certain manner of loving and of behaving with women; it is the natural result of a given temperament, dependent upon birth, wealth, and education, although one could conceive of a purely instinctive Don Juan.... (p. 16)

Many additional elements enter into it, but these are the essential factors: expansiveness, happiness through love; love by conquest; conquest in contempt of any obstacle and consequently of any moral principle.... Beauty, gracefulness, ruse, daring ... constitute the elements of Donjuanism. To these should be added vanity, self-confidence, carefreeness, an eloquence that persuades, irony.... Thus this profound and rare phenomenon comes about as the result of (1) a temperament; (2) the most vivid and least commonly united faculties; (3) an appropriate environment.... (p. 20)

When seduction is not an art, it is mere violence. There are women who surrender without a struggle, and others who surrender after a while. Donjuanism does not primarily concentrate on these. (p. 26)

Young girls generally must be taken and do not surrender. These Don Juan will try to seduce above all, for in their case he has to overcome a resistance which adds spice to his pleasure.... To conquer, to ply wills, to foil virtue—those are the aims of love in Don Juan's manner ... for he knows all about love, all there is to know except the role the heart plays in it.... (p. 27)

There are many ways of seducing women, but there is only one for an individual woman.... With an eagle eye Don Juan must be able to recognize with whom he is dealing and carry out his maneuvers accordingly. The coquettes like being flattered and admired, the proud ones want to be surprised and dominated ... the virtuous ones let themselves be taken while getting ready to fight for their virtue, the "gold-diggers" care only for money.... (p. 31)

Don Juan is curious and bold rather than a voluptuary. The particular kind of sensuousness he thirsts after constantly is to dare, to enjoy the thrill of a new conquest. His sensuousness resides in the novelty of a sensation, not in its intensity.... (p. 33)

Donjuanism starts from the principle that there is no virtue that cannot be overcome, i.e., that there is no such thing as an absolutely virtuous woman. .... (p. 39) He sees in every woman a Manon, more or less. The important thing is not to be taken in by appearances. For that delightful creature appears to Donjuanism always as an enemy of the male, against whom the laws of warfare permit any measure and who continues to be a threat even after she has submitted, perhaps an even greater threat then. (p. 40)

The corruption of Donjuanism is so expert that it attains the highest level and blessings of nature itself. It can educate a girl in a few moments. But the strange thing is that a new world is opened and almost immediately closed again for the unfortunate victim. She has entered a magnificently lit temple and suddenly it turns pitch-dark. The woman in love becomes a penitent.

Don Juan's corruption has struck her, but not mortally. It is as if the Demon had temporarily possessed her. Hence the religious effect of repentance. No other lover could accomplish this. The women the Don Juans leave behind do not turn into street girls. They become nuns, mystics, sometimes saintly women; or else irreproachable wives and mothers. . . . (p. 43)

There is more than one difference between Donjuanism and dandyism. The dandy possesses the art of self-conceit. What matters to him is to make self-conceit appear not only bearable but so lovable, as if it were gracefulness itself. Donjuanism is the science of seduction. Don Juan's concern is to make himself irresistible. The dandy is interested in the effect he produces. Don Juan seeks enjoyment. The dandy wants to be superior to other men; Don Juan wants to make an impression on women only. (p. 114)

While Hayem had exposed the outlines of Donjuanism, Marcel Barrière[7] applied his own theories to depict such a modern Don Juan in his quadrilogy of novels entitled *Le Nouveau Don Juan* (1900).[8] In the manner of Balzac, Barrière attempted to produce a history of the intellectual, moral, political, and artistic life during the late nineteenth century. The interesting aspect of this work is that the author actually points toward Marcel Proust. Well steeped in painting, sculpture, and music, and being moreover a fervent Wagnerian, Barrière makes an effort to join the arts, but what in Proust becomes an intimate union in which literature, painting, and music are fused to create deeper insights, here amounts to scarcely more than a monotonous catalogue of paintings and sculptures, more appropriate to a museum guide than to a novel. The most Barrière will do is to call on a work of art to describe a beautiful woman—his claim to being a forerunner of Proust ends just about there.

The career of the New Don Juan, Prince Baratine, is determined

---

[7] See n. 9 below.

[8] *Le Nouveau Don Juan* contains the following volumes: I. *L'Education d'un contemporain*; II. *Le Roman de l'ambition*; III. *Les Ruines de l'amour*. A fourth volume, *Le Monde noir*, appeared in 1909.

largely by his admiration for Wagner's music: to please him, a woman must appreciate the works of the German musician; in fact, his great love is a Wagnerian singer. But Baratine demands still more. He will not make love unless the surroundings and the atmosphere are just right. It takes all the seductiveness of the great singer and a *Tristan* theme to make him give up his dream of elevated love. In Baratine refinement has reached such an advanced state that it borders on perversion. The possession of the woman, the Burlador's primary goal, has practically become secondary with Baratine. An extreme seemed to have been reached in *Le Nouveau Don Juan*, but it was not yet the end.

The ultimate in Donjuanism is depicted in Henri Lavedan's play *Le Marquis de Priola* (1902). Although the hero's name does not sound Spanish, references to him as the "modern Don Juan" reveal the author's intentions clearly enough. Priola embodies practically all the typical features of the turn-of-the-century seducer: he is noble, handsome, rich, witty, and he knows that no woman is completely secure from seduction. But to this Priola adds a streak of histrionic cruelty which distinguishes him from his rivals. He admits this, moreover, with cynical frankness:

I am a dilettante, and immensely curious. I provide myself with the exciting spectacle of the hesitations, emotional upsets, feverish longings, and deep anguish of the feminine heart. That is my divine comedy. Before my eyes, at the sound of my voice, in my arms I watch them laugh, cry, suffer, lie. And this gives me great pleasure, provided those smiles, those kisses and tears are part of a brilliant performance and always full of beauty. (II, ii)

Priola demonstrates his technique in his attempt to seduce Mme de Valleroy who feigns indifference to his advances:

MME DE VALLEROY: I wonder why you have been courting me so tenaciously during the two months you have known me. Why? You do not love me?

PRIOLA: I? I adore you, madly, as never before a woman has been loved on earth. Only, I know better than to tell you so or to let you see it, because if I told you so you would not believe me, whereas by saying nothing. . . . (I, v)

Although she indignantly rejects his invitation at first, Mme de Valleroy appears at Priola's home, to prove, as she asserts, that a virtuous woman has nothing to fear. This is how the Marquis recounts what happened:

She had come to give herself, that was obvious. I had been sure of it all along. After a quarter of an hour of pretentious bantering, she offered herself, very nicely, in a comradely fashion. But then I no longer wanted her . . . "Ah," I said, "be silent! It would be seventh heaven! But no, . . . surely, I shan't take advantage of you . . . Let's be strong!" And so on, the whole line of friendship! Ah! That lifted me out of this world for five minutes worth more than gold! She was trembling with rage she dared not show; her eyes were two daggers, her smile full of poison, her little hands a vise ready to strangle me. I felt I was being thoroughly execrated, hated as much as possible, and I must say . . . it rather pleased me. (II, iv)

Like his ancestor Mme de Merteuil, the Marquis de Priola suffers a terrible punishment (he is struck by acute ataxia), but once again this is not so much celestial judgment as the author's obligation to see to it that evil shall not triumph.

The contemporary audience certainly did not despise Lavedan's hero as strongly as he deserved. Of course, he is thoroughly evil, far more so than the Burlador or even Valmont, both of whom at least offered the deceived woman a moment of pleasure. But Priola had one advantage over his predecessors: he lived in a society that had practically accepted Don Juan as a full-fledged member who added excitement to an otherwise dull soirée. Accordingly, Don Juan had armed himself with a powerful weapon—entertaining wit. This is, for example, how Dondorf, the hero of Oskar A. H. Schmitz's comedy *Ein deutscher Don Juan* (1909), justifies his fickleness by describing his impression of married life:

Now, you dine with your lady, and afterwards you simply don't leave, you stay! Just try and imagine this: she stays! You go out, you come back, she is still there. You would like to say: "My dear, we'll meet again on Friday." You need not bother saying it; you'll be with her Friday, Saturday, and Sunday. Uninterrupted bliss! Why, are you not bound to tire of even the most gorgeous woman if you are obliged by contract to love her?

By the early twentieth century Don Juan had become such an admired figure that, like a great artist, we find him surrounded by young disciples. In Otto Anthes' drama *Don Juans letztes Abenteuer* (1909) Giovanni greets the group of fops who imitate him with a jovial "Guten Abend, ihr Buben," but then proceeds to chide them: "How you distort the example I have set you! I have become a restless wanderer because I cannot find what I am seeking. . . . You are vice incarnate, I am hapless virtue." In this drama the hero even has a close friend in whom he confides his longings. He does find love at last, but when the young fiancée returns to her bridegroom, Giovanni commits suicide—though not in total despair, for he has experienced love once in his life.

In its portrait of the hero, Donjuanism tried to supply an answer to one of the many problems raised by the romantic interpretation of Don Juan. What is his attraction for women? What makes him irresistible, and how is it possible to explain Hoffmann's assertion that Anna cannot overcome the passion he has kindled in her? Looks alone are not sufficient to justify such a fascination. It is, of course, reasonable to assume that a woman will be attracted by a very handsome, impressive looking man, *le beau ténébreux*, as the French call that type. But unless this man can keep what his looks promise, his success is likely to be of short duration.

To the Burlador this is no problem, for he is not in the least interested in the woman's reaction. All he wants is quick possession, by the easiest and most efficient means possible. Let the woman curse him to her heart's content—he hardly hears her screams as he is off in flight. He arrives like a tempest, leaving the woman crushed, excited perhaps, but certainly unsatisfied. If she clamors for marriage, it is not because of an indelible impression left on her but in order to obtain fulfillment of a broken promise or the restoration of her soiled honor.

Donjuanism is partly an attempt to endow the hero with qualities which seemed indispensable in the perfect lover: wit, education, and amorous savoir-faire. Don Juan thus acquires the skill of satisfying not only his own sexual desires but those of the woman as well. Marcel Barrière, in his essay on Donjuanism,[9] insists particularly on this point: "It can be affirmed that above all he never loves as an egoist. . . . In physical love Don Juan is not concerned with the pleasure he receives." Thus what had begun as a force of nature became a product of utmost refinement and skill. The Burlador, the scourge of women, as Catalinón had called him, was finally turned into woman's benefactor.

But as Don Juan becomes more and more refined and intellectual, he tends at the same time to lose the force of his natural impulses.

---

[9] *L'Art des passions: Essai sur le donjuanisme contemporain* (1904). The quotation is on p. 129 of the 1922 edition.

Whether it is a weakening of the sexual urge or an increase in self-control, the fact remains that from a Burlador who takes his women greedily and almost without discrimination Don Juan is transformed into a sophisticated seducer who demands the proper setting for his love affairs, who eventually sees his greatest triumph in refusing the favors of a woman (an attractive woman) ready to give herself. While this is a "burla" that the Burlador might have admired, it is carried out by a man and in a manner almost diametrically opposed to the character and temperament of Tirso's hero. There remained only one step to complete this development: to have Don Juan run away from a woman who is pursuing him. This was accomplished by G. B. Shaw in his play *Man and Superman* (1901–1903).

The central scene in Shaw's *Man and Superman* has been variously called "Tanner's Dream" or "Don Juan in Hell." Here the principal characters (Tanner, Ann, Ramsden, Mendoza) reappear as Don Juan Tenorio, Ana, the Statue, and the Devil, and some of the numerous themes in the play[10] are discussed from an other-world point of view, as it were.

Shaw's predominant concern revolves around the Life Force theme which, in this play, manifests itself in two ways: (1) the relationship between Man and Woman, in which Woman uses Man as a tool in order to carry out her essential task of procreation; hence she chases him, and not vice versa, as superficial social conventions seem to imply; (2) the creation of the Superman, a goal toward which the Life Force, blind and stupid itself, pushes mankind by direct or devious means.

By the time Tanner has his dream, he has clearly realized that Ann, despite a surface appearance of perfect propriety, has trapped him and that any further resistance would be futile. One might thus conceivably interpret Tanner's dream as an attempt to escape his inevitable fate by calling Don Juan Tenorio to his aid.

Don Juan, however, merely confirms Tanner's worst fears. He reveals that popular conceptions about him are entirely unfounded: he did not seduce women but ran away from them until fatigue and exhaustion overcame him. Nor is Don Juan the great admirer of female beauty and of love—or, at least, if he ever was, he is no longer. Shaw's

[10] Augustin Hamon, *The Twentieth Century Molière: Bernard Shaw*, transl. from the French by Eden and Cedar Paul (London, 1915), 178–79, enumerates ten themes in addition to the main issues.

Don Juan is a supreme realist who wants to leave Hell, the place where beauty and romantic love are worshipped, and go to Heaven, where continued evolution toward the Superman is possible.[11]

Don Juan speaks up as the champion of both the Life Force and the creation of the Superman; but, although supposedly a great master of reality, he does not draw the logical conclusion—that only by submitting to the pursuit of Woman can he aid the Life Force in its efforts to create the Superman. Ana's insistent cry for the father of the Superman shows that she has instinctively realized this.

Shaw is obviously far more concerned with the Life Force theme than with a characterization of Don Juan.[12] In a way, this is regrettable because the author might otherwise have drawn an impressive portrait of Don Juan as the very force that is most strongly opposed to the Life Force, since he wants to enjoy sexual pleasure without regard to procreation or the responsibilities of marriage and family.

In his Epistle Dedicatory, Shaw speaks rather disparagingly of Byron's Don Juan as a vagabond libertine; his own, however (and he is referring to Tanner), he asserts to be a true Don Juan who resists his fate as long as possible. Despite this claim, Shaw does essentially the same thing as Byron: he uses the hero as a vehicle—or rather as a spokesman—for his own ideas; and he accentuates, for reasons of his own, his predecessor's indication that Don Juan is not the huntsman but the prey.

With Shaw the extreme reversal of Tirso's Burlador was accomplished. It is not unreasonable to depict Don Juan as being chased by women, provided he has possessed and abandoned them, possibly after

---

[11] I have considerably simplified the complexities and occasional inconsistencies contained in Don Juan's lines. For these problems, see Arthur N. Nethercot, *Men and Supermen: The Shavian Portrait Gallery* (Cambridge, Harvard University Press, 1954), 278–82.

[12] A first sketch of Shaw's Don Juan can be found in his short story *Don Giovanni Explains* (1887). Mozart's hero, appearing as a ghost to an English lady in a railroad car, relates how he attracted women by his indifferent attitude. He is quite surprised to learn of his fame as a seducer—his list was kept as a joke by Leporello, who added fictitious names to it; the scene with Anna was caused by her mistaking him for his friend Ottavio. This is an outline of Don Juan, the man chased by women; it also contains the mock-debunking interpretation which was later taken up again by Sylvia Townsend Warner, in her short story *After the Death of Don Juan* (1938). Shaw's version of Hell, as contained in *Man and Superman*, is likewise forecast in *Don Giovanni Explains*.

promises of marriage. But when he runs away from a woman he has not possessed, he has lost his *raison d'être*—he has become the anti-Don Juan.

Whereas previously new interpretations, such as Hoffmann's, had created possibilities for expansion and diversification of the Don Juan subject, Shaw's *Man and Superman* led to a dead end from which further developments were practically impossible. Although his influence can be detected in most subsequent English works on Don Juan,[18] as far as the future of the legend was concerned, a new direction was needed.

---

[18] Those writing under Shaw's influence have usually turned out mediocre works. In James Elroy Flecker's play *Don Juan* (1910–11; published 1925) the hero argues with a labor leader and philosophizes most undramatically with the statue. In Benn W. Levy's play *The Poet's Heart: a Life of Don Juan* (1937) 'the hero is a football player who seems to be far better at scoring goals than at seduction. Sylvia Townsend Warner's short story *After the Death of Don Juan* (1938) is a satire that never quite comes off and borders at times on bad taste. In this group, only Ronald Duncan's play *The Death of Satan* (1954) is worthy of notice. In Hell, Don Juan is the only one who suffers; the other inmates (Byron, Wilde, and Shaw) have a thoroughly good time. Satan sends Don Juan back to Seville in order to find out why people no longer suffer in Hell. This mission turns into a grave disappointment for Don Juan, for women do not resist him and husbands no longer are offended. "For there are no virtues now, how can there be sin? / And to sin was both my purpose and my pleasure." (i, iii)

CHAPTER FOURTEEN

The Contemporary Don Juan

Cette vie le comble, rien n'est pire
que de la perdre . . . Don Juan
ne pense pas à "collectionner" les
femmes. Il en épuise le nombre et
avec elles ses chances de vie.[1]

ALBERT CAMUS,
Le Mythe de Sisyphe

Whither Don Juan? That was the problem the legend faced in the early part of the twentieth century. It seemed as if the subject had been hopelessly splintered and various writers were collecting the pieces and turning them into poems, short stories, or one-act plays which recounted isolated adventures of the hero.[2]

As can be seen by the number of versions produced during this period, Don Juan continued to attract authors; but they simply did not know what to do with him once he had loved and fought his way through a series of episodes. This dilemma is illustrated in Otto Carl Bernhardi's play *Don Juan* (1903). Like Lenau's hero, this Don Juan wants to find a woman in whom he can possess all of womanhood. In his search he seduces a nun, kills her brother, conquers Fausta during a shipwreck, takes a bride from her fiancé, and finally kills a former mistress who challenges him in man's clothing. When a philosophical talk with a hermit leaves him still unsatisfied, Don Juan decides to elope with the heroine of a play entitled "Don Juans Abenteuer."

Into the vacuum thus created stepped popularizers and hack writers,

---

[1] "This life gratifies his every wish, and nothing is worse than losing it. . . . Don Juan does not think of "collecting" women. He exhausts their number and with them his chances of life."

[2] For some of these, see Chap. 15, n. 2.

with the result that during the 1920's and 1930's the name of Don Juan can be found in hundreds of titles while the subject itself reached a new low. Any man who has two or more love affairs is called a Don Juan. Hence we find novels such as *El Tenorio de Lavapiés, Le Don Juan de Vincennes, Don Juan de Paris, Der Don Juan der Bella Riva,* and for those who like to travel, *Le Don Juan cosmopolite.*[8]

Gradually, however, the legend began to show signs of recovery as Spanish writers especially rallied to Don Juan's defense. Foremost among these was José Ortega y Gasset, who, in contrast to Marañón, considered Don Juan the epitome of manliness and virility. Far above the common herd, he is disliked by the mass mind because it cannot understand him. If Don Juan seems to have no ideal, says Ortega, it is not, as Maeztu claims, because he seeks momentary pleasure but because he has examined all ideals and has found them wanting.[4]

The first signs of a renaissance of Don Juan versions can be detected in the 1930's when a more vigorous Don Juan appears who returns to his basic traits of seduction and unfaithfulness in the grand manner. This trend is remarkably demonstrated in Jacinto Grau's lively play *El burlador que no se burla* (1930).

At the same time attempts were made to reinterpret the old problem of what the hero's ideal really is.

Manuel Machado y Ruiz depicts the fate of an ideal-seeker in his drama *Juan de Mañara* (1927). The hero is caught between two women—the pure Beatriz and Elvira, his ex-mistress. Unable to decide between the two, Don Juan vacillates from one to the other. Eventually he marries Beatriz, but suddenly Elvira reappears. Under the emotional stress an old wound opens and he dies, seeing Elvira (the *femme*

---

[8] For these and many other titles containing "Don Juan" which are, of course, unrelated to the legend, see A. E. Singer, *A Bibliography of the Don Juan Theme: Versions and Criticism* (Morgantown, 1954).

[4] José Ortega y Gasset frequently refers to Don Juan in his writings, primarily in "Meditación del marco," in *Obras completas,* II (Madrid, 1946), 300–301, and "Introducción a un Don Juan," in *Obras completas,* VI (Madrid, 1947), 121–37. The last article appeared first in *El Sol,* June, 1921.

Ortega's views are seconded by other Spanish and Latin American writers, among them R. Royo-Villanova y Morales, *Redescubrimiento de Don Juan* (Madrid, 1932), Jacinto Grau in his Preface to *Don Juan en el drama* (Buenos Aires, 1944), and Salvador de Madariaga, *Don Juan y la Don Juanía* (Buenos Aires, 1950).

fatale) and Beatriz (the pure woman) united as one. This was his impossible ideal.

Enrique Larreta's play *La que buscaba Don Juan* (1938) seems to imply a lesson similar to Maeterlinck's *Blue Bird*: that one does not have to travel all over the world in order to find happiness because it can be attained right at home. Here Don Juan, who is to be executed because of an abortive rebellion against the dictator Rosas, tries to break through to the cell next to his, which is occupied by an unknown woman. The priest arrives and, while preparing for death, Don Juan explains that he deserted his wife because she could not satisfy his ideal; she turned his pleasures into nausea. His love affairs have not satisfied him either, but now he has found the one he has been seeking: it is the woman in the adjoining cell. Everything about her reveals her uniqueness; she has followed him secretly and has been imprisoned as his accomplice. The priest, overcome by Don Juan's fervor, helps him break through the wall: the woman is Don Juan's wife.

Since the 1940's France has undoubtedly produced the most significant Don Juan versions. Two tendencies stand out: conscious efforts to confront Don Juan with a woman who is his equal, and attempts to turn him into an existential hero.

While we already encountered a *femme fatale* in Machado's *Juan de Mañara* (1927), Claude-André Puget concentrates the action completely on the contest between two powerful antagonists in his play *Echec à Don Juan* (1941). Round One is definitely won by Fabia, who first arouses Don Juan's curiosity by disguising herself as a young man (Fabio) and telling him about a supposed female cousin who is none other than she. The trick she plays on him would have delighted Mme de Merteuil: she first orders her majordomo to let himself be bribed so that Don Juan can hide in her bedroom. Then she puts on a tempting display of her charms (in less literary terms this is known as a strip tease), and when his passion is inflamed, Fabia has her place in bed taken by her old and ugly duenna. As Don Juan is about to embrace the latter, Fabia reenters the bedroom and the deceived lover has to escape under a shower of ridicule.

But Don Juan is not so easily beaten. He quietly has Fabia's household taken prisoners and returns a few hours later. His declarations have no effect on Fabia; even though still searching for love, she is sure it does not exist. What she apprehends most is the day after, when the ungrateful man mockingly disavows all his promises. To overcome her suspicions, Don Juan locks the door, throws a torch on inflammable material under the window and drops the key into the fire. They sink into each other's arms with but little time left and no tomorrow.

At least, so Fabia thinks: but Don Juan has played a trick of his own. The fire was an artificial one that his servant puts out after a while. The next day Fabia returns disguised again as Fabio, and the two draw cards over who is to have Fabia; she loses purposely, but Don Juan's remark that he will not stay long leads to a duel. She wounds him mortally, but he does not regret dying, for he, who has feared love like slavery, flees it for the last time.[5]

The most interesting development in the Don Juan legend so far during the twentieth century may well turn out to be the use of the hero as an illustration of certain contemporary existential tendencies. It is not, however, a Sartrian character we encounter in these efforts[6] but a type of personage whom Albert Camus calls the "absurd" hero in his series of essays entitled *Le Mythe de Sisyphe* (1942). We are, of course, still too close to this new trend to make any accurate predictions as to its importance, but it would not be surprising if some day Camus's brief essay were to occupy a place in the legend analogous to Hoffmann's short story, for it has already inspired various noteworthy attempts to embody the author's concept of the hero in dramatic works.

[5] In Carlos Salvaño Campos' play *Don Juan derrotado* (1927), Don Juan actually suffers a complete reversal at the hands of a *femme fatale*. This one has already caused the suicides of two husbands and, before leaving for Europe with her third, she challenges Don Juan (a lawyer, married, and father of a boy) to a love duel.

Five years later, having disposed of her third husband, the woman returns to face Don Juan. But instead of dominating her like a superman, as she had hoped, he begs for her love and understanding; she turns away from him with contempt. Only the return of his wife, who announces she will bear him another child, saves him from breaking down after this crushing defeat.

[6] It is somewhat surprising that Jean-Paul Sartre has not written a Don Juan play as yet. The hero could either serve to illustrate "bad faith" (in this case: assumption of complete liberty but refusal to accept the responsibility that goes with it); or else he could be depicted as a tragic figure caught in the web of existential love, a possibility already indicated by Kierkegaard in his "Diary of a Seducer" (cf. Chap. 13 above, especially the quotation identified in n. 4).

I shall not try at this place to give any but the most cursory indications about the traits of Meursault, the narrator in Camus's novel *L'Etranger* (1942), but some idea of this work is necessary in order to understand Camus's interpretation of Don Juan. What strikes us most in this "Stranger" is an obstinate adherence (not reasoned but rather natural and instinctive throughout most of the novel) to concrete phenomena and an indifference to such abstract temptations as ambition, religion, or love. As for the latter, Meursault quite frankly (naïvely, not cynically) answers the pleading question of his mistress by stating that he does not love her and that anyway the expression does not mean anything. Even when during his stay in prison (after having killed an Arab "because of the sun," as he vainly tries to explain to the court) Meursault thinks about his mistress, he can only remember her body, her clothing—all the rest is meaningless to him. Condemned to death for his crime, Meursault gradually becomes aware of his role and in a talk with the prison chaplain he pours out the vision he has gained: only one thing matters—death. It matters little what we do in life; the same fate awaits all of us, and it is the only thing to be feared. Thus, embracing the absurd life consciously, Meursault, the little clerk, rises to the heights of Sisyphus, who was so attached to earthly life that the gods condemned him to the absurd task of rolling a heavy stone up a mountain only to have it roll down again once he has reached the top. But when Sisyphus, conscious of his fate, descends the mountain to recommence his useless labors, he is superior to the gods who have punished him.

In his essay "Le Don Juanisme,"[7] Camus exposes his view of Don Juan as an "absurd" hero, a sort of Sisyphus in matters of sexual relations:

It is not through lack of love that Don Juan goes from woman to woman. It is ridiculous to represent him as a mystic in quest of total love. But it is indeed because he loves them with the same passion and each time with his whole self that he must repeat this gift and his profound quest. Whence each woman hopes to give him what no one has ever given him. Each time they are utterly wrong and merely manage to make him feel the need of that repetition. "At last," exclaims one of them, "I have given you love." Can we be surprised that Don Juan laughs at this? "At last? No," he says,

[7] From *The Myth of Sisyphus and Other Essays*, transl. by Justin O'Brien (New York, Alfred A. Knopf, 1955), pp. 69–77. Quoted by permission of the publisher.

"but once more." Why should it be essential to love rarely in order to love much? . . .

. . . Molina's *Burlador* ever replies to the threats of hell: "What a long respite you give me!" What comes after death is futile, and what a long succession of days for whoever knows how to be alive! Faust craved worldly goods; the poor man had only to stretch out his hand. It already amounted to selling his soul when he was unable to gladden it. As for satiety, Don Juan insists upon it, on the contrary. If he leaves a woman it is not absolutely because he has ceased to desire her. A beautiful woman is always desirable. But he desires another, and no, this is not the same thing.

This life gratifies his every wish, and nothing is worse than losing it. This madman is a great wise man. . . .

. . . He is not like Milosz's Mañara, who damns himself through a desire to be a saint. . . . Don Juan can be properly understood only by constant reference to what he commonly symbolizes: the ordinary seducer and the sexual athlete. He *is* an ordinary seducer. Except for the difference that he is conscious, and that is why he is absurd. . . . What Don Juan realizes in action is an ethic of quantity, whereas the saint, on the contrary, tends toward quality. Not to believe in the profound meaning of things belongs to the absurd man. As for those cordial or wonder-struck faces, he eyes them, stores them up, and does not pause over them. Time keeps up with him. The absurd man is he who is not apart from time. Don Juan does not think of "collecting" women. He exhausts their number and with them his chances of life. "Collecting" amounts to being capable of living off one's past. But he rejects regret, that other form of hope. He is incapable of looking at portraits. . . .

For him it is a matter of seeing clearly. We call love what binds us to certain creatures only by reference to a collective way of seeing for which books and legends are responsible. But of love I know only that mixture of desire, affection, and intelligence that binds me to this or that creature. That compound is not the same for another person. I do not have the right to cover all these experiences with the same name. This exempts one from conducting them with the same gestures. The absurd man multiplies here again what he cannot unify. Thus he discovers a new way of being which liberates him at least as much as it liberates those who approach him. There is no noble love but that which recognizes itself to be both short-lived and exceptional. . . .

I think at this point of all those who absolutely insist that Don Juan be punished. Not only in another life, but even in this one. I think of all those tales, legends, and laughs about the aged Don Juan. But Don Juan is already ready. To a conscious man old age and what it portends are not a surprise. Indeed, he is conscious only in so far as he does not conceal its horror from himself. . . . He would consider it normal to be chastised. That is the rule of the game. And, indeed, it is typical of his nobility to have accepted all the rules of the game. Yet he knows he is right and that there can be no question of punishment. A fate is not a punishment. . . .

. . . it was the fact of living that assured his innocence. It was from death alone that he derived a guilt now become legendary.

What else does that stone Commander signify, that cold statue set in motion to punish the blood and courage that dared to think? . . . No, it was not under a stone hand that Don Juan met his death. I am inclined to believe in the legendary bravado, in that mad laughter of a healthy man provoking a non-existent God. But, above all, I believe that on that evening when Don Juan was waiting at Anna's the Commander didn't come, and that after midnight the blasphemer must have felt the dreadful bitterness of those who have been right.

It is this "absurd" Don Juan, a true "master of reality," who has tempted several present-day playwrights. In almost all these portraits it is not difficult to detect some aspect of the interpretation Camus had proposed. Don Juan, contrary to the Stranger, is at all times conscious of the absurdity of human existence. In this world in which nothing matters except death, he has decided to enjoy himself with the most concrete object life has to offer him—women. Of course, at the end of the road there are old age and death, but he is ready for that.

André Obey's drama *L'Homme de cendres* (1949)[8] contains a scene in which Don Juan (very much like the Stranger in his talk with the prison chaplain), facing the Inquisitor, unburdens his mind:

I am not afraid of anything. First of all, there is nothing. Nothing on earth. Nothing in Heaven. . . . But I forget; of course, there is something. . . . There is death. . . .

What if, at the end of your life, you were to suspect that the only thing that matters, that is of value, in even the longest life, is to die a good death, and that you have failed in this? . . . What if, at the end of the road, too late to turn back, you were to know, Cardinal, that God is a mistake, that the world is a mistake, that man is a mistake, that everything is monstrous, haggard, fortuitous, absurd! . . . That man has only one duty . . . one single duty . . . at the end of a life filled with restraints, rules, orders, laws, senseless dogmas—to absolve the world . . . for being incomprehensible, to absolve himself, born to understand and having understood nothing; then,

---

[8] This is actually the third Don Juan version by Obey, the two previous ones being *Don Juan* (1934) and *Le Trompeur de Seville* (1937).

about to be cast into nothingness, . . . to lift the veil of the enigma and—
pure at last, and great, and just, and man at last as one should be at birth,
Cardinal—to die. (Act II)

Obey does not break altogether with previous trends of the legend,
however. His Don Juan is both irresistible and an ideal-seeker. He
does not tire of proclaiming that he is looking for "the countenance of
life." This last trait, it would seem, is out of harmony with the "absurd"
philosophy the hero professes.[9] One can hardly be surprised that he
does not find this vague ideal in the numerous beds he occupies, so that
finally, burnt out by passion and time, he chooses to be killed by his
friend in a duel.

It is noteworthy that two of France's most important playwrights
have recently produced Don Juan plays: Jean Anouilh and Henry
de Montherlant. The very name of the hero in Anouilh's *Ornifle ou
le Courant d'air* (1955) indicates that the author has consciously modeled his play on Molière's *Dom Juan*. Not only is the seventeenth-
century atmosphere preserved thanks to a costume ball, but Molière's
essential characters reappear, even though under different disguises:
Ornifle is Dom Juan-Tartuffe-Onuphre; Sganarelle, the voice of his
conscience, turns out to be a sighing, weeping, hysterical female secretary named Supo; the Commander's place is taken by Ornifle's illegitimate son Fabrice, a close relative of Thomas Diafoirus from *Le Malade*

---

[9] This makes also for rather poor drama, for Don Juan has to be a philosophical
realist and a passionate idealist at the same time. Here is, for example, how Obey's
hero conquers Anna, his friend's fiancée:
   DON JUAN: Everything people are interested in—love, money, glory,
   ideas—all that leaves me cold as ice. . . . All of life is but a grimace. And
   I feel that life has a countenance. . . . I was seeking it tonight, all alone
   . . . in the coldness of the night, the coldness of the world. Then you
   appeared, warm, golden, young, everything. You bore exactly the countenance of life. So I shouted (*he shouts*) "Anna."
   ANNA (*she shouts*): Juan.
Another hero who refuses to be swayed by abstract values is the protagonist of
Michel Poissenot's drama *Don Juan* (written in 1941–42; published in 1950):
   "I have *flirted* quite a bit with God. I have frequently gone to churches where
the women were ugly. . . . Underneath the smoke of the incense, I have sought
the celestial fire. And my human warmth called for supernatural warmth. That
call remained unanswered. When I touch the body of a girl, I feel under my warm
hands the contact of a warm body; and I am far too much alive to think of death."

imaginaire; Ornifle's wife resembles Elvire very much; and even religion is represented, not by a humble beggar this time but by the
worldly-wise and all-too-indulgent Father Dubaton. But how small
everything has become in the hands of the modern author! One has
the impression of looking at Molière's play through the wrong end of
one's opera glasses. The result, however, is miniature in the best sense
of the word, for Anouilh's sparkling and clever lines compensate considerably for a lack of dimension.

Ornifle de Saint-Oignon is a poet who, after a brilliant start, has
become a rhymester for the music hall. Surrounded by his adoring
secretary, his tolerant wife, and the *nouveau riche* Machetu, for whose
shows he composes facile lyrics, Ornifle, who must be around forty-
five, has a long list of conquests to his credit and seems still at his best.
His latest adventure has resulted in a pregnancy, but he is already tired
of the woman and arranges for Machetu to marry her.

The shock which disturbs this pleasant existence is the arrival of
Fabrice, Ornifle's illegitimate son by a mistress whom he abandoned
twenty-five years ago. Fabrice has become a medical student and has
sworn vengeance, which he is ready to carry out now that his mother
has died. The attempt fails, because Fabrice's fiancée Marguerite has
emptied his revolver; nevertheless, Ornifle falls to the floor and
Fabrice diagnoses his illness as Bishop's disease. Once revived, Ornifle
seems to be deeply concerned with the souls of those he has until then
treated as objects: he reunites Fabrice and Marguerite, who have quar-
reled, he tries to prevent the marriage so cynically arranged for
Machetu, and he even makes a sort of confession to Father Dubaton.
But as soon as two specialists have assured him that Fabrice's diagnosis
was incorrect, Ornifle returns to his old ways with renewed vigor. This
time he makes elaborate plans for what looks like a difficult seduction—
that of his future daughter-in-law. Upon arriving at the hotel where
he is to meet the young couple, Ornifle suffers a fatal attack—Fabrice
had diagnosed his illness correctly.

Like Camus's Don Juan, Ornifle is convinced of the absurdity of
life, but he has willingly and desperately embraced this absurd life in
order to squeeze out of it every pleasure it has to offer. And his greatest
pleasure is women. Everything abstract (art, morality, philosophy),
constantly proposed to him by his wife and by Supo, is rejected as
unimportant, even in bad taste. This is his view of love:

We play the little ballet of desire like the doggies. I smell you, you smell me, I turn away, I turn around, I don't want to, yes! I do want to. And since I am willing, it is for life. . . . And then someone (who it is we do not know) suddenly pulls on the leash and the doggy who was dreaming of happiness is snatched away . . . until chance or the master, who is musing about his little worries some five feet nine above, happens to lead the doggy to another doggy. Then the ballet begins all over again with the same vows until the next time the leash is pulled, which interrupts everything once more. (Act II, pp. 95–96)

To serious warnings and objections, Ornifle retorts with a phrase reminiscent of the Burlador's "¡Qué largo me lo fiáis!" His motto is: "Our purpose in this world is to dance." For Ornifle, as for Meursault, only the present moment matters. "Pleasures," he counsels Fabrice, "are never futile, at least not during the moment we enjoy them." But, unlike the Burlador, the "absurd" Don Juan is ready for the inevitable denouement of his comedies. To him the eventual vengeance of Heaven is not a punishment but a destiny.

I know what Heaven has in store for me. It is no doubt preparing my punishment. It is patiently polishing its thunderbolt, it is already lubricating the wheels of the little cart to which I shall be nailed when my day comes. On that day I shall not expect anyone to pity me. I shall pay the price of my pleasures. (Act II, p. 89)

One of the main reasons why Ornifle cannot rise to more than a miniature of Molière's Dom Juan is the lack of opposition, which can be noticed in several contemporary Don Juan versions. Supo is far weaker than Sganarelle at his most ridiculous; Ornifle's wife never dares chastise her husband the way Elvire did; Fabrice is a silly fool unworthy of the Commander's role; and Father Dubaton seems to be more interested in pleasing Ornifle than in saving his soul.

Another feature almost inevitable in the "absurd" Don Juan is that he is somewhere between thirty-five and forty-five. While this deprives him of the attractiveness of youth, it provides a new tragic possibility: only a man past the age of the Burlador will take that last desperate leap at pleasure which subordinates all other considerations; only a mature Don Juan can consciously formulate a view of life and still be believable.

Henry de Montherlant's play *Don Juan* (1958) is the most recent version on the subject. The author, who had previously demonstrated a profound understanding of the Spanish character, seemed ideally suited to produce a work that might be epoch-making in the history of the Don Juan legend; yet his play was almost unanimously condemned by the critics.

As a play, indeed, *Don Juan* is disappointing, especially when compared to such previous successes by the same author as *La Reine morte* and *Le Maître de Santiago*. Neither public nor critics are likely to applaud a Don Juan who is sixty-six years old: the notion of the young and dashing Don Juan is simply too strong in people's minds for that. The play lacks consistency of mood, a difficulty of which Montherlant is fully aware, as seen in his notes appended to the published edition of the play. There are also unnecessary scenes that only certain specialists are likely to appreciate.[10]

The most serious shortcoming of the play, however, is the weakness of the supporting characters. They are either caricatures (such as the Commander, his wife, Le Marquis de Ventras, Don Basile, La Double Veuve, and the three "thinkers") or colorless (Don Alcacer, Linda, and even Ana). It is therefore not so much the predominance of Don Juan that detracts from the effectiveness of the play as the virtual absence of opposition to him; what opposition there is has been purposely reduced to ridiculous characters. There is, nevertheless, a powerful and terrifying opponent in the play, but he is not contained in the list of characters, as will be seen below.

Although Montherlant's *Don Juan* suffers considerably from the disproportionate importance of the hero, this very defect enabled the author to define his Don Juan as fully as possible; and in this respect Montherlant's achievement is far greater than the critics have given him credit for.

It has previously been pointed out that contemporary authors seem to prefer to depict Don Juan in his forties. Montherlant boldly fixes his hero's age at sixty-six. This, of course, entails the usual disadvantages of an aged Don Juan (how can he attract and seduce young

---

[10] Especially the scene featuring the three "thinkers who have ideas about Don Juan" (III, ii). The first claims Don Juan needs God (the way Toinette claims that the would-be invalid Argan has a bad lung); the second insists that Don Juan is seeking an absolute similar to that sought by an artist; the third presents Otto Rank's view that the servant (whose role is here taken by Don Alcacer) is the double of Don Juan. There are also oblique references to André Obey's play *L'Homme de cendres* in II, iv and III, i.

girls?),[11] but it adds one important feature: he is facing death, the one opponent he cannot defeat and hence his drama, his last desperate fling at pleasure, becomes intensified.

Montherlant has not only portrayed the aged Don Juan more keenly than anyone else—he also has bridged the gap that separated the romantic Don Juan from his first ancestor: Tirso's Burlador. "I have unburdened my hero," Montherlant writes in his notes, "of what the nineteenth century had made of him. Don Juan, in my play, is a simple character; he has no depth. I wanted him to be that way. He runs after all women. He does not wish them any ill. On the contrary: he is not wicked." And later on: "What he says is never carefully weighed, polished, substantiated, *thought out*: it is *spontaneous*."

Montherlant's Don Juan is Tirso's Burlador grown old. Instead of ending his career at the height of his power, he has outlived his role by many years; and what began as a youthful game now has become an obsession. "And I have to do it every day," the old Don Juan confesses; "for me, it's like bread. The only trouble with women is that, while you do it with one, you can't do it with others, nor even chase after others." (1, i) Even buckets of water from windows above will not make him leave the hiding place where he is waiting for young Linda. And when she finally arrives (late, of course), he tries the means of seduction to which an old man is reduced: offering her an expensive pin, telling her she reminds him of his daughter who died young, etc.; in fact, her repugnance upon seeing his wrinkled face adds spice to his desire.

With Ana, however, matters are different. She loves Don Juan as the man who has made a woman out of her; her love is that of the proud and apparently cold virgin whose first lover appears to her as the only man capable of giving her happiness. The fact that he has killed her father, whether intentionally or not, an age difference of fifty years—all this matters very little to her.

Aside from his age, Don Juan differs from the Burlador in two aspects. While Tirso's hero will never speak a true word to a woman, the old Don Juan never lies to them. He refuses to flatter Linda, for he admits that his love for her will last but one morning; and his declarations of love to Ana are sincere, even if not durable.

[11] Robert Kemp (*Le Monde*, November 14, 1958) refers to Montherlant's aged hero as a "sugar grand-daddy."

Death, too, appears in different forms to the two heroes. To the Burlador it comes as a horrible surprise; Montherlant's Don Juan, by contrast, has faced it for so long that it has become part of him. And when, in the last scene, he puts on a mask so that he will not be recognized in Seville, it is the mask of death which he cannot remove.

Montherlant's Don Juan, nevertheless, exhibits the basic traits of the Burlador: simplicity, naturalness, a craving for women, fickleness. But the author has set himself an additional and difficult task. He has attempted to imbue his hero with a temperamental make-up he considers typically Sevillian: mobility, fluctuation of character. "The word 'Seville,'" Montherlant explains, "is, first of all, synonymous with gaiety. The *sevillana* is a dance full of liveliness. But the Sevillian *cuadro flamenco* derives its inspiration from pain and death. This mixture of lightness and poignancy typifies Seville as well as Don Juan, the Sevillian."

Thus Don Juan appears in turn (or even within one speech) serious and humorous, light-hearted and melancholy, pitiful and impressive. If we add to this that the first act is light, the second farcical, and the third (at least scenes 4 to 7) serious, then it becomes apparent that Montherlant's *Don Juan* is a very difficult wager, namely: to produce a play that lacks unity of mood and whose principal character is inconsistent, at least in the sense in which that term is used in theater criticism.

Montherlant has undoubtedly lost his wager, but his defeat is a glorious one, for he has thrown out a challenge to future creators of Don Juan and to the theater in general. He has shown that certain characters may be true only to the extent they are inconsistent. Whether the theater can successfully deal with this problem, that is another question. But if experiments in this direction are to be made, Don Juan would serve as an ideal instrument, and Montherlant may have opened up new and fruitful possibilities for further development of the eternal Burlador.

CHAPTER FIFTEEN

Epilogue

Questa è il fin, di chi fa mal,
E dì perfidi la morte
Alla vita è sempre ugual.[1]

MOZART,
Don Giovanni

In the preceding chapters we have followed the fate of a dramatic concept which, by capturing the imagination of age after age, has become one of the great themes in Western literature. We have observed the ups and downs of the hero, the worship and condemnation, the glory and abuse that each new generation has heaped upon him according to its ideals and attitudes. Truly, no literary figure has gone through more metamorphoses than Don Juan.

Drawn probably in part from medieval folklore and in part modeled on theatrical trends of the time, the Don Juan legend finds its first complete dramatic expression in Tirso de Molina's morality play *El Burlador de Sevilla*, published in 1630. The subject apparently aroused initial interest mainly because of its supernatural elements, but its lasting success has been due primarily to the personality of Don Juan and the moral, religious, and psychological aspects of the subject.

In Italy these features were replaced by comic elements, effected by the buffooneries of the *commedia dell'arte*. After being introduced into France by Italian actors, the subject had its dignity restored by Molière, who presented a penetrating psychological portrait of the hero as a "grand seigneur méchant homme." During the eighteenth century Don Juan was almost completely eclipsed by the *roué* in the manner of Lovelace and Valmont, until Mozart and Da Ponte created

---

[1] "Such is the end of him who doeth ill. And the death of the wicked is always in keeping with their lives."

a brilliant synthesis of preceding trends in their opera *Don Giovanni*, which led to a renaissance of the legend.

The first half of the nineteenth century is dominated by Hoffmann's interpretation of Mozart's opera and by Zorrilla's drama *Don Juan Tenorio*—the former because it sketched the transfiguration of the hero and proposed a concept which is still very influential; the latter because it saved Don Juan from condemnation and, as a matter of statistics, has been the most popular Don Juan play for over one hundred years. As the century progresses, the Faust and Mañara legends exert their influence on the Don Juan subject. Following a period of attacks on and criticisms of the hero, Donjuanism concentrates on the over-refined maneuvers of high-society seducers.

The twentieth century opens with Shaw's reversal of Don Juan's most basic trait by making him the prey rather than the huntsman. After becoming the stamping grounds of popularizers and hack writers, the legend finally comes back into its own: first through the hero's rehabilitation by Spanish writers, then by works which create new interest by opposing Don Juan with a *femme fatale*, and most recently by existential and "absurd" interpretations of the hero, as proposed by Albert Camus.

This history of the Don Juan legend has, of course, not exhausted the subject. Since my effort was to present the most significant trends in the development of the legend, only those works were studied which, in my judgment, made an important contribution to the legend or developed a certain trend. Consequently a number of works that may be of interest in themselves but do not particularly affect the evolution of the legend have not even been mentioned. These include a number of short stories and poems,[2] farcical plays,[3] adventurous versions,[4] ambitious but rather muddled philosophical interpretations,[5] or simply mixtures of various trends that offer nothing particularly new.[6]

---

[2] Examples: Jules Barbey d'Aurevilly, *Le plus Bel Amour de Don Juan* (1874); Ramón de Campoamor, *Don Juan* (poem, 1887); Ernst Kratzmann, *Don Juan in Venedig* (about 1940).

[3] Examples: W. T. Moncrieff, *Giovanni in London, or the Libertine Reclaimed* (1820); Paul Eudel, *La Statue du Commandeur* (1892).

[4] Examples: Richard Mansfield, *Don Juan* (play, 1891); Carl Sternheim, *Don Juan* (tragedy, 1909); Giuseppe Pagliari, *Don Giovanni* (drama, 1911).

[5] Examples: Sigismund Wiese, *Don Juan* (tragedy, 1840); Ferdinand von Hornstein, *Don Juans Höllenqualen* (drama, 1901).

[6] Example: August Lembach, *Don Juan* (drama, 1912).

An entire book could also be devoted to the Don Juan type outside of the legend. A character as powerful as Don Juan has, of course, made his influence felt on almost any work dealing with a seducer or a ladies' man.[7] A similar study might be made of the female Don Juan, the Doña Juana type.[8]

Another aspect of the legend to which little attention has been paid in the preceding chapters is the nationality of the authors involved. It might therefore be in order to make a few summary remarks on that topic for whatever such generalities may be worth.

Of the principal countries concerned (Spain, Italy, France, Germany, and England), Italy has produced the smallest number of Don Juan versions. Her contribution to the legend has been most important in the operatic field. In literature Italy has primarily served as a liaison agent between Spain and France.

England ranks next to the last in fertility of production. Byron and Shaw occupy, of course, the first places among English contributors to the Don Juan legend. Whatever the merits of their respective works, so far as the legend is concerned they have not been among the most fruitful. Byron divorced himself completely from his predecessors, thus opening the way for complete anarchy in treatments of the subject; Shaw, although far better acquainted with the tradition of the legend, chose to reverse the role of the hero, which led to a dead end.

Considering the remaining English versions, I find them inferior to the French, German, and Spanish ones, and I believe the reason is

---

[7] Examples: Anton Chekhov's untitled play (1881), variously translated as *That Worthless Fellow Platonov* (by John Cournos, 1930) and *Don Juan (in the Russian Manner)* (by Basil Ashmore, 1952); Alexander Pushkin, *Eugene Onegin* (novel in verse, 1831); Hermann Sudermann's play *Das Glück im Winkel* (1895; character Baron von Röcknitz); Hugo von Hofmannsthal's comedy *Christinas Heimreise* (1910; character Florindo); George Meredith's novel *The Egoist* (1879; character Sir Willoughby Patterne); Charles Dickens' novels *Nicholas Nickleby* (1838–39; character Mantalini) and *David Copperfield* (1849–50; character Steerforth); Gabriele d'Annunzio's novel *Piacere* (1889; character Count Andrea Sperelli); Luigi Pirandello's play *Ma non è una cosa seria* (1918; character Memmo Speranza); Gustave Flaubert's novel *Madame Bovary* (1857; character Rodolphe); Henry de Montherlant's novel *Pitié pour les femmes* (1936; character Pierre Costals); Albert Camus's novel *La Chute* (1957; the narrator); and innumerable French plays and novels dealing with *viveurs* and *lions*. (See Singer, *A Bibliography of the Don Juan Theme*, under these categories.)

[8] Example: Marcel Prévost's novel *Les Don Juanes* (1922).

that the English author writing a Don Juan version has to deal with certain preliminaries which the others usually can dispense with. To the Spanish and French, sex has been, at most periods of their history, an accepted part of life. A Don Juan to them is not a person basically different from the normal man except in so far as he may carry his desires to an excess. The French or Spanish writer can therefore begin his story *in medias res*.

The English author has to start at a different level, because he has to take a stand on the basic issue of sex, which English morality cannot face squarely but is inclined to look at through stealthily spread fingers, as it were. Like Hoffmann the romantic, the English author discovers in Don Juan a figure that is capable of expressing his own rebellion against his hypocritical environment; yet, unlike Hoffmann, the English did not transcend this subjective starting point in order to arrive at the essense of Don Juan's character or impose a new interpretation on it. Instead they expended all their energy in using the hero as a means of attacking or satirizing their society—and thus, so far as the development of Don Juan's personality is concerned, they stopped at the point where they should have begun. In England, Don Juan becomes an eccentric; such a person is representative not of general humanity but of a very small minority. While elsewhere Don Juan is punished for excesses of otherwise normal impulses which threaten to upset the natural order of society, in England the hero represents an essentially foreign attitude that can be used for satire but not for much else. Moreover, when the celestial punishment by the statue is introduced in an English version, it is out of place, not only because it does not fit into the English moral framework but also because one clearly senses that the English mind is ill at ease in an atmosphere of miraculous and supernatural events.

Spain, France, and Germany have been the most active countries in Don Juan productions, each of them having produced about one hundred versions.

The Germans have, in general, tended to lend more philosophical and sentimental depth to the Spanish hero. We have had occasion to note the central position in the legend of Hoffmann's short story. Grabbe and others attempted to oppose Don Juan and Faust or to instill some of the philosophical weight of the German magician into the light-hearted pursuer of women. On the other hand, German authors have at times carried tendencies implicit in the hero to the point of ridiculous exaggeration. The German contribution to the legend has consistently declined during the present century.

French authors have generally followed the pattern established by Molière: the psychological portrait of the hero in his social milieu. In France, therefore, more than anywhere else, Don Juan mirrors faithfully the various literary and intellectual tendencies of the times. This is perhaps why at present the subject is most alive in that country, where Don Juan continues to receive significant attention. We should also mention the contributions of Mérimée and Milosz in their versions of the Mañara legend.

The most striking weakness in French Don Juan versions is the loquaciousness of the hero in many instances.[9] This is perhaps unavoidable in psychological studies which require speeches of self-explanation and in versions dealing with an existential or "absurd" hero. Yet a talkative Don Juan seems a misconception.

One of the fascinating features in Don Juan is exactly that he talks very little but acts constantly. Tisbea, in Tirso's *Burlador*, describes this aspect of the hero in a striking phrase: "You say much—even without words." (1, 609) Kierkegaard expressed the same view in *Either-Or* when he wrote: "A seducer, therefore, ought to be possessed of a power Don Juan does not have—the power of eloquence"; and Mozart lifted this interpretation to new heights by having his entire opera centered about Don Giovanni yet without giving him any major arias. The loss of this "immediate erotic," as Kierkegaard calls it, in modern Don Juan versions is truly deplorable. It does not suffice to create a sexually loaded atmosphere, as contemporary French writers (Puget, Poissenot, Obey) evoke in the opening scenes of their plays—this impression must radiate from Don Juan himself, and with a minimum of verbiage. A difficult task, but one that seems imperative in order to capture one of the great secrets of Don Juan.

Spain occupies, of course, a special place in this summary of national contributions to the Don Juan legend. Regardless of academic disputes about the origins of the legend, the hero and his environment are Spanish. Two plays stand out: Tirso de Molina's *El Burlador de Sevilla*, which, for all practical purposes, is the first literary work on the subject; and José Zorrilla's *Don Juan Tenorio*, which continues to

---

[9] The most talkative of all is probably the hero of Michel Poissenot's tragedy *Don Juan* (1950), but he is not far ahead of his closest rivals.

enjoy immense popularity. Next to these two great works, most of the remaining Spanish Don Juan versions pale considerably. We might, however, mention two interpretations of the Mañara legend: José de Espronceda's dramatic poem *El estudiante de Salamanca,* and Gregorio Martínez Sierra's play *Don Juan de España.* Contemporary Spanish and Latin American writers continue to show great interest in the Don Juan legend, as witnessed by the contributions of Ortega y Gasset, Jacinto Grau, and Salvador de Madariaga.

In an over-all view of the legend, among the vast number of Don Juan works five are in a class by themselves: those of Tirso de Molina, Molière, Mozart, Hoffmann, and Zorrilla. After these five giants, at a respectable distance, might be placed the versions and interpretations of Mérimée, Kierkegaard, Grabbe, Lenau, and Camus.

It is indeed difficult to choose among these great creations. Mozart's *Don Giovanni* is perhaps the most perfect expression the hero has ever received, for, as Kierkegaard maintains so persuasively, only music can convey the inexpressible attractiveness and power of that great figure. Among the four outstanding literary works, my choice goes to Tirso de Molina's *El Burlador de Sevilla.* In my opinion this first Don Juan play has never been equaled or surpassed by another literary work in the history of the legend. Tirso's hero is incomparably alive, active, youthful, dynamic. He speaks relatively little, but what he says is significant and revealing. He has one more advantage which no other Don Juan ever since has enjoyed or will enjoy: he has read no definitions of himself—he does not even know that one day he will be famous. Only a Don Juan who is unaware of what others have written about him, who is far too busy *being* Don Juan to formulate a program or a philosophy of life or an apology for his actions—only such a personage can possess the natural vitality of Tirso's hero. It is indeed essential that the author should know what his hero represents, but it is not at all essential that his Don Juan should spell it out so completely as to leave nothing to our imagination. The inexorable consistency of Tirso's moral and religious attitude and his presentation of the statue are likewise without equal among literary Don Juan versions. In addition, *El Burlador de Sevilla* is an exciting and moving drama.

Finally, Tirso has succeeded in making his Burlador more representative of general male psychology than most of his successors. His hero embodies in the most direct manner possible certain tendencies, desires, and (often unavowed) ambitions that are active, in varying degrees, in practically every male during a more or less protracted period of his life. We did not have to wait for the Kinsey Report, for example, to know that men are basically inconstant and that even a marriage vow does not prevent them from being strongly tempted by every pretty woman they pass. The Burlador incorporates this male fickleness, this curiosity and appetite for variety. Along with this, he possesses a quality which constitutes a male ideal: inexhaustible sexual energy and hence unflagging desire for new adventures. Finally, the Burlador represents the wish-fulfillment of another male ambition: the quick enjoyment of a desired woman with practically no preliminary courting or subsequent obligation. Certainly, there is much truth in Stendhal's statement:

The error of their [the Don Juans'] life consists in the belief that they are able to conquer in two weeks what a frightened lover scarcely obtains in six months. . . . They do not want to see that what they obtain, even if it were accorded by the same woman, is not the same thing.[10]

But this is the kind of wisdom that comes with experience and in retrospect—no young lover will agree with this while his unsuccessful courtship frustrates him. The Burlador is this eternal young lover who has read no treatises on love but is driven only by two forces: male concupiscence and the vanity of being admired for his successes. He manages to possess the woman he desires yet limits his relations with her to the sole satisfaction of his sexual urge. Thus the Burlador obtains without charge from a decent woman what can normally be bought only from a prostitute.[11]

To interpret Don Juan as an ideal-seeker is still valid, for the desire to find an ideal woman is generally present in men, even though most of them are probably less difficult than Don Juan. As an irresistible lover he continues to symbolize a male wish image, but this interpretation entails some grave dramatic problems. Once Don Juan no longer encounters obstacles, either from the women he desires or from religious and social opponents, the dramatic interest decreases and we watch the monotonous surrender of women and his repeated: "No, she

---

[10] *De l'Amour*, Chap. lix.

[11] The fact that the Burlador will just as readily deceive prostitutes does not affect the validity of this view.

was not the one," which is featured in only too many modern Don Juan versions.

Although the individualization of the hero was inevitable, the result has been that the legend became subject to all kinds of minor sequels: Don Juan meets the Ideal Woman; Don Juan meets the Irresistible Woman; Don Juan's Last Adventure, etc.

This splintering of the Don Juan legend has been especially noticeable since the beginning of the twentieth century. It is all the more gratifying to observe that the contemporary effort to have the hero represent an existential or "absurd" attitude returns the subject to a more universal plane. Thus the legend has once more proved its vitality by serving as an expression for the philosophical and psychological preoccupations of the mid-twentieth century. While the subjects of Faust, Don Quixote, and Hamlet have shown relatively little development in recent times, the legend of Don Juan, like the great Greek legends that have been interpreted anew by each generation, promises to go on indefinitely.

Bibliography[1]

Aby, Robert-Peter. "The Problem of Crébillon *fils*." Unpublished Ph.D. dissertation, Stanford, California, Stanford University, 1955.

Agustin, Francisco. *Don Juan en el teatro, en la novela y en la vida*. Madrid, Editorial Paez-Bolsa, 1932.

Auster, John. *The Story of Don Juan: A Study of the Legend and of the Hero*. London, Martin Secker, 1939.

Azorín: see *Martínez Ruiz, José*

Baldensperger, Fernand. *Goethe en France*. Paris, Hachette, 1904.

Barrière, Marcel. *L'Art des passions: Essai sur le donjuanisme contemporain*. Paris, Editions du Monde Nouveau, 1904. Reissued in 1922 with shortened title, *Essai sur*, etc.

Beyle, Henri. *De l'Amour*. Paris, Le Divan, 1927.

———— *Mémoires d'un touriste*. 2 vols. Paris, Michel Lévy frères, 1854.

Bianquis, Geneviève. *Faust à travers quatre siècles*. Paris, Droz, 1935.

Blaze, François Henri J., called Castil-Blaze. *Molière musicien; notes sur les œuvres de cet illustre maître* . . . , Vol. I. Paris, Castil-Blaze, 1852.

Boelte, J. "Über den Ursprung der Don-Juan Sage," *Zeitschrift für Vergleichende Literaturgeschichte*, XIII (1899), 374–98.

Boyd, Elizabeth French. *Byron's Don Juan: A Critical Study*. New Brunswick, Rutgers University Press, 1945.

Brachfeld, F. Oliver. *Inferiority Feeling in the Individual and the Group*. Transl. from the French by Marjorie Gabain. New York, Grune and Strutton, 1951.

Breuillac, Marcel. "Hoffmann en France," *Revue d'Histoire Littéraire de la France*, XIII (1906), 427–57; XIV (1907), 74–105.

Caillard, Maurice. "Don Juan et les poètes," *Gemmes d'Art*, No. 1 (June, 1921).

---

[1] The books and articles listed here are those which were consulted for this study only. For an exhaustive list of works on the Don Juan subject, the reader is referred to the bibliographies of Everett W. Hesse and Armand E. Singer, listed below.

Calvet, J. *Les Types universels dans la littérature française.* 2ᵉ série. Paris, F. Lanore, 1928.

Camargo y Marín, César. *Un tríptico sobre Don Juan.* Madrid, Javier Morato, 1934.

Camus, Albert. "Le Don Juanisme," in *Le Mythe de Sisyphe.* Paris, Gallimard, 1942, pp. 97–106. Transl. by Justin O'Brien as *The Myth of Sisyphus and Other Essays.* New York, Knopf, 1955.

———— *L'Etranger.* Paris, Gallimard, 1942.

Cárdenas, Juan de. *Breve relación de la muerte, de la vida y virtudes de Miguel Mañara.* Seville, M. Gómez Imaz y J. Mª. Valdenebro, 1903.

Casalduero, Joaquín. "Acotaciones al *Burlador de Sevilla* de Tirso de Molina," *Die Neueren Sprachen,* XXXVII (1929), 594–98.

———— *Contribución al estudio del tema de Don Juan en el teatro español.* Northampton, Mass., 1938. Smith College Studies in Modern Languages, Vol. XIX, Nos. 3–4.

Castellane, Maurice. *Die grossen Don Juans und das Geheimnis ihres Lebens.* Leipzig, M. Wendel, 1908.

Castro, Américo. Introduction and notes in his edition of *El Burlador de Sevilla,* in *Tirso de Molina, Obras I. Clásicos castellanos,* 5th ed. Madrid, Espasa-Calpe, 1952.

———— See *Cinco ensayos sobre Don Juan*

Cesari Rocca, Colonna di. "Don Juan (Miguel Mañara); sa famille, sa légende, sa vie d'après des témoignages contemporains," *Mercure de France,* CXIX (1917), 193–220.

Cinco ensayos sobre Don Juan (con un prólogo de Américo Castro). Santiago de Chile, Editorial Cultura, 1937. Contains essays by Gregorio Marañón, Ramiro de Maeztu, José Ingenieros, Azorín, and Ramón Pérez de Ayala, listed separately under the names of the authors.

Cockain, Sir Aston. *The Tragedy of Ovid.* London, For Phil. Stephens, Jr., 1662.

Coquelin, Constant. "The Don Juan of Molière," *International Quarterly* (Burlington, Vt.), VIII (December, 1903), 60–92.

Costanzo, Luigi. *Don Giovanni Tenorio nel teatro spagnolo e romeno.* Naples, A. Guida, 1939.

Cotarelo y Mori, Emilio. *Tirso de Molina.* Madrid, Impr. de E. Rubiños, 1893.

———— "Ultimos estudios acerca de *El Burlador de Sevilla,*" *Revista de Archivos, Bibliotecas y Museos,* XVIII (1908), 75–86.

Crébillon [fils], Claude-Prosper Jolyot de. *Les Egarements du cœur et de l'esprit.* Paris, Le Divan, 1929.

———— *La Nuit et le moment.* Paris, Le Divan, 1929.

———— *Le Sopha.* Paris, Le Divan, 1929.

Dahmen, Hans. "E. T. A. Hoffmanns Weltanschauung," *Beiträge zur Deutschen Literaturwissenschaft*, No. 35 (1929). A monograph of eighty-six pages.

Deffoux, Léon. "Le Comte de Gobineau: 'Don Juan' et les 'Cousins d'Isis,'" *Mercure de France*, CLXIX (January 15, 1924), 402–9.

Denslow, Stewart. "Don Juan and Faust," *Hispanic Review*, X (1942), 215–22.

Despois, Eugène, and Paul Mesnard. *Œuvres de Molière*. Vols. IV, V. Paris, Hachette, 1880.

Díaz-Plaja, Guillermo. *Nuevo asedio a Don Juan*. Buenos Aires, Editorial Sudamericana, 1947.

Douglas, Sir G. B. S. "Don Juan in Literature and Music," *The Cornhill Magazine*, new series, LI (July, 1921), 96–104.

Dumesnil, René. *Le Don Juan de Mozart*. Paris, Librairie de France, 1927.

Ellinger, Georg. *E. T. A. Hoffmann: Sein Leben und seine Werke*. Hamburg and Leipzig, L. Voss, 1894.

Engel, Karl. *Die Don-Juan Sage auf der Bühne*. Oldenburg, Schulze, 1887; Dresden, Pierson, 1887.

Estève, Edmond. *Byron et le romantisme français*. Paris, Hachette, 1907.

Espinosa, Aurelio M. "La leyenda de Don Juan y las doce palabras retorneadas," *Boletín de la Biblioteca Menéndez y Pelayo* (Santander), XV (1933), 216–19.

Faligan, Ernest. *Histoire de la légende de Faust*. Paris, Hachette, 1888.

Farinelli, Arturo. "Cuatro palabras sobre Don Juan y la literatura donjuanesca del porvenir," in *Homenaje a Menéndez y Pelayo*, Vol. I (Madrid, 1899), pp. 205–22.

———— "Don Giovanni, note critiche," *Giornale Storico della Letteratura Italiana*, XXVII (1896), 1–77; 254–326.

———— *Don Giovanni*. Milan, Fratelli Bocca, 1946. "Letteratura Moderna," No. XXVI.

Finck, Henry T. *Richard Strauss: The Man and his Work*. Boston, Little, Brown, 1917.

Fitz-Gerald, Thomas. "Some Notes on the Sources of Zorrilla's *Don Juan Tenorio*," *Hispania*, V (1922), 1–7.

Franquesa y Gomis, José. "*La venganza en el sepulcro*, comedia inedita de D. Alonso de Córdoba y Maldonado," in *Homenaje a Menéndez y Pelayo*, Vol. I (Madrid, 1899), pp. 253–68.

Fuà, Franco. *Don Giovanni attraverso le letterature spagnuola ed italiana*. Turin, S. Lattes, 1914.

Gauchez, Maurice. "Essai sur Don Juan," *Flandre Littéraire*, Cahier No. VIII (Ostende-Bruges, 1926). A twenty-page monograph.

Gautier, Théophile. "Italiens. *Don Giovanni*," in *Histoire de l'art dra-*

matique en France depuis vingt-cinq ans (4ᵉ série, January 27, 1845), IV, 35–38. Paris, Ed. Hetzel, Librairie Magnin, Blanchard et Compagnie, 1858–59.

Gendarme de Bévotte, Georges. *Le Festin de Pierre avant Molière.* Paris, Connely et Cie., 1907. "Société des textes français modernes," Vol. V.

―――― *La Légende de Don Juan: Son évolution dans la littérature des origines au romantisme.* Paris, Hachette, 1906. Volume I of the 1911 edition is a slightly abridged reproduction of this book.

―――― *La Légende de Don Juan.* 2 vols. Paris, Hachette, 1911.

Giuliano, W. "A Spanish Version of the Authentic Don Juan," *Hispania,* Vol. XXXIV, No. 3 (August, 1951), 256–60.

Goncourt, Edmond and Jules de. *La Femme au dix-huitième siècle.* Paris, G. Charpentier, 1907.

Grau, Jacinto. Preface to *Don Juan en el drama.* Buenos Aires, Editorial Futuro, 1944. This volume contains plays by Tirso de Molina, Molière, Goldoni, Pushkin, Dumas, Zorrilla, and Rostand.

―――― *Don Juan en el tiempo y en el espacio: Análisis historicopsicológico,* seguido de una serie de *Estampas* diversas. Buenos Aires, Editorial Raigal, 1953. Don Juan is discussed on pp. 21–46.

Grimsley, Ronald. "The Don Juan Theme in Molière and Kierkegaard," *Comparative Literature,* VI, No. 4 (Fall, 1954), 316–34.

Hamon, Augustin. *The Twentieth Century Molière: Bernard Shaw.* Transl. from the French by Eden and Cedar Paul. London, Allen and Unwin, 1915.

Harich, Walter. *E. T. A. Hoffmann: Das Leben eines Künstlers.* Berlin, Erich Reiss, 1920.

Hayem, Armand. *Le Donjuanisme.* Paris, A. Lemerre, 1886.

Hazañas y La Rúa, Joaquín. *Génesis y desarrollo de la leyenda de Don Juan Tenorio.* Seville, Izquierdo, 1893.

Heckel, Hans. *Das Don-Juan Problem in der neueren Dichtung.* Stuttgart, J. B. Metzler, 1915.

Heimann, Erhard. *Tristan und Isolde in der neuzeitlichen Literatur.* Ph.D. dissertation, Rostock, 1930.

Helbig, Fr. "Die Don-Juan-Sage, ihre Entstehung und Fortentwicklung," *Westermann's Illustrierte Deutsche Monatshefte,* XLI (March, 1877), 637–50.

Hesse, Everett W. "Catálogo bibliográfico de Tirso de Molina (1648–1948), incluyendo una sección sobre la influencia del tema de Don Juan," *Estudios* (Madrid), V (1949), 781–889.

Hoffmann, Werner. *E. T. A. Hoffmanns Lebensgefühl und Weltanschauung.* Ph.D. dissertation, Würzburg, 1929.

Huszár, Guillaume. *Molière et l'Espagne: Etude de littérature comparée*, II. Paris, Champion, 1907.

Ingenieros, José. "Werther y Don Juan," in *Cinco ensayos sobre Don Juan*. Santiago de Chile, Editorial Cultura, 1937.

Jahn, Otto. *W. A. Mozart*. Vol. II. Leipzig, Breitkopf und Härtel, 1891.

Jost, Walter. *Von Ludwig Tieck zu E. T. A. Hoffmann: Studien zur Entwicklungsgeschichte des romantischen Subjektivimus*. Ph.D. dissertation, Frankfurt a.M., 1920.

Kahlert, August. "Die Sage vom Don Juan und ihre Vergleichung mit jener vom Faust," in Johann Scheible, *Das Kloster*, III (cell II), 667–95. Stuttgart, J. Scheible, 1846.

Kahn, Gustave. "Les Types littéraires: Don Juan," *Revue Encyclopédique*, VIII (April 16, 1898), 326–29.

Kierkegaard, Søren. *Enter-Ellen (Either-Or)*. Transl. by David F. Swenson and Lillian M. Swenson. 2 vols. Princeton, Princeton University Press, 1946.

Krauss, Werner. "El concepto del Don Juan en la obra de Tirso de Molina," *Boletín de la Biblioteca Menéndez y Pelayo* (Santander), V (1923), 348–60.

Kroll, Erwin. *E. T. A. Hoffmanns musikalische Anschauungen*. Ph.D. dissertation, Königsberg, 1909.

Laclos, Choderlos de. *Les Liaisons dangereuses*. In *Œuvres complètes*. Paris, Bibliothèque de la Pléiade, 1951.

Lafora, Gonzalo R. *Don Juan and Other Psychological Studies*. Transl. by Janet H. Perry. London, Thornton Butterworth, 1930.

La Hire, Jean de. *Mémoires d'un Don Juan et physiologie du donjuanisme*. Paris, Librairie Universelle, 1905.

Lancaster, H. Carrington. "Don Juan in a French Play of 1630," *PMLA*, XXXVIII (1923), 471–78.

Laun, Adolf. "Molière und Téllez als Bearbeiter des Don Juan," *Archiv für Literaturgeschichte*, III (1873–74), 367–90.

Laverdant, Désiré. *Les Renaissances de Don Juan: Histoire morale du théâtre* moderne. 2 vols. Paris, J. Hetzel, 1864.

Lemaître, Jules. *Impressions de théâtre*. Vol. I. Paris, H. Lecène et H. Oudin, 1888.

Leslie, J. K. "Towards the Vindication of Zorrilla: the Dumas-Zorrilla Question again," *Hispanic Review*, XIII (1945), 288–93.

Loo, Esther van. *Le Vrai Don Juan: Miguel de Mañara*. Paris, SFELT, 1950.

López Núñez, Juan. *"Don Juan Tenorio" en el teatro, la novela y la poesía*. Madrid, Prensa Castellana, 1946.

Lorenzi de Bradi, Michel. *Don Juan, la légende et l'histoire*. Paris, Librairie de France, 1930.

McKay, Dorothy E. *The Double Invitation in the Legend of Don Juan*. Stanford, California, Stanford University Press, 1943.

Madariaga, Salvador de. *Don Juan as a European Figure*. Nottingham, England, 1946. Byron Foundation Lecture, No. 22.

——— *Don Juan y la Don-Juanía*. Buenos Aires, Editorial Sudamericana, 1950. Besides the one-act play (see Appendix), this book contains seven general studies (pp. 11–42) on Byron, Molière, Pushkin, Zorrilla, Tirso, and Mozart.

Maeztu, Ramiro de. "Don Juan o el poder," in *Cinco ensayos sobre Don Juan*. Santiago de Chile, Editorial Cultura, 1937.

——— *Don Quijote, Don Juan y la Celestina; ensayos de simpatía*. Madrid, Espasa-Calpe, 1926.

Magnabal, J.-G. *Don Juan et la critique espagnole*. Paris, Leroux, 1893. Contains translations into French of Manuel de la Revilla, Picatoste, and Pí y Margall, listed under authors' names below.

Manning, Clarence A. "Russian Versions of Don Juan," *PMLA*, XXXVIII (1923), 479–93.

Marañón, Gregorio. "Biología de Don Juan," *El Universal Ilustrado* (1924).

——— *Don Juan: ensayos sobre el origen de su leyenda*. Buenos Aires, Espasa-Calpe, 1940.

——— "Notas para la biología de Don Juan," in *Cinco ensayos sobre Don Juan*. Santiago de Chile, Editorial Cultura, 1937.

——— "Les Origines de la légende de Don Juan," *Revue Hebdomadaire*, 48th year (January 21, 1939), pp. 263–87.

Martinenche, Ernest. *Molière et le théâtre espagnol*. Paris, Hachette, 1906.

Martínez Ruiz, José [Azorín]. "Don Juan," in *Cinco ensayos sobre Don Juan*. Santiago de Chile, Editorial Cultura, 1937.

Menéndez Pidal, Ramón. "Sobre los orígines de *El convidado de piedra*," in *Estudios literarios*. Madrid, Atenea, 1920. Contains combination of two articles first published in *Cultura Española*, May and August, 1906.

Menéndez y Pelayo, Marcelino. *Estudios de crítica literaria*. 2d series. Madrid, Est. tipográfico "Sucesores de Rivadeneyra," 1895.

Mersenne, le P. Marin. *La Vérité des sciences contre les septiques* [sic] *ou pyrrhoniens*. Paris, T. Du Bray, 1625.

Nethercot, Arthur N. *Men and Supermen: The Shavian Gallery*. Cambridge, Harvard University Press, 1954.

Nettl, Paul. "Casanova and Don Giovanni," *Saturday Review*, XXXIX, No. 4 (January 28, 1956), 44 and *passim*.

Northrup, George T. *An Introduction to Spanish Literature*. Chicago, University of Chicago Press, 1925.

Nozick, Martin. "The Don Juan Theme in the Twentieth Century." Unpublished Ph.D. dissertation, New York, Columbia University, 1954.

────── "Some Parodies of *Don Juan Tenorio*," *Hispania*, XXXIII (1950), 105–12.

────── "Unamuno, Ortega and Don Juan," *Romanic Review*, XL (1949), 268–74.

Olivier, Paul. "En marge de l'histoire—La Canonisation de Don Juan," *Revue de France*, I (March 15, 1921), 214–22.

Ortega y Gasset, José. "Las dos ironías: Socrates y Don Juan (El tema de nuestro tiempo)," in *Obras completas*, III, 174–78. Madrid, Revista de Occidente, 1946–47.

────── "La estrangulación de Don Juan," in *Obras completas*, V, 238–46. Madrid, Revista de Occidente, 1946–47. Originally in *El Sol* (Madrid), November 17, 1935.

────── "Introducción a un 'Don Juan,' " in *Obras completas*, VI, 121–37. Madrid, Revista de Occidente, 1946–47. Originally in *El Sol* (Madrid), June, 1921.

────── "Meditación del marco," in *Obras completas*, II, 300–301. Madrid, Revista de Occidente, 1946–47.

Pérez de Ayala, Ramón. "Don Juan," in *Cinco ensayos sobre Don Juan*. Santiago de Chile, Editorial Cultura, 1937.

────── *Las máscaras*. Buenos Aires, Espasa-Calpe, 1940.

Peter, Franz. *Die Literatur der Faustsage systematisch zusammengestellt*. Leipzig, H. Hartung, 1857.

Pfandl, Ludwig. *Spanische Kultur und Sitte des 16. und 17. Jahrhunderts; eine Einführung in die Blütezeit der spanischen Literatur und Kunst*. Kempten, J. Kösel, F. Pustet, 1924.

Pí y Margall, Francisco. "Observaciones sobre el carácter de Don Juan," in *Comedias de Tirso de Molina y Don Guillen de Castro*. Madrid, Imprenta da Fortanet, 1878. Transl. into French in Magnabal, *Don Juan et la critique espagnole*.

Picatoste, Felipe. "Estudios literarios. Don Juan Tenorio," in Magnabal, *Don Juan et la critique espagnole*.

Praz, Mario. *The Romantic Agony*. Transl. from the Italian by Angus Davidson. London, Oxford University Press, 1933.

Puibusque, Adolphe de. *Histoire comparée des littératures espagnole et française*. 2 vols. Paris, G-A. Dentu, 1843. Don Juan discussed, II, 236–71.

Radoff, M. L., and W. C. Salley. "Notes on the *Burlador*," *Modern Language Notes*, XLV (1930), 239–44.

Rank, Otto. *Don Juan: Une étude sur le double.* Traduite d'une nouvelle version allemande par S. Lautmann. Paris, Denoël et Steele, 1932. The German original is probably *Der Doppelgänger* (Vienna, 1925).

———— *Die Don-Juan Gestalt.* Leipzig, Vienna, and Zurich, Internationaler Psychoanalytischer Verlag, 1924.

———— *Seelenglaube und Psychologie.* Vienna, F. Deuticke, 1930.

Rauber, A. *Die Don-Juan Sage im Lichte biologischer Forschungen.* Leipzig, A. Georgi, 1899.

Rétif [Restif] de la Bretonne, Nicolas-Edme. *Monsieur Nicolas.* 14 vols. Paris, Isidor Liseux, 1883.

Revilla, Manuel de la. "El tipo legendario de Don Juan Tenorio y sus manifestaciones en las modernas literaturas," in Magnabal, *Don Juan et la critique espagnole.*

Rey, E. "Don Juan et 'l'Homme à la Rose,' " *Revue de Paris,* XXVIII (January 15, 1921), 402–15.

Reynaud, Louis. *Français et Allemands: Histoire de leurs relations intellectuelles et sentimentales.* Paris, Fayard, 1930.

———— *L'Influence allemande en France au XVIIIe et XIXe siècle.* Paris, Hachette, 1922.

———— *N. Lenau, poète lyrique.* Paris, G. Bellais, 1922.

Reynier, Gustave. "Les Origines de la légende de Don Juan," *Revue de Paris,* XIII, Part 3 (May 15, 1906), 314–38.

Riccoboni, Luigi. *Histoire du théâtre italien depuis la décadence de la comédie latine.* 2 vols. Paris, A. Cailleau, 1731.

Richardson, Samuel. *Clarissa, or the History of a young lady, comprehending the most important concerns of private life and particularly shewing the distress that may attend the misconduct both of parents and children in relation to marriage.* 8 vols. London, printed for J. and F. Rivington, 1774.

Ríos de Lampérez, Blanca de los. "Don Juan en la literatura y en la musica," *España Moderna,* XII (December, 1889), 5–13.

———— "Don Juan y sus avatares," *Revista Nacional de Educación,* VIII, No. 77 (1948), 37–41.

———— "El viaje de Tirso a Santo Domingo y la génesis del 'Don Juan,' " *Raza Española,* VI, No. 67 (1924), 4–35.

———— *El enigma biográfico de Tirso de Molina.* Madrid, Alberto Fontana, 1928.

Ristelhuber, P. *Faust dans l'histoire et dans la légende.* Strasbourg, Impr. de V^re Berger-Levrault, 1863.

Rougemont, Denis de. "Don Juan," *Nouvelle Revue Française,* LIII (1939), 62–68.

Royo Villanova y Morales, Ricardo. *Redescubrimiento de Don Juan.* Madrid, Javier Moreta, 1932.

Said Armesto, V. *La leyenda de Don Juan: Orígines poéticos de* El Burlador de Sevilla y Convidado de piedra. Madrid, Sucesores de Hernando, 1908.

Sauvage, Micheline. *Le Cas Don Juan.* Paris, Editions du Seuil, 1953.

Schade, Oscar. *Faust vom Ursprung bis zur Verklärung durch Goethe.* Berlin, K. Curtius, 1912.

Scheible, Johann. *Das Kloster.* Vol. III. Stuttgart, J. Scheible, 1846.

Schönherr, Kurt. *Die Bedeutung E. T. A. Hoffmanns für die Entwicklung des musikalischen Gefühls in der französischen Romantik.* Ph.D. dissertation, Munich, 1931.

Schröder, Theodor A. "Die dramatischen Bearbeitungen der Don-Juan Sage in Spanien, Italien und Frankreich bis auf Molière einschliesslich," *Beihefte zur Zeitschrift für Romanische Philologie,* XXXVI (1912), 1–215.

Schurig, Arthur. *Wolfgang Amadeus Mozart.* Leipzig, Insel-Verlag, 1913.

Sedwick, Frank. "*El Burlador, Don Giovanni* and the Popular Concept of Don Juan," *Hispania,* XXXVIII (1955), 173–77.

Sender, Ramón. "Three Centuries of Don Juan," *Books Abroad,* XXIII (1949), 227–32.

Simone-Brouwer, F. de. "Ancora Don Giovanni (osservazioni ed appunti)," *Rassegna Critica della Letteratura Italiana,* II (1897), 55–66, 145–65.

────── *Don Giovanni nella poesia e nell'arte musicale. Storia di un dramma.* Naples, Regia Università, 1894.

Singer, Armand E. *A Bibliography of the Don Juan Theme: Versions and Criticism.* West Virginia University Bulletin (Morgantown, West Virginia), Series 54, No. 10-1 (April, 1954).

────── "Flaubert's *Une Nuit de Don Juan,*" *Modern Language Notes,* LV (1940), 516–20.

Spitzer, Leo. "En lisant 'El Burlador,' " *Neuphilologische Mitteilungen,* XXXVI (1935), 282–90.

Stendhal: see *Beyle, Henri*

Tailhade, Laurent. *Masques et visages: Essais inédits.* Paris, T. Rombaldi, 1925. Don Juan is discussed on pp. 148–80.

Thompson, John A. *Alexandre Dumas Père and Spanish Romantic Drama.* Baton Rouge, Louisiana State University Studies, 1938, pp. 160–74.

Turnell, Martin. *The Novel in France.* New York, New Directions, 1950.

Turner, W. J. *Mozart: The Man and his Works.* Doubleday Anchor Book A 24, 1954.

Unamuno, Miguel de. "Sobre Don Juan Tenorio," in *Mi religión y otros ensayos breves*. Buenos Aires-Mexico, Espasa-Calpe, 1945. This essay is dated "1908."

Viardot, Louis. *Etudes sur l'histoire des institutions, de la littérature, du théâtre et des beaux-arts en Espagne*. Paris, Paulin, 1835.

Waxman, Samuel M. "The Don Juan Legend in Literature," *Journal of American Folk-Lore*, XXI (1908), 184–204.

Weinstein, Leo. "A Critical Study of the Don Juan Legend." Unpublished Ph.D. dissertation, Stanford, California, Stanford University, 1951.

—— "The Don Juan of Téllez and Molière." Unpublished Master's thesis, Stanford, California, Stanford University, 1948.

Worthington, Mabel P. "Don Juan: Theme and Development in the Nineteenth Century." Unpublished Ph.D. dissertation, New York, Columbia University, 1953.

Zeidler, M. "Beiträge zur Geschichte des Klosterdramas," *Zeitschrift für Vergleichende Literaturgeschichte*, IX (1896), 88–132.

Zorrilla, José. *Recuerdos del tiempo viejo*. Barcelona, Sucesores de Ramirez y Cª., 1880–82.

Catalogue of Don Juan Versions

The following list of works is neither complete nor free of possible error. Many of the items have been taken from previous compilings of Don Juan versions, especially from Armand E. Singer, *A Bibliography of the Don Juan Theme: Versions and Criticism*; however, I have been able in some cases to add items to, and correct errors in, the existing Don Juan catalogues. The arrangement of the Catalogue offers a complementary view of the development of the Don Juan legend, since it is presented chronologically by language groups and separated into the various art forms.

In general, the following categories have been omitted:

(1) Puppet shows, children's plays, and the like, which were especially popular during the eighteenth and nineteenth centuries in Germany, Italy, Austria, and Hungary. For information on these items, see Gendarme de Bévotte, *La Légende de Don Juan* (both the 1906 and the 1911 editions), Farinelli's *Don Giovanni* (1946), and Scheible, *Das Kloster*, Vol. III, all listed in the Bibliography above.

(2) Straight translations, continuations, and parodies of works by well-known authors, unless of special interest. Those most frequently involved are Molière, Mozart, Byron, and Zorrilla. For information on these items, see Singer's *Bibliography*. For parodies of Zorrilla, see also Martin Nozick, "Some Parodies of *Don Juan Tenorio*," *Hispania*, XXXIII (1950), 105–12.

(3) Scenarios for Italian *commedia dell'arte* performances. For these, see Singer's *Bibliography*.

(4) Works containing the name "Don Juan" or references to the Don Juan legend in their title but having no real connection with the legend. I may not always have been consistent in my choice.

(5) Works having neither any connection with the Don Juan legend nor containing the name of any of the traditional characters in their title but dealing with seducers or "fatal women" (*viveurs*, female Don Juans, etc.). For these, see Singer's *Bibliography*.

A. LITERARY DON JUAN VERSIONS
I. · SPAIN, PORTUGAL, AND LATIN AMERICA[1]

1. Tirso de Molina [pseud. of Gabriel Téllez]. *El Burlador de Sevilla y convidado de piedra*. Play. Printed in 1630. Written at some time

---

[1] Unless otherwise stated, the works listed below were published in Spain.

between 1613 and 1630. Usually considered first Don Juan play, but see next entry.

2. *Tan largo me lo fiáis.* Play. Found in 1878. It has been attributed to Tirso de Molina, Andrés de Claramonte, and Calderón. Considered by most critics to be a recast of (1), by others as the earliest play.

3. Don Alonso de Córdoba y Maldonado. *La venganza en el sepulcro.* Comedia. Not printed. Probably second half of seventeenth century.

4. Antonio de Zamora. *No hay deuda que no se pague y convidado de piedra.* Comedia. Printed 1744.

5. Anon. *O convidado de pedra.* Also called *Don João Tenorio o dissoluto.* Play. Portugal. 1783. Inspired by (117). Another date suggested: 1775.

6. Rafael Vives y Aspiroz. *Don Juan.* One-act verse play. 1783. Unverified reference.

7. José Zorrilla y Moral. *El capitán Montoya. Leyenda.* Originally in Vol. IV of his *Obras* (Madrid, 1840). Version of the Mañara story.

8. José de Espronceda. *El estudiante de Salamanca.* Dramatic poem. 1840.

9. José Zorrilla y Moral. *Don Juan Tenorio.* Drama. Part I: four acts; Part II: three acts; in verse. First performance: March 28, 1844.

10. Estéban Echeverría. *El ángel caído.* Dramatic poem. Argentina. 1844–46.

11. Anon. *Don Juan de Marana.* "Novela española." 1848. 2 vols.

12. José Gutiérrez de la Vega. *Don Miguel de Mañara.* Traditional tale, found in his *Semanario pintoresco.* 1851.

13. Manuel Fernández y González. *Don Juan Tenorio.* Novel. 1851. Title later changed to *Aventuras de Don Juan Tenorio.*

14. Manuel Bretón de los Herreros. *Cosas de Don Juan.* Three-act zarzuela. Music by Rafael Hernando y Palomar. 1854.

15. Anon. *Don Juan Tenorio, leyenda tradicional.* Seville, between 1850 and 1866, cited in Hazañas y La Rúa, *Génesis y desarrollo de la leyenda de Don Juan Tenorio* (Seville, 1893), pp. 45–46.

16. José Simões Dias. *O bandolim de D. Juan.* Set of eleven lyric poems. Portugal. 1863. In his *O mundo interior,* 2d ed. (Coimbra, 1867). The 3d ed. of *O mundo interior* is included in *As peninsulares,* Vol. I (Vizeu, 1876). Here, the section that corresponds to what he called *O bandolim* has been enlarged from eleven to twenty-two poems, though not all of the original eleven are included, and the title has been abandoned.

17. *Idem.* "Xacara de D. João." Poem. Portugal. 1863(?). In his *As peninsulares* (Lisbon, 1899), in the set called "Canções."
18. *Idem.* "A guitarra de D. João." Poem. Portugal. Located as preceding entry.
19. Theofilo Braga. *A ondina do lago.* "Poema de cavalleria." Portugal. 1866. Don Juan appears in Part II, Chap. xxxviii, and in the interpolated poem "A barcarolla do remador."
20. Manuel Fernández y González. *Don Miguel de Mañara, memorias del tiempo de Carlos V. Leyendas nacionales.* 1868.
21. Antonio de Castro Alves. *Don Juan ou A prole dos saturnos.* Unfinished, three-part drama. Brazil. *Ca.* 1870.
22. Claudio José Nunes. *D. João e Elvira.* A dialogue in verse. Portugal. In his *Scenas contemporaneas.* Lisbon, 1873.
23. Manuel Cano y Cueto. *Don Miguel de Mañara.* Verse *leyenda.* 1873.
24. *Idem. Los rosales de Mañara.* Lyrical dramatic *leyenda.* 1874.
25. Guerra Junqueiro. *A morte de Don João.* Poem. Portugal. 1874.
26. Rafael del Castillo. *El convidado de piedra.* Three-act *zarzuela* in verse. Music by Nicolás Manent. Barcelona, 1875.
27. José Simões Dias. "D. Juan." Poem. Portugal. In the "Canções meridionales" section of Vol. II of his *As peninsulares* (Vizeu, 1876).
28. *Idem.* "A hostia de oiro." Poem. Portugal. In his *As peninsulares,* Vol. I (Vizeu, 1876).
29. Juan de Alba. *Las mocedades de Don Juan Tenorio.* Two-act drama in verse. 1877.
30. Ramón de Campoamor. *Don Juan.* Poem. 1887.
31. João Saraiva. "D. João e Elvira." Short poem. In his *Lyricas* (Lisbon, 1890). Portugal. Poem undated.
32. Jacinto Benavente. *El criado de Don Juan.* Dramatic sketch. In his *Teatro fantástico.* 1892.
33. José Zorrilla y Moral. *La leyenda de Don Juan Tenorio.* Fragment of a *leyenda.* Issued posthumously, Barcelona, 1895. Part of a very extensive work on the Tenorios which he projected but never finished.
34. Manuel Cano y Cueto. *La última aventura de don Miguel de Mañara.* Verse *leyenda.* Revision and expansion of (23). 1897.
35. A Careta y Vidal. *El audaz Don Juan Tenorio.* Five-act verse drama. 1897. Adaptation of (9).
36. Manoel Antonio de Álvarez de Azevedo (1831–52). *Lyra dos vinte annos.* Poetry. Brazil. Part III contains the poem "Sombra de D. Juan," in six short sections, the third of which carries the additional title "A canção de Don Juan."

37. Guilhermo de Azevedo (1839–82). *O último D. João.* Poem(?). Portugal.
38. Antonio Hurtado (1825?–1878?). *Monólogo de ultratumbe. Leyenda.*
39. Luiz Osorio (1860?–?). *A morte de Don João.* Poem. Portugal. Unverified reference.
40. Pedra Badenelli. *La cuna de Don Juan.* n.d.
41. Vincente de Carvalho (1866–1922). *Uma impressão de D. Juan.* Sonnet. Brazil. Date uncertain.
42. Rafael Guerrero, *Don Juan Tenorio.* Novel. No place or date cited.
43. Luis Araquistain (1886–). *La salvación de Don Juan.* A sketch in the form of a dialogue.
44. Carlos María de Vallejo (1890–). *La capa de Don Juan.* Poem(?). Uruguay.
45. Anon. *Las hazañas de Tenorio.* Play. Performed in Barcelona(?), autumn 1900.
46. Joaquín Arqués. *Tenorio en Nápoles.* "Humorada trágico bufo cómico lírico bailable en un acto y cuatro cuadros, original." Music by Liñán and Videgain. 1900.
47. Enrique Menéndez y Pelayo. *Las noblezas de Don Juan.* Three-act play. 1900.
48. Felipe Pérez Capo. *Don Miguel de Mañara.* One-act *zarzuela* in verse. Music by J. Serrano. 1903.
49. Joaquín Dicenta. *La conversión de Mañara.* "Comedia dramática." 1905.
50. Manuel da Silva Gaio. *Don Juan.* Poem. Portugal, 1906. Translated into French by Raymond Bernard in 1929.
51. Emilio Gutiérrez-Gamoro y Romate. *La derrota de Mañara.* Play(?). 1907.
52. Alfonso Hernández Catá. "Un triumfo de Don Juan." Story. In his *Cuentos pasionales.* Cuba. 1907.
53. Manuel Machado. *Don Miguel de Mañara.* Short poem. 1910.
54. Carlos Arniches y Barrera. *La locura de Don Juan.* Three-act "tragedia grotesca." 1913.
55. Jacinto Grau. *Don Juan de Carillana.* Play. 1913.
56. Joaquín Belda. *Tenorio contra Sherlock Holmes.* Novel. 1915.
57. Alberto Insúa. *El alma y el cuerpo de Don Juan.* Novel. Cuba. 1915.
58. Enrique Calonge. *Don Juanito y su escudero.* "Sainete lírico." 1916.
59. José L. Alcaraz. *Les conquistes de Don Juan.* "Aproposit en un acte." Valencia, Spain. 1917.

60. Ruy Chianca. *A alma de D. João*. Play. Portugal(?). 1918.
61. João de Barros. *D. João*. Poem. Portugal. 1920.
62. Francisco Pati. *Fausto e Don Juan*. Poem. Brazil. 1920.
63. Juan Pérez Zuñiga. *Lo que cuenta Don Juan*. "Manojo de cuentos festivos para niños menores de cincuenta años." Stories. 1920.
64. Gregorio Martínez Sierra. *Don Juan de España*. Play. 1921.
65. Belisario Roldán. *El burlador de mujeres*. Dramatic poem in three acts, in verse. Argentina. 1922. Act I is called "Don Juan."
66. Leopoldo Lugones Argüello. *El secreto de Don Juan*. Story. In his *Cuentos fatales*. Argentina. 1924.
67. Antonio Patricio. *D. João e a mascara*. "Uma fábula tragica." Portugal. 1924.
68. Juan Ignacio Luca de Tena. *Las canas de Don Juan*. Three-act play. 1925.
69. Ricardo Miró Denis. "El miedo de Don Juan." Poem. Panama. Found in *Antología de Panamá* (ed. Demetrio Korsi, Barcelona, 1926). Also in *El libro de oro de la literatura hispanoamericana* (ed. Miguel Rivas and Juan Balagué, Barcelona, 1928).
70. Emilio Lascano Tegui. "El amor de Don Juan." Sonnet. Argentina. Found in *Los mejores poetas de la Argentina* (ed. Eduardo de Ory, Madrid, 1927). Poem undated.
71. Manuel and Antonio Machado y Ruiz. *Juan de Mañara*. Three-act drama in verse. First performance: March 17, 1927, at Teatro Reina Victoria, Madrid.
72. José Martins Fontes. "Don Juan e as mulheres que elle amou" (sonnet) and "Madrigal de Don Juan" (poem). Brazil. In *Verão*, section called "Palavras romanticas." 1927(?).
73. Carlos M. Noel. *La boda de Don Juan*. Novel. Argentina. 1927.
74. Carlos Salvaño Campos. *Don Juan derrotado*. Play in three acts. Uruguay. 1927.
75. Francisco Villaespesa. *El Burlador de Sevilla*. Play. 1927.
76. Arturo Casinos Moltó. *Tenorio a la forsa*. "Aproposit en un acte y dos cuadros en prosa." Valencia, n.d. First performed October 30, 1928.
77. Paulo Menotti del Picchia. *A angustia de Don João*. Long poem. Brazil. 1928.
78. Frederico Oliver y Crespo. *Han matado a Don Juan*. Farce. 1929.
79. Manuel Soriano. "La marcha de Don Juan." Poem. In *Nuevo Mundo*, Nov. 29, 1930.
80. Jacinto Grau. *El burlador que no se burla*. ". . . escenas tragicomicos de una vida y muerte en cinco cuadros, prólogo y epílogo." Play. 1930.

81. José Puig Pujades. *La fi de D. Juan.* Play(?). Sabadell, 1930. (Transl.: "The Faith of Don Juan.")
82. Carlos Sabat Ercasty. *El demonio de Don Juan.* Dramatic poem. Uruguay. 1934.
83. Miguel de Unamuno. *El hermano Juan o El mundo es teatro.* Play. 1934.
84. Enrique Larreta. *La que buscaba Don Juan.* "Poema dramático estrenado en Buenos Aires bajo el título *La Luciérnaga.*" Play. Argentina. 1938.
85. Dionisio Ridruejo. *Don Juan.* "Ensayo dramático." Three-act play in prose. 1945. Modeled loosely on (1) and (9).
86. Fernando de Araujo Lima. *A última noite de D. João.* Play. Portugal. 1948. Not a translation of Rostand, despite the title.
87. Salvador de Madariaga. *Don Juan y la Don-Juania, o Seis Don Juanes y una dama.* One-act play. 1950.

II. ITALY

88. Anon. *Il convitato di pietra. Commedia dell'arte.* Performed in Italy after 1620. Contained in *Notes de Biancolelli* (see below, 91).
89. Giacinto Andrea Cicognini. *Il convitato di pietra.* Opera esemplare. Before 1650. Oldest known printing: 1671.
90. Onofrio Giliberto. *Il convitato di pietra.* 1652. Lost.
91. Domenico Biancolelli. Author of notes of scenario played by Italian *commedia dell'arte* actors in Paris. The scenario was translated into French by Thomas Simon Gueulette, and published in the Elzevier ed. of *Les Œuvres de Molière* (Amsterdam, 1675), Vol. II.
92. Andrea Perucci. *Il convitato di pietra.* Opera tragica. 1678.
93. Enrico Prendarca. *Il convitato di pietra.* Recast of preceding entry under name of Prendarca. 1690.
94. Carlo Goldoni. *Don Giovanni Tenorio ossia il dissoluto.* Performed 1736. Printed 1760.
95. Girolamo Rovetta. *La moglie di Don Giovanni.* Drama. 1877.
96. Enrico Panzacchi. "Don Giovanni." Sonnet. In his *Lyrica, Romanze e canzoni.* 1877.
97. G. A. Cesareo. *Don Juan.* Fragment of a poem. 1883.
98. Domenico Bassi. *La cena di Don Giovanni.* Farce. "Riduz. di D. Bassi senza nome di autore." 1884.
99. Enrico Panzacchi. "Accanto al fuoco." Poem. In his *Nuove liriche,* 1888(?). Another date given is 1847.
100. M. Fazzio [or Faccio]. *La morte di Don Giovanni.* 1889.
101. Fernando di Giorgi. "La fine di Don Giovanni." *Novella.* In his *La prima donna.* 1895.

102. Arturo Graf. *La dannazione di Don Giovanni.* Poem. 1905.
103. Giuseppe Pagliara. *Don Giovanni.* Four-act drama in verse. 1911.
104. Carola Prosperi. *La conquista di Don Giovanni.* Short novel. Appeared in *La Stampa* (Turin), April 20, 1913.
105. Romualdo Pantini. *La morte di Don Giovanni.* Poem. 1916.
106. Alessandro Varaldo. *Intermezzo: Don Giovanni si pente.* Short play. 1922. In his *Donne, profumi e fiori; novelle* (Milan, *ca.* 1922). Despite the title, this item is a play.
107. Mario Pensuti. *La seconda vita di Don Giovanni.* Novel. 1924.
108. Pietro Solari. "Don Juan and the Statues." Short story. Appeared in transl. in *Living Age*, CCCXXXIV (Feb. 15, 1928), 347–51. Taken from *900* (an international French-language literary and artistic quarterly), issue No. 3.
109. Lorenzo Giusso. *Don Giovanni ammalato.* Poems. 1932.
110. Alberto de Angelis. *Don Giovanni ovvero l'elogio della volubilità.* Prose fantasy. In *Rassegna Nazionale*, August-September, 1936.
111. F. Nissolino. *Don Giovanni.* Novel. 1937.
112. Vitaliano Brancati. *Don Giovanni in Sicilia.* Novel. 1943.
113. Emilio Jadius. "Don Giovanni." Poem. In *Inventario* (Milan), III, No. 3 (1950), 55–59.
114. Carlo Terron. *La moglie di Don Giovanni.* Three-act play. 1953.

III. FRANCE AND VERSIONS IN FRENCH

115. Dorimon. *Le Festin de Pierre ou le Fils criminel.* Tragi-comédie. Written 1658; printed 1659.
116. Claude Deschamps, Sieur de Villiers. *Le Festin de Pierre ou le Fils criminel.* Tragi-comédie. Written 1659; printed 1660.
117. Molière. *Dom Juan ou le Festin de Pierre.* Comédie. First performance: February 15, 1665. First printing: 1682.
118. Claude Rose [or La Rose], Sieur de Rosimond [pseud. of Jean-Baptiste Du Mesnil]. *Le Nouveau Festin de Pierre, ou l'Athée foudroyé.* Tragicomedy. 1669.
119. Thomas Corneille. *Le Festin de Pierre.* Comédie. Recast in verse of (117). 1677.
120. Fr. Kick. *Le Spectre de D. Pedro ou la Témérité châtiée.* Amsterdam, 1720. Unverified work, listed in previous bibliographies.
121. Jules Lefèvre-Deumier. *Fragments de Don Juan.* An unfinished poem. 1825. Found in *Le Clocher de Saint Marc* (Paris, 1825), 123–34.
122. Honoré de Balzac. *L'Elixir de longue vie.* Novelette. 1830.
123. Alfred de Musset. *Namouna.* Poem. 1832.
124. *Idem. Une Matinée de Don Juan.* Fragment. 1833.

125. George Sand. *Lélia*. Novel. 1833. Chap. lxii is entitled "Don Juan."
126. Blaze de Bury [Hans Werner, pseud.]. *Le Souper chez le Commandeur*. Dramatic poem. In *Revue des Deux Mondes*, June 1, 1834.
127. Prosper Mérimée. *Les Ames du purgatoire*. Novel. In *Revue des Deux Mondes*, August 15, 1834.
128. Alexandre Dumas père. *Don Juan de Marana ou la Chute d'un ange*. Mystery play. First performance: April 30, 1836, at the Théâtre de la Porte Saint-Martin.
129. Roberge. *Don Juan de Marance, ou la Chute d'un ange*: "Drame en dix tableaux raconté par Robert Macaire et Bertrand." 1836. Parody of (128).
130. Eugène Robin. *Livia*. Dramatic poem. 1836.
131. Théophile Gautier. *La Comédie de la mort*. Poem. 1838.
132. Joseph-Arthur Gobineau. "Les Adieux de Don Juan." Dramatic poem. In *Les Cousins d'Isis*.
133. Charles Baudelaire. "Don Juan aux enfers." Poem. In *Les Fleurs du mal*. First published in 1846.
134. Gustave Levavasseur. *Don Juan barbon*. Drama. 1848.
135. George Sand. *Le Château des désertes*. 1851. Chaps. ix–xiii contain an account of a performance of a *Don Juan*, a mixture of Molière, Mozart, and others, in which the actors improvise as they go along.
136. Gustave Flaubert. *Une Nuit de Don Juan*. Sketch for a novel. *Ca.* 1851.
137. Pierre-Jean Félicien Mallefille. *Mémoires de Don Juan*. Novel. 1852. Another suggested date: 1847, but earliest edition noted is 1852.
138. Jules Viard. *La Vieillesse de Don Juan*. Drama. 1853.
139. Eliacim Jourdain [pseud. of Séraphin Pélican]. *Don Juan*. Fantastic drama. 1857.
140. Villiers de l'Isle-Adam. "Hermosa." In his *Premières Poésies*. 1859.
141. Ernest Dutouquet. *Une Aventure de Don Juan*. Poem. 1864.
142. Désiré Laverdant. *Don Juan converti*. Drama. 1864.
143. Paul Verlaine. "A Don Juan." Sonnet. It may be found in his *Œuvres posthumes, vers et prose* (Paris, Vannier, 1903), p. 143, but not in subsequent editions of the posthumous works. A note at the foot of p. 143 reads: "Sonnet de jeunesse douteux, publié sous la signature Fulvio." The sonnet appeared originally in *L'Art*, in 1866.
144. Louise Victorine Choquet Ackermann. *L'Idéal*. Poem. Especially Stanza II on Don Juan. *Ca.* 1871.

145. Jules Barbey d'Aurevilly. "Le plus Bel Amour de Don Juan." Short story. In his *Les Diaboliques.* 1874.

146. Jules Ferrand. *Le Mariage de Don Juan.* Narrative poem. 1883.

147. Paul Verlaine. "Don Juan pipé." Poem. In his *Jadis et naguère.* 1884.

148. Anon. "L'Homme des foules: Don Juan Tenorio." A satirical essay attacking the morality of modern women, in narrative form. In *La Vie Moderne* (Paris), May 8, 1886, pp. 292–95; a weekly magazine.

149. Armand Hayem. *Don Juan d'Armana.* Drama. 1886.

150. Charles Baudelaire. *La Fin de Don Juan.* Projected drama. First published in 1887.

151. Philibert Audebran. *La Sérénade de Don Juan.* Novel. 1887.

152. Jean Aicard. *Don Juan 89.* Dramatic poem in five acts and an epilogue. 1889. Alternate title: *Don Juan 1889.* Also issued in 1893 with new title: *Don Juan ou la Comédie du siècle.*

153. Paul Eudel. *La Statue du Commandeur.* Pantomime in three acts. Music by E. Mangin. Score by Adolphe David. First staged in 1892.

154. Jean Richepin. *L'Inconnue.* Short play, or "saynète," in one act. 1892.

155. *Idem. Mille et quatre.* Short play, or "saynète," in one act. 1892. Richepin calls this and the preceding item "Don Juaneries." They are contained in his *Théâtre chimérique* (Paris, 1896).

156. Maurice Montégut. *Don Juan à Lesbos.* Short story. 1892.

157. Henry Roujon. *Miremonde.* Short novel. 1895.

158. Armand Masson. "La Cave de Don Juan." Poem. In *Supplément Littéraire du Figaro*, November 23, 1895.

159. José [Gabriel Jules Delarue] de Strada. *Don Juan.* Dramatic poem. 1897.

160. Edmond Haraucourt. *Don Juan de Mañara.* Five-act drama in verse. Incidental music by Paul Vidal. First performance: March 8, 1898, at Théâtre de l'Odéon.

161. Loriot-Lecaudey and Charles de Bussy. *Don Juan au cloître.* Dramatic poem. 1898.

162. Edmond Lepelletier and Clément Rochel. *Les Amours de Don Juan.* Novel. Adaptation of (9). 1898.

163. Marcel Barrière. *Le Nouveau Don Juan.* Novel. Vol. I: *L'Education d'un contemporain*; Vol. II: *Le Roman de l'ambition*; Vol. III: *Les Ruines de l'amour*; Vol. IV: *Le Monde noir.* Vols. I–III, 1900; vol. IV, 1909.

164. Catulle Mendès. "Le Cauchemar de Don Juan." Poem. In his *Braises du cendrier.* 1900.

165. Jean Richepin. "Don Juan sauvé." Story. In his *Contes espagnols* (Paris, 1901).

166. Henri Lavedan. *Le Marquis de Priola*. Play in three acts. First performance: February 7, 1902, at the Comédie Française.

167. Durel. *Pierrot Don Juan*. Pantomime. 1905.

168. Camille Debans. "La Vieillesse de Don Juan." Novel. In *Le Roman Romanesque* (November, 1905), pp. 296–384.

169. Jean Mounet-Sully and Pierre Barbier. *La Vieillesse de Don Juan*. Drama in verse. First performance: April 27, 1906, at the Théâtre de l'Odéon.

170. Emile Bruni. *Les Deux Nuits de Don Juan*. Short story. 1907.

171. Anne-Elisabeth, Comtesse de Noailles. "Don Juan de Maraña." Poem. In her *Eblouissements*. 1907. Based on (127).

172. Fernand Sarnette. *La Fin de Don Juan*. In his *Collier des heures* . . . (Paris, 1908).

173. Henri de Régnier. *Les Scrupules de Sganarelle*. Play. 1908.

174. *Idem.* "Don Juan au tombeau." Poem. In *Revue de Paris* (January 15, 1910), pp. 314–20.

175. J.-E. Fidao-Justiniani. *Le Mariage de Don Juan*. Novel. 1909.

176. Pierre Grasset. "Le Pauvre Don Juan." Short story. In *Vers et Prose*, XXIX (1912), 81–92. About Don Juan de Mañara.

177. O. V. de Lubicz-Milosz. *Miguel Mañara*. "Mystère en six tableaux." 1912.

178. Louis Dumur and Virgile Josz. *Don Juan en Flandre*. One-act play. In *Vers et Prose*, XXXIII (1913), 75–83.

179. Guillaume Apollinaire. *Les Trois Don Juans: Don Juan Tenorio d'Espagne, Don Juan de Maraña de Flandres, Don Juan d'Angleterre*. Novel. 1914.

180. Michel Zévaco. *Don Juan*. Novel. 1916.

181. Henri Bataille. *L'Homme à la rose*. Drama. 1920.

182. Jean Roc. *Don Juan et* . . . Short stories. 1920–21.

183. Edmond Rostand. *La Dernière Nuit de Don Juan*. Dramatic poem in prologue and two acts. Written before World War I; published 1921.

184. H.-R. Lenormand. *L'Homme et ses fantômes*. Drama. First performance: June 11, 1921, at the Théâtre de l'Odéon.

185. J. Reboul. "Don Juan." Poem. In *Mercure de France*, CXLIX (July 15, 1921), 345–46.

186. Max Jacob. "Poème dans un goût qui n'est pas le mien." In his *Le Carnet à dés* (Paris, 1923). Don Juan and Faust speak briefly.

187. Albert T'Serstevens. *La Légende de Don Juan*. Novel. 1923.

188. José Ferba. *Le Carnet de Don Juan, ou Don Juan au repos*. Short novel. Nîmes, 1925.
189. Paul Renaudin. "Don Juan dépité ou le Rival imprévu." Comedy in three scenes. In *Revue des Deux Mondes*, Année 96, 7ᵉ période (1926), 270–97.
190. Georges Le Faure. *Don Juan*. Novel. 1927.
191. Michel de Ghelderode. *Don Juan*. Play. In *La Renaissance d'Occident*, XXVII (1928).
192. Martial Perrier. *L'Adieu à Don Juan*. Poems. 1929.
193. Joseph Delteil. *Don Juan*. Novel. 1930.
194. Jean Suberville. *La Passion de Don Juan*. Drama in three acts. Performed, 1932.
195. André Obey. *Don Juan*. Drama in four acts. First performance: January 12, 1934, at the Palais des Beaux-Arts, Brussels.
196. B. Taladoire. *Don Juan*. Act II (fragment). In *Cahiers du Sud* (Marseille), 1936, pp. 817–30.
197. A. Carot. *Don Juan*. Four-act play. 1936. In his *Mariages*.
198. Georges Oltramare. *Don Juan ou la Solitude*. Play. First performed, 1936.
199. Charles Desbonnets. *Une Nuit de Don Juan*. One-act play. Brussels, 1937.
200. André Obey. *Le Trompeur de Séville*. Prologue and three acts. New version of (195). First performance: January 28, 1937, at Porte Saint-Martin Theater.
201. Claude-André Puget. *Echec à Don Juan*. Drama in three acts. Music by Roland Manuel and Roger Désormières. First performance: December 18, 1941, at Théâtre des Ambassadeurs. Can be found in his *Théâtre* (Paris, 1944), Vol. I.
202. Claude Henri Fresch. *Triptyque de Don Juan*. Casablanca, 1942.
203. Maurice Hebert. *Le Cycle de Don Juan*. Long poem. French Canadian. Large sections of it appeared in the *Proceedings and Transactions of the Royal Society of Canada*, Ser. 3, Vol. XXXVII, Sect. I (1943), 39–44; Vol. XXXIX, Sect. I (1945), 89–102; Vol. XL, Sect. I (1946), 37–49; Vol. XLIII, Sect. I (1949), 39–49.
204. Flor C. Mielants [Herwig Hensen, pseud.]. *Don Juan*. Play. Brussels, 1943.
205. Paul-Henri Tribouillet. *Don Juan*. Poem. Hanoi, Indochina. 1943.
206. Suzanne Lilar. *Le Burlador*. Three-act play. Brussels, 1945.
207. Charles Bertin. *Don Juan*. Play. Brussels, 1947.
208. Marcel Jouhandeau [pseud. of Marcel Provence]. *Carnets de Don Juan*. Short novel. 1947. More commonly titled simply *Don Juan*. The trade edition appeared in 1948.

209. Georges Krassovsky. *Les Maximes de Don Juan.* Paris, 1947. Also in German as *Aphorismen eines Don Juan*, 1948.
210. Maurice Dekobra. *Don Juan frappe à la porte.* Short story. 1948.
211. André Obey. *L'Homme de cendres.* Prologue and three acts. Third version of (195). First performance: December 22, 1949, at Comédie Française (Salle Luxembourg).
212. Michel Poissenot. *Don Juan.* Three-act tragedy. 1950.
213. Jean Anouilh. *Ornifle ou le Courant d'air.* Play. Performed 1955, at Comédie des Champs-Elysées.
214. Marie Noël [pseud. of Marie Mélanie Rouget]. *Le Jugement de Don Juan.* Miracle play. 1955.
215. Saint-Paulien. *Aurélia: Scènes de la vie fantastique.* Short stories. 1957. Contains section entitled "La Séduction de Don Juan."
216. Henry de Montherlant. *Don Juan.* Play in three acts. First performance: November 4, 1958, at the Théâtre de l'Athénée.

IV. HOLLAND AND VERSIONS IN FLEMISH

217. Adriaan Peys. *De maeltyt van Don Peedros geest of de gestrafte vrijgeest.* Amsterdam, 1699. (Transl.: "The Meal of Don Pedro's Guest, or the Libertine Punished.")
218. Leon de Fuyter. *Don Jan, of de gestrafte ontrouw.* Five-act tragedy in verse. Earliest ed. known is 1716. (Transl.: "Don Juan, or Infidelity Punished.")
219. G. van Maater. *Don Jan, of de gestrafte vrijgeest.* Morality play. Haarlem. 1719. (Transl.: "Don Juan or the Libertine Punished.")
220. F. Seegers. *De gestrafte vrijgeest.* Tragedy. Leiden, 1721. (Transl.: "The Libertine Punished.")
221. J. van Rijndorp. *De gestrafte vrijgeest.* Morality play. Leiden, 1721. (Transl.: "The Libertine Punished.")
222. F. Rijk. *Don Pedroos geest of de gestrafte baldaadigheit.* Drama. Amsterdam, 1721. (Transl.: "Don Pedro's Ghost, or Temerity Punished.")
223. Frederik Chasalle and C. J. Kelk. *De Terugkeer van Don Juan of de Alcalá'sche moordverwarring.* Play. Amsterdam, 1924. (Transl.: "The Return of Don Juan or the Alcalá Murder Muddle.")
224. Elisabeth Reitsma. *Don Juan.* "Een moderne legende. Zilveren verpoosingen. Een keur van kunst en letteren." Anthology(?). Amsterdam, 1935. (Transl.: "A modern legend. Silver relaxations. A selection from art and letters.")
225. Hubert Lampo. *Don Juan en de laatste nimf.* Short novel. Brussels, 1943. Part I of a "Triptiek von de onvervulde liefde." (Transl.:

"Don Juan and the Last Nymph." "A Triptych of Unfulfilled Love.")

226. Luisa Treves. *De brief van Don Juan*. One-act play. Amsterdam, about 1949. (Transl.: "Don Juan's Letter.")

227. Jaap Romijn. *Rechtvaardigung van Don Juan*. Novel. Utrecht. 1954. (Transl.: "Don Juan's Justification.")

V. ENGLAND AND THE UNITED STATES

228. Sir Aston Cockayn [Cockain, Cokain, Cockayne]. *The Tragedy of Ovid*. Play. 1662. Contains episode of invitation of, and vengeance by, a dead man.

229. Thomas Shadwell. *The Libertine*. Tragedy. 1676.

230. Anon. *Don Juan; or the Battle of Tolosa*. Poem in three cantos. 1816. In it, Don Juan steals Inez from her home near the Guadalquivir, puts her on his fiery steed and makes away with her. They are pursued by her brother. Juan is a typical Romantic, ardent but not basically evil. He marries the girl eventually. It might well have served Byron as a source for some of the adventures of his own Don Juan. (Singer, *Bibliography*.)

231. George Gordon, Lord Byron. *Don Juan*. Epic poem. 1818–23.

232. Anon. *Don Giovanni in Ireland*. Burlesque play. 1821.

233. Washington Irving. "Don Juan; a Spectral Research." Short story. In *Crayon Miscellany*. Probably written in 1826; published in 1835, and collected as part of *Wolfert's Roast and Other Papers* (New York, 1855), 322–33.

234. Anon. *Don Giovanni in New York*. Play. Given in New York, 1841.

235. John Clare. *Don Juan*. Poem. 1841. In *Poems of John Clare's Madness* (London, 1949).

236. Anon. *Don Giovanni in Gotham*. Play. Given in New York, 1842.

237. Henry Morsford. *The Rest of Don Juan*. Poem. 1846.

238. Anon. *Don Juan*. Farce. Given November 22, 1870, at Theatre Royal, Bradford, England.

239. Robert Browning. *Fifine at the Fair*. Poem. 1871–72.

240. George Bernard Shaw. *Don Giovanni Explains*. Short story. 1887. Can be found in his *Short Stories, Scraps and Shavings* (New York, 1934), 95–118.

241. Richard Mansfield. *Don Juan*. 1891. It was registered for copyright in the United States as *The Adventures of Don Juan*, in 1890.

242. John P. Wilson. *Don Juan ad Lib*. Spectacular burlesque in three acts. *Ca*. 1896. United States.

243. John Martin Harvey. *Don Juan's Last Wager*. "Dramatic Comp."

London, copyright 1900. A typewritten copy is held in the Library of Congress. Apparently never published.

244. G. B. Shaw. *Man and Superman.* Play. 1901–1903.

245. Lee Fairchild. *Don Juan's Bouquet.* Poems. New York, 1903. Singer lists this item as "Don Juan's Banquet."

246. W. A. Brannan. *Don Juan Tenorio.* "Blank verse version of the legend of Don Juan from the Spanish." 1906. Apparently never published.

247. James Elroy Flecker. *Don Juan.* Three-act play. Written, 1910–11. Published, 1925.

248. Maurice Baring. "Don Juan's Failure." Playlet. In his *Diminutive Dramas.* 1911.

249. Algernon Boyesen. *Don Juan Duped.* One-act play. In *Smart Set,* XXXIII (April, 1911), 131–40.

250. Arnold Bennett. *Don Juan de Marana.* Play. Adaptation of (128). Privately printed, 1923, but finished in 1913.

251. Florence Wilkinson. "Don Juan in Portugal." Poem. In *Poetry,* XIX (November, 1921), 78–79.

252. Harry Kemp. *The Love-Rogue.* "Poetic drama in three acts." 1923. A very free adaptation of (1), with additions and omissions.

253. *Idem. Don Juan's Christmas Eve; a Miracle.* One-act play. 1924. Contained in his *Boccaccio's Untold Tale, and Other One-Act Plays* (New York, ca. 1924).

254. *Idem. Don Juan in a Garden.* One-act play. Located as last entry.

255. Leonard L. Cline. "Don Juan in Baltimore." Short story. In *Scribner's Magazine,* LXXIX (May, 1926), 467–76.

256. Harry Kemp. *Don Juan's Note-Book.* Poem in 101 short stanzas. New York, privately printed. 1929.

257. Robert Nicholas. *Don Juan the Great.* Poem. A selection from it, called "Song of the Jester Dwarf," appeared in *Best Poems . . . of 1932.*

258. Leonard A. G. Strong. "Don Juan and the Wheelbarrow." Short story. Appeared in the *Yale Review,* new series, Vol. XXI (March, 1932), 581–89; then in *Don Juan and the Wheelbarrow, and Other Stories* (New York, 1933).

259. Louis How. *The Other Don Juan.* Poem. New York, 1932. This is Miguel de Mañara. Based on (127).

260. Christina Stead. "Don Juan in the Arena." Short story. In her *Salzburg Tales* (New York, 1934).

261. Robert Nicholas. "Don Juan's Address to the Sunset." Short poem. It may be found in the *Oxford Book of Modern Verse,* 1890–1935.

262. Henry Bertram Lister. *A Renaissance Gangster, or Adventures of Don Juan.* Unpublished drama. Mimeographed by the La Bohême Club, San Francisco. 1935. Based on (128).

263. Walter Greenwood. "Don Juan." Short story. In his *Cleft Stick.* 1937.

264. Benn W. Levy. *The Poet's Heart: A Life of Don Juan.* Play. 1937.

265. Sylvia Townsend Warner. *After the Death of Don Juan.* Short story. 1938.

266. Michael O'Donovan [Frank O'Connor, pseud.]. "Don Juan (Retired)." Short story. In his *Common Chord.* 1947.

267. *Idem.* "Don Juan's Temptation." Short story. In his *Common Chord.* 1947.

268. John F. A. Heath-Stubbs. "Don Juan Muses." Poem. In *Harper's Magazine,* CXCVII (November, 1948), 103.

269. Richardson Savell. *Don Juan.* Poem. 1949.

270. Christopher La Farge. *Don Juan Miscarried.* Short story. In *Esquire,* October, 1952.

271. Ronald Duncan. *Don Juan.* Drama. Performed July 13, 1953, at Palace Theater, Bideford, England. Adaptation of (9).

272. V. S. Pritchett. "A Story of Don Juan." Short story. In *A Book of Modern Ghosts* (New York, 1953).

273. Ronald Duncan. *The Death of Satan.* Play in two acts, in free verse. First performance: August 5, 1954, at Palace Theater, Bideford, England.

274. Gwyn Thomas. *The Love Man.* Novel. 1958.

VI. GERMANY AND AUSTRIA

275. Anon. *Don Juan oder der steinerne Gast.* Performed 1716 in Vienna.

276. Anon. *Schrecken im Spiel ruchloser Jugend oder das lehrreiche Totengastmahl des Don Pedro.* 1735. On schedule of Caroline Neuberin.

277. Joseph Felix von Kurz-Bernardon. *Das steinerne Gastmahl, oder die redende statua, samt Arie welche von Hans Wurst singet nebst denen Versen des Eremiten und denen Verzweiflungversen des don Juan bey dessen unglückseligen Lebens-Ende.* 1740(?).

278. Justinus Knecht. *Don Juan oder das klägliche Ende eines verstockten Atheisten.* Musical farce. Performed, 1772.

279. Karl Marinelli. *Don Juan oder der steinerne Gast.* Vienna. 1783. Date of first performance given as 1781 as well as 1783; printed, 1783.

280. Friedrich Schiller. *Don Juan*. Ballad fragment. *Ca.* 1797.
281. Christian August Vulpius (ascribed to). *Don Juan der Wüstling*. Novel. 1805.
282. Christian E. K., Graf von Benzel-Sternau. *Der steinerne Gast, eine Biographie*. Four-volume novel. 1808.
283. Nicolas Vogt. *Der Färberhof oder Die Buchdruckerei in Mainz*. Three-act play-opera-ballet, in verse, unfinished. 1809. It is Part II of his poem *Die Ruinen am Rhein*. He uses the music from Mozart's *Don Giovanni, Requiem*, and *Die Entführung aus dem Serail*; from Haydn's *The Creation*; and from Salieri's *Asur*. Vogt himself arranged this mixture. He also utilized as backgrounds for the action paintings by Raphael, Michelangelo, etc.
284. Anon. *Don Juan*. Pantomime. Vienna, 1811. Given in Hungary after being translated into Hungarian.
285. *Der Laufner Don Juan*, so called. Salzburg. End of eighteenth century. The text as we have it was written in 1811 by a group of actors called the "Schiffsleute von Laufen." A folk play, or *Hauptaction*. *Der Donn Joann*; "ein Schauspill in 4 Aufzigen" is the same play. It has been wrongly attributed to Metastasio.
286. E. T. A. Hoffmann. *Don Juan. Eine fabelhafte Begebenheit, die sich mit einem reisenden Enthusiasten zugetragen*. Short story. Appeared first in *Allgemeine Musikalische Zeitung*, March 31, 1813.
287. Adolf Bäuerle. *Moderne Wirtschaft und Don Juans Streiche*. Farce, with songs. Austria. 1818.
288. Robert Ludwig. *Der todte Gast*. Drama. 1828.
289. Christian Dietrich Grabbe. *Don Juan und Faust*. Tragedy. 1829.
290. A. Kahlert. *Donna Elvira*. Short novel. First appeared in *Gesellschafter*, 1829; then in his *Novellen*, 1832.
291. Karl von Holtei. *Don Juan*. Dramatic fantasy in seven acts. 1834.
292. W. Langewiesche. *Don Juan und Faust*. Poem. 1834.
293. Theodor Creizenach. *Don Juan*. Poem. 1836.
294. A. Brockhaus. *Don Juan*. Drama. 1840.
295. Sigismund Wiese. *Don Juan*. Tragedy in five acts. 1840.
296. Karl Braun von Braunthal. *Don Juan*. Drama. 1842.
297. Nikolaus Lenau. *Don Juan*. Dramatic poem. 1844.
298. Georg Hesekiel. *Faust und Don Juan*. Novel. 1846.
299. R. Hörnigk. *Don Juan*. Five-act tragedy, in verse. 1850.
300. Viktor Precht. *Don Juan*. Poem. In *Düsseldorfer Künstleralbum*. 1853.
301. Friedrich Spiesser. *Don Juan oder: Der steinerne Gast. Seine Thaten und sein furchtbares Lebensende*. "Mit einem Anhange von Liedern, welche Don Juan sang." Play. Kassel, 1857(?).

302. A. Widmann. *Don Juan de Maraña.* Romantic play in five acts. 1858. Appeared in his *Dramatische Werke* (Leipzig, 1858), Vol. II.
303. Alfred Friedmann. *Don Juans letztes Abenteuer.* Drama. 1881.
304. Julius Hart. *Don Juan Tenorio.* Four-act tragedy. 1881.
305. Paul Heyse. *Don Juans Ende.* Five-act tragedy. 1883.
306. Prinz Emil von Schönaich-Carolath. *Don Juans Tod.* Dramatic poem. 1883.
307. Johannes Proelsz. *Don Juans Erlösung.* Poem. In his *Gedichte* (Frankfurt a.M., 1886), pp. 210–18.
308. Adalbert Rudolf. *Don Juan.* Poem. 1888. Fills in the lacunae in (280).
309. Rud. von Gottschall. *Der steinerne Gast.* Play. 1890.
310. A. Ritter. *Don Juan auf dem Turnfest.* Two-act comedy with songs and acrobatics. 1893.
311. Günther von Freiberg [pseud. of Ada Pinelli]. *Don Juan de Marana.* Music by A. Boczek. "Monodrama." 1894.
312. Franz Herzfeld [Franz Held, pseud.]. *Don Juans Ratskellerkneipen.* Humorous poem. 1894.
313. Wilhelm Weigand. *Don Juans Ende.* Comedy. 1894 or 1896.
314. Ad. Böttiger. "Don Juan und Maria." Dramatic poem. In his *Düstere Sterne.* Date uncertain.
315. Landau. *Don Juan.* Unverified reference. No date or place indicated.
316. Oskar A. H. Schmitz. *Don Juan und die Kurtisane.* Three scenes. 1900.
317. Ferdinand von Hornstein. *Don Juans Höllenqualen.* Fantastic drama. 1901.
318. R. Strauss. *Die Waffe des Don Juan.* Comedy. Vienna, 1901.
319. J. van C. *Der Mond und der Mai oder Don Juan.* "Lose Blätter und Wandelbilder aus dem Leben. Dichtung von J. van C. Herausgegeben von P. Valentin." Dresden, 1902.
320. Otto Carl Bernhardi. *Don Juan.* Play. 1903.
321. H. Franz. *Don Juan.* Tragedy. 1904.
322. Liská Bürger. *Don Juan and Company.* ". . . farcical comedy, three acts, after the German . . ." 1905, U.S. Copyright Office. German original could not be located.
323. Jakob Lippmann. *Don Juans Ende.* "Zukunftsposse mit Gesang." 1908.
324. Oskar A. H. Schmitz. *Don Juanito.* Comedy. 1908.
325. *Idem. Ein deutscher Don Juan.* Comedy in three acts. First performance: 1909, in Mannheim.
326. Carl Sternheim. *Don Juan.* Tragedy. 1909.

327. Otto Anthes. *Don Juans letztes Abenteuer.* Three-act drama. 1909.
328. Thaddäus Rittner. *Unterwegs.* A Don-Juan drama in three acts. 1909.
329. Hans Bethge. *Don Juan.* Three-act tragicomedy. 1910.
330. Martin Langen. *Don Juan.* Tragedy. 1910.
331. August Lembach. *Don Juan.* Three-act drama. 1912.
322. Carl Leyst [pseud. of Carl Küchenmeister]. *Don Juans Mission.* Three-act drama. *Ca.* 1912.
333. Rich. Zoozmann. *Don Juan.* Drama. 1913.
334. Waldemar Bonsels. *Don Juan.* Epic poem. Published 1919. The last four cantos of the poem appeared in 1910 under the title *Don Juans Tod.* The poem was begun in 1906 and finished in 1914.
335. Arthur Brausewetter. *Don Juans Erlösung.* Novel. 1915.
336. Otto Bierbaum. *Don Juan Tenorio.* Short novel. 1918.
337. Friedrich Sebrecht. *Don Juan und Maria.* Play in three acts. 1919.
338. Rainer Maria Rilke. "Don Juans Kindheit." Poem. 1920. In his *Gesammelte Werke* (Leipzig, 1927), Vol. III.
339. *Idem.* "Don Juans Auswahl." Poem. 1920. Located as previous entry.
340. Franz Scott. *Der Don Juan.* Novel of manners. 1920.
341. Robert Heymann. *Don Juan und die Heilige.* "Roman aus dem Mysterium des verlorenen Paradieses." Novel. 1921.
342. Willem van Vloten. *Don Juan empor.* Novel. Basel, 1922.
343. Egon Kees. *Don Juan.* Epic in five cantos. 1923.
344. Friedrich Wencker. *Don Juans erste Liebe.* Story. 1923.
345. Rudolf Ehrenberg. *Don Juans Duell mit Gott.* Drama. 1924.
346. Franz K. Becker. *Don Juans Anfang.* Short play. 1925.
347. Werner von der Schulenburg. *Don Juans letztes Abenteuer.* 1925. Unverified reference, contained in Wilhelm Kosch, *Deutsches Literatur-Lexikon* (Bern, 1949), I, 364. Singer, *Bibliography*, lists a novel by the author, *Don Juan im Frack*, 1912.
348. Franz Karl Becker. *Don Juans Anfang.* Play in eight scenes. 1925.
349. Willy Drucker. *Don Juan und sein Sohn.* 1928. Unverified reference, contained in Wilhelm Kosch, *Deutsches Literatur-Lexikon* (Bern, 1949), I, 364.
350. Erica Grupe-Lörcher. *Der wiedererstandene Don Juan.* Novel. 1928.
351. Siegfried von der Trenck. *Don Juan-Ahasver; eine Passion der Erde.* Poem. 1930.
352. Rudolf Hans Bartsch. *Die Schauer im Don Giovanni.* Novel. 1931.
353. Alfred Schirokauer. *Don Juan auf der Flucht.* Novel. 1932.

354. Alf. Heimerdinger. *Don Juan.* "Balladen-Zyklus." Berlin, 1933.

355. Stephan von Hartenstein. *Don Juan. Ein Leben Liebe, Laster, Heiligkeit.* Story. 1934.

356. Franz Adam Beyerlein. *Don Juans Überwindung.* Short novel. 1938.

357. Heinrich Tiaden. *Don Juan ist unschuldig.* Novel. 1939.

358. Ernst Kratzmann. *Don Juan in Venedig.* Short novel. Published with his *Regina Sebaldi* (Vienna, ca. 1940).

359. Hans G. Brenner. *Drei Abenteuer Don Juans.* (1) "Das Gartenfest"; (2) "Der Stierkampf"; (3) "Leporellos Rache." Three tales. 1941.

360. Franz Zeise. *Don Juan Tenorio; ein Lebensbild.* Novel. 1941.

361. Christian Schneller. *Der Sturz.* A Don Juan tragedy with choirs. Music by Reinhard Raffalt. 1948.

362. Georg Trakl. *Don Juans Tod.* Fragment. Published 1948. Unverified reference, contained in Kosch, *Deutsches Literatur-Lexikon* (Bern, 1949), I, 364.

363. Frank Thiess. *Don Juans letzte Tage.* Novel. 1950. Based on (407), as told by Leporello.

364. Max Frisch. *Don Juan; oder die Liebe zur Geometrie.* Drama. 1953.

VII. SCANDINAVIAN COUNTRIES

365. Ludwig von Holberg. *Don Juan.* Drama. 174–(?). Denmark. Unverified reference.

366. Johann Ludwig Heiberg. *Don Juan.* "Romantisk comedie i 4 Acter." Denmark. 1814. Modeled rather loosely on (117).

367. Johann Carsten Hauch. *Don Juan.* Five-act tragedy. Denmark. Before 1836.

368. C. J. L. Almquist. *Ramido Marinesco.* Play. Sweden. 1845.

369. Per August L. Hallström. "Don Juans rubiner." Short story. In his *Reseboken.* Sweden. 1898. Transl. into English by F. J. Fielden, in Hallström's *Selected Short Stories* (London, 1922), pp. 155–88. (Transl.: "Don Juan's Rubies.")

370. M. Lie. *Don Juan.* Drama. Denmark. 1899.

371. Annie F. Quidling Akerhielm. *Don Juan Tenorio.* Four-act play. Sweden. 1909.

372. Artur Möller. *Don Juans synd. Novelle.* Sweden. 1915. (Transl.: "Don Juan's Sin.")

373. Karin Michaelis. *Don Juan—efter Døden.* Short novel. Denmark. 1919. Translated into German as *Don Juan im Tode* (1921), and

into Spanish by Jacinto Vidal as *Pasiones y muerte de Don Juan* (1941).

374. Sigurd Hoel and Helge Krog. *Don Juan.* Play. Norway. 1930.

375. Ulla Bjerne. *Don Juan i Tarbusch.* Sweden. 1935. (Transl.: "Don Juan in Tarboosh.")

376. Svend Borberg. . . . *Synder og helgen.* Tragedy. Denmark. 1939. (Transl.: "Sinner and Saint.") Concerns Don Juan and Don Quixote.

VIII. OTHER COUNTRIES

377. Alexander Pushkin. *Kamenyi Gost.* Dramatic poem. Russia. 1830. (Transl.: "The Stone Guest.")

378. Aleksei Konstantinovich Tolstoi. *Don Juan.* Dramatic poem. Russia. 1860.

379. János Bulla. *Don Juan.* Unfinished epic. Hungary. Cantos I and VI appeared in 1880 and 1882 respectively.

380. Stanislas Rzewuski. *Ostatni dzien Don Juana.* Drama. Poland. 1888. (Transl.: "Don Juan's Last Day.")

381. Gyula Reviczky. *Don Juan a másvilágon.* Lyric poem. Hungary. 18—. (Transl.: "Don Juan in the Other World.")

382. Andor Kozma. *Egy Don Juanhoz.* Lyric poem. Hungary. 1902. (Transl.: "To a Don Juan.")

383. Marcel Benedek. *Don Juan feltámadása.* Novel in verse. Hungary. 1904. (Transl.: "The Resurrection of Don Juan.")

384. Valeska von Stradtwitz. *Don Juans Dressur zur Ehe.* Story(?). From the Russian. Bratislava, 1906. Title of Russian original not available.

385. Larisa Petrovan Kosach [pseud.: Lesya Ukrainka]. *Kamenny Hospodar.* Play in six short acts or scenes. Ukraine. 1912. (Transl.: "The Stone Host.") Transl. into Russian by M. Aliger, 1941.

386. Lajos [Ludwig] Biró. *Don Juan három éjszakája.* Novel. Hungary. 1917. (Transl.: "Don Juan's Three Nights.") Transl. into German by Leo Lazar as *Don Juans drei Nächte* (1917).

387. Victor Eftimiu. *Don Juan.* Drama in verse. Romania. 1922.

388. Vladimir Piotrovski. *Smert Don Zhuana.* Play. Berlin, 1929. Published with three other plays under the title *Beatrice.* (Transl.: "The Death of Don Juan.") The author's name is ordinarily a Polish name, but the language in which the play is cited is Russian.

389. Mirko Jelusich. *Don Juan: die sieben Todsünden.* Novel. Croatia. 19—(?). The title is from a German translation in a 1936 edition.

390. Karel Capek. "Don Juan's Confession." Short story. Czechoslovakia. Transl. in his *Apocryphal Stories* (1949).

B. MUSICAL DON JUAN VERSIONS

I. SPAIN, PORTUGAL, AND LATIN AMERICA

391. Manuel Ferreira. Incidental music for (4). Eighteenth century.

392. Domenico Rossi. *Don Juan Tenorio o por otro nombre El combidado de piedra.* "Bayle trágico pantomimo." Ballet. *Ca.* 1790–1800.

393. Ramón Carnicer y Battle. *Don Giovanni Tenorio ossia il convitato di pietra.* Opera. Librettist unknown; the libretto is in Italian but the composer is Spanish. First performance: June 20, 1822. Another suggested date: Barcelona, 1818.

394. Ángel Rubio, 1846–1906. *Don Gonzalo de Ulloa.* Light opera. Unverified work. Date uncertain.

395. Luis Alonso. *Don Juan y la estatua del comendador.* Opera. 1901(?). Libretto by A. Berlioz; from (9).

396. Amadeo Vives Roig. *Don Juan.* Zarzuela(?). Libretto by Eduardo Marquina. 1905. A fusion of (1) and (9).

397. Luis Alonso. *Don Juan Tenorio.* Opera. 1914. Libretto by A. Berlioz. Apparently a reworking of (395).

II. ITALY[2]

398. Filippo Acciaiuoli. *Il empio punito.* Opera. Libretto and music by Acciaiuoli, although some critics have credited Alessandro Melani with the music. Probably earliest Don Juan opera. First staged February 17, 1669, in Rome.

399. Angelo Mingotti. *La pravità castigata.* Opera. Performed 1734 in Brünn. Unverified reference.

400. Vincenzo Righini. *Don Giovanni ossia il convitato di pietra.* Opera. Librettist either unknown, or A. de Filistri da Caramondani. First staged in Vienna, August 21, 1777. Other dates suggested: 1776 and 1779. Other possible location for première: Prague. Other title: *Il convitato di pietra ossia il dissoluto.* It has been called the first opera on the Don Juan theme, although Acciaiuoli's (398) is over one hundred years older.

401. Guiseppe Calegari. *Il convitato di pietra.* Opera. Performed 1777 in Venice.

402. Domenico Cimarosa. *Il convitato di pietra.* It is not certain that Cimarosa wrote such an opera. He did compose *Il convito* in 1781, which has no connection with Don Juan.

---

[2] Mozart's *Don Giovanni* has been included in this section, because of its close relationship—in libretto, at least—to Italian operas of that period.

403. G. Tritto. *Il convitato di pietra*. Musical farce in one act. Text by Giambattista Lorenzi. Performed 1783 in Naples.

404. Onorato Viganò. *Il convitato di pietra*. ". . . ballo semi-tragico pantomimo." Music by Luigi Mareschalchi. Performed 1784 in Rome.

405. Giovacchino Albertini. *Il convitato di pietra*. Opera. Performed 1784 in Venice. Librettist unknown. First performance in Warsaw, 1783, with a Polish libretto.

406. Giuseppe Gazzaniga. *Il Don Giovanni ossia il dissoluto*. One-act opera. Text by Giovanni Bertati. Performed 1787 in Venice. Other titles reported: *Il convitato di pietra, Don Giovanni Tenorio*. Other places and dates of performance suggested: Bergamo, 1788; Lucca, 1792. It has also been doubted whether Bertati really wrote the libretto, or whether it should be considered anonymous.

407. Wolfgang Amadeus Mozart. *Il dissoluto punito ossia il Don Giovanni*. Dramma giocoso in two acts. Text by Lorenzo Da Ponte. First performance: October 29, 1787, in Prague.

408. Francesco Gardi. *Il nuovo convitato di pietra*. Dramma tragicomico. Text by Giuseppe Foppa. Performed 1787 in Venice.

409. Vincenzo Fabrizi. *Don Giovanni Tenorio ossia il convitato di pietra*. Opera buffa. Text by Giuseppe Maria Diodati, or by Giambattista Lorenzi. Performed 1788 at Fano.

410. Lorenzo Da Ponte. *Il Don Giovanni*. One-act tragicomic opera. It was concocted from his own libretto for Mozart's *Don Giovanni* with parts of Bertati's libretto (406) added. The music was Gazzaniga's (406) with extra airs by Giuseppe Sarti, Francesco Federici, and Pietro Guglielmi. It was produced in London, on March 1, 1794.

411. Pietro Raimondi. *Il dissoluto punito*. Opera. *Ca.* 1818.

412. Giovanni Pacini. *Il convitato di pietra*. Comic opera in one act. Performed once in Viareggio, 1832. Pacini claims in his *Memorie artistiche* to have composed such an opera for a performance in a private family theater. There seems to be no reason to doubt his word, although the opera was never performed before the public.

413. Michele Ruta (1827–1896). Musical interludes for (128). There is supposed to be one composition for each of the first four acts. Unverified. Date uncertain.

414. Benedetto(?) Palmieri. *Il nuovo Don Giovanni*. Comic opera. Supposedly played *ca.* 1887. Unverified reference.

415. Franco Alfano. *L'Ombra di Don Giovanni*. Opera in three acts. Libretto by Ettore Moschino. First performance: April 2, 1914, at Teatro alla Scala, Milan.

416. Felice Lattuada. *Don Giovanni.* Opera. Libretto by A. Rossato. First performed May 18, 1929, in Naples. Based on (9).

417. Franco Casavola. *L'Alba di Don Giovanni.* Pantomime. Performed 1932, in Venice.

418. Franco Alfano. *Don Juan de Manara.* Opera. Libretto by Ettore Moschino. Revised version of (415). First performance: May 10, 1941, in Florence.

III. FRANCE

419. Le Tellier. *Le Festin de Pierre.* Vaudeville, or comic opera. 1713. It was the basis for many succeeding works of similar nature, on into the nineteenth century, and a good example of the *théâtre de la foire* pieces which were very popular during the eighteenth century in France.

420. Rivière. *Le Grand Festin de Pierre.* Musical drama. Music arranged by Cunissy. 1811.

421. Edouard Barthélemy Byron d'Orgeval. *Le Don Juan de village.* Comic opera in one act. Libretto by Chazot. First performed in Brussels, in 1863.

422. Henri de Saint-Georges. *Les Amours de Don Juan.* Ballet-pantomime. 1865.

423. Edmond J. M. M., Prince de Polignac. *Don Juan et Haïdée.* Libretto by Edmond Delière. 1877. Based on (231). Not exactly an opera. It has been described as a "scène lyrique" and a "cantata dramática."

424. Edouard V. A. Lalo. *Namouna.* Ballet with music in two acts. From (123). Continuity ("suite") by A. Messager. 1882.

425. Robert N. C. Bochsa. *Fantasie and Variations on a Theme from the Opera of Don Juan.* From (407). Philadelphia, 18—. The composer is French.

426. Antoine de Choudens. *La Jeunesse de Don Juan.* Opera. Libretto by Louis Gallet. 18—.

427. Charles Dancla (1818–1907). *Souvenir de Mozart.* Opus 156. For violin, cello, and piano. Six pieces. Nos. 2, 3, and 5 are called "Don Juan."

428. Marguerite Canal. *Don Juan.* "Scène dramatique." Piano accompaniment by M. Canal. Words in verse by E. Adenis. 1920 Grand Prix de Rome. Published in Paris, 1922.

429. Reynaldo Hahn. *L'Homme à la rose.* Opera. Paris, 1920. After (181)?

430. Henri Tomasi. *Don Juan de Mañara.* "Mystère en six tableaux." Opera. 1949–52. Based on (177).

431. Juan Morata. *Les Amours de Don Juan.* Performed at Théâtre Mogador. 1956.

IV. GERMANY[8]

432. Christoph Willibald Gluck. *Don Juan oder das steinerne Gastmahl.* Ballet in four acts. Palermo, 1758.

433. J. L. Schröder. *Don Juan oder der steinerne Gast.* Ballet. 1769.

434. Justinus Heinrich Knecht. Incidental music for his musical farce (278). 1772.

435. Haydn, Joseph(?). *Don Juan oder das steinerne Gastmahl.* Ballet. 1804. Neither Franz Joseph Haydn nor his brother Michael is credited with this work which is listed in previous bibliographies. Joseph did compose *Il Sganarello*, now almost entirely lost, in 1762, but 1804 is really too late for any composition by him.

436. Albert Lortzing. Overture and entr'acte for (289). 1829. Not printed.

437. Richard Strauss. *Don Juan.* Tone poem based on (297). Op. 20. 1888.

438. A. Boczek. *Don Juan de Marana.* Music for (311). 1894.

439. Moritz Moszkowski. *Don Juan und Faust.* Opus 56. Music for (289). 1896. Consists of an overture, entr'actes, etc.

440. J. Blumenthal. *Don Juan.* Unverified reference. 1901.

441. Paul Graener. *Don Juans letztes Abenteuer.* Opera. Performed: June 11, 1914, in Leipzig. Based on (327).

442. Walter Braunfels. *Don Juan.* "Eine klassisch-romantische Phantasmagorie für grosses Orchester." Opus 34. Vienna and New York, 1925.

443. Hermann Wunsch. *Don Juans Sohn.* Opera. Performed February 1928, in Weimar.

444. Herman Reutter. *Don Juan und Faust.* Opera. Based on (289). Performed 1950 in Stuttgart.

V. ENGLAND AND THE UNITED STATES

445. Henry Purcell. Incidental music for (229). 1692(?).

446. Anon. *Don Juan, or the Libertine Destroyed.* Pantomime. Songs, choruses, duets, etc., by William Reeve. Music by Gluck. 1787. In the preface, Delpini says that the pantomime was produced by Garrick several years before, at the Drury Lane Theatre, and Garrick died in 1779. Gendarme de Bévotte thinks that Garrick may even have written it. It is commonly thought to be based on (229), but Gendarme de Bévotte (I, 200–201) denies it.

[8] For Mozart's *Don Giovanni*, see note at head of Section II: Italy.

447. Henry Rowley Bishop. *Don John or The Libertine.* Two-act opera. 1817. Music by Mozart, adapted to the English stage by Bishop. Libretto is by Isaac Pocock, based on (229).

448. Thomas John Dibdin. *Don Giovanni or A Spectre on Horseback!* Two acts. London, 1817. Burlesque of (407).

449. William Thomas Moncrieff. *Giovanni in London, or the Libertine Reclaimed.* An operatic extravaganza in two acts. 1817. Another suggested date: 1820. Burlesque of (407).

450. Robert Reece. *Don Giovanni in Venice.* "An operatic extravaganza in two acts and in prose." 1860(?).

451. Granville Bantock. *Fifine at the Fair.* Orchestral drama. Based on (239). 1912.

452. Dennis Arundell. *Don Juan.* Opera. 1926. Based on (247).

453. Eugène Goossens. *Don Juan de Mañara.* Opera. Libretto based on (250). Performed: June 24, 1937, at Covent Garden Theatre, London.

454. Frederick Ashton. *Don Juan.* One-act ballet. Choreography by Ashton; music by R. Strauss. 1948.

VI. OTHER COUNTRIES

455. Aleksandr Sergievich Dargomyzhsky. *Kamennyi Gost.* Opera in three acts. Libretto uses Pushkin's poem (377) unaltered. Completed after the composer's death by Cui, and orchestrated by Rimski-Korsakov. First performed: May 16, 1856, at St. Petersburg. Another date given: 1872, which may be the performance of the completed work. (Transl.: "The Stone Guest.")

456. Pëtr Ilich Tchaikovsky. *Don Juan's Serenade.* Song. Op. 38, No. 1. 1877. The words are taken from (378).

457. Aleksandr Boris Shell [or Sheel, Schell, Scheel]. *Don Juan Tenorio.* Opera. Libretto by A. Tolstoi. First performance: 1888, in St. Petersburg.

458. Arseny Nikolayevitch Koreshchenko. *Don Juan.* Cantata. Opus 5. *Ca.* 1890.

459. Nicolai Aleksandrovich Sokolov. Incidental music for (378). Opus 5.

460. Eduard F. Nápravnik. *Don Juan.* Opus 54. Music for (378). Czechoslovakia. Incidental music, with choral and solo parts. 1891. Another suggested date: 1893.

461. August Enna. *Don Juan Maraña.* Opera in three acts. Denmark. 1925.

462. Jaroslav Jezek. *Don Juan and Comp.* Musical revue. Czechoslovakia. *Ca.* 1931.

C. PAINTINGS AND ILLUSTRATIONS ON THE DON JUAN SUBJECT[*]

463. Juan de Valdés Leal (1622–90). *Miguel de Mañara*. Painting. Spain. About 1672. Displayed in the Hospital de la Caridad, in Seville.

464. François Boucher. *Don Juan Invites the Statue of the Commander to Supper*. Engraving. France. Illustration for (117). See Molière, *Œuvres* (Paris, Prault, 1734), III, 189.

465. Jean-Michel Moreau (le jeune). *Le Festin de Pierre*. Drawing for an etching done by J. P. Le Bas in 1770. Appeared as an illustration for Molière, *Œuvres* (Paris, Compagnie des Libraires Associés, 1773), III, 211. Also found on the inside cover of the "Classiques Larousse" edition of *Dom Juan*.

466. Francisco de Goya. *Don Juan and the Comendador*. Painting. 1798. Variously titled. Size of canvas: 43 × 30 cms.

467. De Novelli. *The Statue of the Commandant*. Unverified reference. Possibly Pietro Antonio Novelli (1729–1804), or Francesco Novelli (1764–1836).

468. Alfred Johannot. *Don Juan naufragé trouvé par Haïdée*. Painting. France (Johannot was born in Germany but spent most of his life in France). Exhibited at Paris Salon, 1831. Last reported in Museum of Besançon.

469. Alexandre-Marie Colin. *Don Juan and Haïdée*. Painting. France. See next entry.

470. *Idem. Don Juan Disguised as a Girl*. Painting. This and the preceding item were reproduced as etchings by Réveil, *Historical Illustrations of Lord Byron's Works*. . . . Appeared in London in 1832 and the following year in Paris.

471. Eugène Devéria. *The Abduction of Doña Inés*. France. Probably the same as either one or both of the following.

472. *Idem. Episode de Don Juan*. Painting(?). Sold as late as 1931. Mentioned in Bénézit, *Dictionnaire des peintres*. . . . (1950 ed.).

473. *Idem. Don Juan, 1835*. Aquarelle. Same as preceding entry or entries?

474. Louis Boulanger. *Don Juan*. Lithograph. Scene from (407). France. Reproduced in *L'Artiste*, Series I, Vol. X (1837), opposite p. 238.

475. Eugène Delacroix. *La Barque de Don Juan*, or, more commonly, *Le Naufrage de Don Juan*. Painting. 1840. Size of canvas:

[*] This section is at best representative, since there are probably a great number of additional paintings and illustrations on the Don Juan subject.

4 ft. 3 in. × 6 ft. 4 in. Exhibited Paris Salon, 1841, Exposition Universelle, 1855. Given to French State by Mme Adolphe Moreau in 1853. Last reported in Louvre, Paris. It is usually considered to represent an episode from (231). There has been a claim, however, that the title should read "du," not "de," and that the subject was inspired by the sinking of a boat named the "Don Juan," a news item mentioned in the press at that time.

476. Emile-Jean-Horace Vernet (1789–1863). *The Shipwreck of Don Juan*. Lithograph. Undated.

477. Ford Madox Brown. *Haidée and Don Juan*. Aquarelle. England. Ca. 1865–70. Now in Melbourne, Australia.

478. Moritz von Schwind. Sketches for (407). Austria. 1870. Last reported in possession of von Ravenstein family in Karlsruhe, Germany.

479. Charles [or Carlos] Ricketts (1866–1931). *Don Juan and the Statue*. Painting. England. Date uncertain. Last reported in Tate Gallery, London.

480. Jean-André Rixens. *Don Juan*. Painting. France. *Ca.* 1888.

481. *Idem. Don Juan*. Painting. Exhibited in 1922. Either a second depiction by Rixens of the same subject, or else a re-exhibition of his earlier work.

482. Giacomo Grosso. *Ultimo convegno* (also titled: *Le donne alla tomba di Don Giovanni*). Italy. Exhibited in Venice, 1895. Reported as having fallen victim to fire about 1900, in New York. This painting, when first exhibited, aroused angry protests from the clergy, but the painter was awarded the "Grand Prize of the People" (1,000 Lire). It represented a church in which Don Juan's body lies in state in a half-opened coffin. Around it, four or five naked women carry on a witches' dance while expressing their emotions in highly passionate gestures.

D. MOTION PICTURES ON THE DON JUAN SUBJECT

483. *Don Juan et Faust*. 1922. Produced by Marcel L'Herbier. Société des Etablissements Gaumont. Copyright July 17, 1922.

484. *Don Juan*. 1926. From (231). Screen play by Bess Meredyth. Directed by Alan Crosland. Music by William Axt. Warner Brothers. John Barrymore as Don Juan.

485. *Don Juan's Three Nights*. 1926. From (386). Presented by Henry M. Hobart. Produced by John Francis Dillon. Screen play by Clara Beranger. Copyright August 12, 1926, by First National Pictures, Inc. No evidence that this film was actually released.

486. *The Private Life of Don Juan.* 1934. Based on (181). Screen play by Frederick Lonsdale and Lajos Biró. Produced in England by London Films. Douglas Fairbanks in the role of Don Juan. Opened in London, September, 1934.

487. *The Adventures of Don Juan.* 1949. From a story by Herbert Dalmas. Screen play by George Oppenheimer and Harry Kurnitz. Errol Flynn as Don Juan. Little connection with the Don Juan legend. Warner Brothers.

488. *Don Giovanni.* 1956. Based on (407). Produced and directed by Paul Czinner. With Cesare Siepi (Don Giovanni), Lisa Della Casa (Donna Elvira), and Anton Dermota (Don Ottavio). Harmony Films.

489. *Don Juan.* 1956. Based on (407). Directed by H. W. Kolm-Veltee. With Cesare Danova (Don Giovanni) and Marianne Schoenauer (Donna Anna). Produced by Akkord Films of Vienna.

490. *Don Juan.* 1956. Color film. On an idea by Maurice Clavel. Collaborators: Jacques-Laurent Bost and Bardem. Directed by John Berry. Stars Fernandel. Plot hinges on exchange of clothing between Don Juan and Sganarelle, which makes the latter become irresistible.

Index[1]

[1] This index lists all titles and authors mentioned in the text. For additional authors and titles, see Catalogue of Don Juan Versions, pp. 187–214.